Reading Poetry

AN ANTHOLOGY OF

POEMS

Reading Poetry

AN ANTHOLOGY OF
POEMS

Robert DiYanni

Pace University, Pleasantville

 Random House School Division · New York

First Edition
987654321

Project Editor: Charles Roebuck
Senior Production Associate: Venessa Martin
Cover Design: DanielsDesign, Inc., New York

Text Development, Design, and Production: Keim Publishing, New York
Designer: Claudia DePolo

Library of Congress Cataloging-in-Publication Data

Reading poetry : an anthology of poems / [compiled by] Robert DiYanni.
— 1st ed.
    p. cm.
    Includes index.
    Summary: A textbook anthology of poems by international authors both classic and contemporary, presented with commentary to develop the ability to read and analyze poetry perceptively.
    ISBN 0-676-35882-9
    1. Readers (Secondary)   2. Poetry.   3. English language-
-Composition and exercises.   4. Criticism—Authorship.   [1. Poetry-
-Collections.]   I. DiYanni, Robert.
PE1127.P57R44   1989
808.1—dc19   88-19149
                                                     CIP
                                                     AC

International Standard Book Number: 0-676-35882-9
Manufactured in the United States of America

Copyrights and Acknowledgments appear on pages 447–456.

For Magnhild

AUTHOR'S ACKNOWLEDGMENTS

For encouraging me to undertake this project, and for supporting me generously and graciously, I would like to thank Charles Roebuck, Gerry Gabianelli, and Barbara Darga of Random House. For her expert work on the Teacher's Edition of *Reading Poetry,* with its wealth of practical classroom applications, I would like to thank Judith A. Stanford of Rivier College, who, like me, has also taught high school students. To my wife, Mary, I owe more than this brief acknowledgment can convey.

Preface

꙳

Reading Poetry is a textbook. No attempt has been made to disguise that fact. But it is a textbook that offers many hours of reading pleasure because it contains poems that, quite simply, are enjoyable to read. Some are humorous, others serious, still others both surprising and thought provoking. Some are unforgettable. The poems were chosen because they are well crafted and wide ranging in vision. They are written in a wide variety of styles and voices, and they reflect varying perspectives. Some are long and complex; others are short and more accessible. Classic poems balance contemporary works by poets whose reputations are still growing. Poems by women complement others by men; poems by American poets stand alongside those from other countries.

The book is designed to prepare you to read poetry thoughtfully and perceptively. Chapter One, Reading and Responding, provides an overview of the reading process. It describes what you do as you read, and it explains how you can improve your ability to interpret and evaluate poems. Chapter Two, Elements of Poetry, identifies and explains basic poetic characteristics such as imagery, figures of speech, irony, allusion, structure, symbolism, rhythm, meter, and sound effects. The critical vocabulary introduced in this chapter will enable you to discuss poems and analyze them carefully and well.

An appendix—Writing about Poetry—has also been included. In it you will find guidelines for writing, including making notes, drafting, organizing, and revising papers. The appendix also suggests topics for papers.

A glossary of poetic terms has been included to provide a convenient way to check the meanings of critical terms.

An ability to read perceptively, with understanding, is one sign of an educated person. An ability to read appreciatively, with enjoyment, is a source of lifelong pleasure. *Reading Poetry* can bring you both.

Robert DiYanni

Contents

卍

PART TWO   ANTHOLOGY OF POEMS

Part One

❧

INTRODUCTION TO POETRY

Chapter One

ॡ

READING AND RESPONDING

The Pleasures of Poetry

We read poetry for the many pleasures it offers—pleasures of sound and sense, pleasures of image and symbol, pleasures of speech and feeling and thought. Some of these pleasures are intellectual, as when we enjoy a poet's witty wordplay or we understand a poem's central idea. Other pleasures of poetry are emotional, as when we are moved by a poem to feel sorrow or pity, fear or joy. Still other pleasures are physical, as when our skin tingles or we feel the impulse to tap our feet or nod in time to a poem's rhythmic beat. Emily Dickinson once remarked that she could tell she was reading poetry when she felt as if the top of her head were coming off. Although our own ways of acknowledging the power of poetry may not be as extravagant as Dickinson's, we will arrive, nonetheless, at some distinctive apprehension of poetry's pleasures.

At times particular poems may seem puzzling or mysterious. Yet mystery and confusion are not essential attributes of poetry. Nor is poetry simply dressed-up prose, statements that have been made to look good (by being organized in stanzas) and sound good (by being arranged in patterns of rhythm and rhyme). Even though we can discuss the ideas in poems, poems can never be reduced to their intellectual content. Poems present experiences in language, experiences created by the poet to be re-created by the reader. In reading poetry our experience involves more than considering the meanings of words, for it includes their sounds as well as their sense. Our experience in reading poetry also includes our apprehension of a poem's form, its organized patterns of sound and sense, its controlled structure of thought. The meaning of any poem involves our total experience of reading it, an experience that includes intellectual understanding but which is not restricted to it.

Reading poetry can bring us intellectual, emotional, and aesthetic pleasure. Poetry sharpens our perception of the world around us, since it draws its energy from the fresh observation of life. Poetry increases our understanding of our world and ourselves, making us aware of things we didn't know or knew only vaguely. In fact, poetry can excite our capacity for wonder, and it can enlarge our appreciation of beauty. It can make us feel more acutely and deeply, and it can make us more receptive to imaginative experience. Reading poetry also improves our ability to use and understand language, since poems are made of words—at their best, the choicest words in the best possible order. These pleasures are there for the taking. All we have to do is seize and enjoy them.

Although you will not necessarily experience all or even most of these pleasures of poetry in reading any single poem, you will almost certainly experience some of them. You can test your experience of poetry by reading and responding to the following poem.

ROBERT FROST

[1874–1963]

♦

Dust of Snow

The way a crow
Shook down on me
The dust of snow
From a hemlock tree

Has given my heart   5
A change of mood
And saved some part
Of a day I had rued.

Part of our enjoyment of this poem comes from its brevity. It captures an experience and recreates it for us in just a few words. The poem's quick stab of reality engages us, very likely sending us back almost immediately for a second look. We may be struck by the nature of the poem's action—a crow's jouncing a tree limb, which unloads its dusty snow on a person beneath it. We may smile, considering that the crow's action may have been intentional. And we may reflect on the person's response—not anger or frustration but a shift of feelings, "a change of mood" (presumably from sorrow to something more joyous, elation perhaps).

Our pleasure in "Dust of Snow" may include a consideration of our own experience—whether or not that experience duplicates either the poem's external action or the speaker's internal change. We may find ourselves thinking about how our moods can and do change and about what prompts those changes. We may enjoy the surprising reversal of our expectations in reading how Frost's speaker responds to the situation, perhaps comparing what our own imagined response might be.

These experiential or imaginative pleasures, moreover, might very well be supplemented by the pleasure we take in the poem's sound—especially its rhythm and rhyme. And they may extend to other details we observe about its structure and language. We may enjoy noticing, for example, that although "Dust of Snow" is a single sentence, it is cast as two separate nearly symmetrical stanzas. And we might ask ourselves why the poem occurs in two stanzas rather than one, or why it appears as a single sentence—and how it would differ if it were arranged as one stanza or constructed of two sentences. Furthermore, we might enjoy Frost's use of the word "rued," which stands out in a context of more common and familiar language. And we may take pleasure in discovering the related implications of the following details: that it is a "crow" (not an owl or a woodpecker) that shakes down the "dust" of snow from a "hemlock" tree (not a maple or an apple tree).

The poem may also lead us to speculate not only about the little narrative incident it recounts but about its larger significance. We might think about the relationship between human beings and the natural world that "Dust of Snow" implies. (That is, that nature can affect man in beneficial ways; that it can make us feel better about our experience.) And we may derive pleasure from considering this idea in general or from considering other poems by Frost and other writers whose works seem to confirm or perhaps contradict the impression of Frost's poem. We may thus find ourselves considering the larger implications of "Dust of Snow" along with a set of attitudes toward nature and its relationship to our human world. This too may provide us with a kind of pleasure.

Taken together, these and similar pleasures are available when we read any poem. Our enjoyment is composed partly of understanding the poem's language and form, partly of responding to the experience it describes, and partly of relating its implied values to what we believe and think and feel.

The Act of Reading

Learning to read poetry well and to savor its pleasures involves learning to ask questions about its elements—its speaker and situation, diction and imagery, symbols and figures of speech, syntax and structure, rhythm and sound effects. These poetic elements are discussed in chapter two, which provides a critical vocabulary for explaining how poems create meaning and convey feeling. But reading poetry involves learning to ask other kinds of questions as well. Such questions include the following:

1. What feelings does the poem evoke? Or alternatively: How am I affected by this poem? How do I feel as I read it?
2. What ideas does the poem express? Or alternatively: What sense do I make of it?
3. What values does the poem endorse? Or alternatively: What do I think about the beliefs, attitudes, and values it displays?

We will divide our discussion of understanding poetry into three parts: reading, interpreting, and evaluating. By *reading* we mean primarily our subjective experience of the poem; by *interpreting* we mean the process of analysis we engage in to understand the poem; by *evaluating* we mean our estimation of the attitudes it conveys and the values it endorses. All three aspects of reading poetry can be used in measuring the extent to which any poem moves or touches us, stimulates us to see and think and wonder.

Reading   When we read a poem something happens to us. We experience the poem both intellectually and emotionally. This experience involves our feelings about the poem's speaker and situation, and it includes our desire to see how its poetic action works out in the end. In reading, therefore, we are concerned with our personal and subjective involvement in the poem. Instead of immediately asking ourselves what the poem means, we consider what it does to us, how it affects us—and why. To examine this dimension of our experience of poetry, we will read the following poem about a man looking at a photograph of his father. As you read, consider the thoughts and feelings the poem gives rise to.

RAYMOND CARVER

[b. 1939]

♦

Photograph of My Father in His Twenty-second Year

October. Here in this dank, unfamiliar kitchen
I study my father's embarrassed young man's face.
Sheepish grin, he holds in one hand a string
of spiny yellow perch, in the other
a bottle of Carlsbad beer.   5

In jeans and denim shirt, he leans
against the front fender of a 1934 Ford.
He would like to pose bluff and hearty for his posterity,
wear his old hat cocked over his ear.
All his life my father wanted to be bold.   10

But the eyes give him away, and the hands
that limply offer the string of dead perch
and the bottle of beer. Father, I love you,
yet how can I say thank you, I who can't hold my liquor
    either,
and don't even know the places to fish?   15

The poem describes a photograph of the speaker's father holding
a bottle of beer in one hand and a string of fish in the other. We may
not have ever seen a photograph of our father holding either of
these, but we probably have looked at a photograph of someone
important to us holding something. Carver's poem may trigger our
thoughts and feelings in remembering them. Or perhaps in listening
to the speaker describe his father's photograph, we may think less
about the photograph and more about the man. Perhaps feelings
about our own fathers will emerge as we listen to the speaker.

We might be struck by particular details such as the father's lack
of boldness or by the way he seems to pose for posterity. Such observations may stimulate us to make connections with our own experience. Very likely by the time we complete the last stanza, we will
respond to the speaker's direct expression of love for his father and
perhaps also to the speaker's confession of his own inadequacy.
Carver's poem, that is, may raise questions about how we "see" our
own fathers, and it may stimulate additional reflection about how
we measure ourselves in relation to them. It might, moreover, tap a
well of memories, thoughts, and feelings we didn't know we had.

Suppose, however, that we can't relate the poem to a relationship
between a father and son. Does the poem's focus on males deny female readers access to its pleasures? Not really, since in reading literature we typically make adjustments to accommodate such
differences. Women experience strong feelings about their fathers,
and they also judge them. Moreover, a female reader who didn't
directly relate Carver's poem to her own father might easily trans-
pose it to reflect her way of seeing her mother. Such adaptations and
adjustments form a normal part of our experience in reading poetry.

We should also make a final point. Our experience in reading this
or any poem will almost inevitably change on subsequent readings.
There are a number of reasons for this. First, we may have thought
or talked about the poem since our initial reading. Second, in the

interval between the two readings we may have changed in some significant way ourselves. And third, we may have read other works or undergone other experiences that relate in some way to our reading of the poem. Since our experience of reading a poem changes as we change, we should remain open to this possibility. We should not be too quick, therefore, to dismiss a poem we don't like on first reading. We may even discover that with more knowledge or experience our response may change.

Interpreting   When we interpret a poem we explain it to ourselves. We make sense of it. If *reading* is viewed primarily as a subjective experience in which we satisfy our personal needs as readers, then *interpreting* directs us to more objective considerations. When we interpret a poem, we concern ourselves less with how it affects us and how it makes us feel than with what it means or suggests. Interpretation, in short, aims at understanding; it relies on our intellectual comprehension and rational understanding rather than on our emotional response.

The act of interpreting involves essentially four things: observing, connecting, inferring, and concluding. To understand a poem, we first need to observe its details. For example, we hear its rhythm and rhyme; we notice its pattern of organization; we envision the objects or experiences it describes. As we do these things, we begin formulating a sense of the poem's focus, emphasis, and point. We arrive at this formulation, however tentative it may be, largely by making connections among the many details we observe. On the basis of these connections we make inferences or interpretive hypotheses about their significance. Finally, we come to some kind of provisional conclusion about the poem's meaning based on our observations, connections, and inferences. Our act of interpretation continues as we read. We don't delay making inferences, for example, until after we have made and connected all our observations. Instead, we develop tentative conclusions *as* we read and observe, *while* we make observations and develop inferences. We may change and adjust our inferences and provisional conclusions both *during* our reading of a poem and *afterward* as we think back over its details. We do not separate this intellectual process, however, from our subjective reactions and emotional responses. Although they have been separated here for convenience, the way we actually

9

read combines emotional response and intellectual analysis. In the same way, the four interpretive actions of observing, connecting, inferring, and concluding occur together, sometimes simultaneously, and not in a series of neatly separated sequential stages.

Whether you were aware of it or not, you were performing this complex act of reading-interpreting-responding when you read "Dust of Snow" and "Photograph of My Father in His Twenty-second Year." In fact, our discussion of each poem was based partly on an implicit interpretation. Now that you better understand the interpretive process, reread these poems and develop an interpretation for each. In doing so, you would find it useful to proceed slowly and deliberately. Make a list of the details you observe in each poem. Then relate some of the details to one another, looking for connections among them. Once you establish a few connections among the details, you can then make inferences or hypotheses about what the related details imply. Finally, from your inferences you can develop an interpretation or explanation of the poem's meaning.

Once you have developed an interpretation for either or both of the poems in the reading section, follow the same approach in working out an interpretation of the following poem.

EMILY DICKINSON

[1830–1886]

♦

Much Madness is divinest Sense

Much Madness is divinest Sense—
To a discerning eye—
Much Sense—the starkest Madness—
'Tis the Majority
In this, as All, prevail—   5
Assent—and you are sane—
Demur—you're straightway dangerous—
And handled with a Chain—

How can you begin to interpret this poem? First, notice the way sense and madness are the dominant issues. Although they are opposites, Dickinson asserts their apparent equality, perhaps even their identity. To be more precise, she ascribes the condition of one state to the other. Madness, the lines suggest, may not be what it *appears* to be. Although madness might look insane, it might really be quite sensible. Conversely, something may appear sane and sensible, but upon closer inspection turn out, instead, to be madness.

So far we have been unpacking Dickinson's tightly compressed lines, clarifying our sense of what her words mean, of what the lines suggest. We have not yet asked why or how madness can be sense and sense can be madness. Nor have we considered whether we agree with such an assertion. Our purpose when we interpret is to read patiently and reflect deliberately on the meaning of the words.

You may have noticed, however, that in interpreting lines 1–3, we left out a few important details. First, the lines assert that "much" madness (not all) is or may be sensible, and that "much" sense may also be madness. Dickinson's lines do not insist that what appears to be madness never is, or that what appears sensible is never so. The word "much" qualifies her assertion to suggest that "sometimes" madness and sense masquerade as one another. Second, her lines also indicate that when madness is really sense, it is "divinest" sense; and when sense is really madness, it is "starkest" madness. The superlative form of each word suggests that when madness and sense are interchanged, the reversal is complete, thorough, absolute.

Dickinson's poem is based on *paradox,* a poetic device that describes an apparent contradiction: that madness can be sense and that sense can be madness. In a paradox, the apparent contradiction disappears with a shift in perspective. Thus, from the standpoint of worldly wisdom, sacrificing everything else in life for money or power or prestige may be very sensible. From a religious standpoint, whether that of Buddhism or Christianity, for example, such behavior is madness. To use another example, from the standpoint of finding employment upon graduating college, to major in business, perhaps in accounting or management, may seem eminently sensible. However, from an alternative standpoint that an undergraduate course of study should promote broad learning and develop an ability to learn, a major in a liberal arts subject such as history, English, or philosophy would be the better choice.

The second part of the poem (lines 4–8) moves on to something else—to how sense and madness are defined by social majority. The lines suggest that if you go along with the crowd, with majority opinion, you will be considered sane; if not, you may be considered a threat to the majority and branded as odd, different, perhaps even crazy. As in the first part of the poem, Dickinson employs a pair of contrasting words to accentuate these contradictory responses: "Assent" (agree) and "Demur" (disagree). Dickinson's poem suggests that it is dangerous to disagree, to diverge from the conventional ways of seeing and doing things. While recognizing this as a fact of life, the poem nevertheless questions the validity of such a view, and in fact undermines it by suggesting that it is often the majority in their seeming sensibleness who are mad and the individual in his seemingly eccentric madness who is really right and sane. By means of paradox and wit Dickinson invites us to think about such serious, important, and inescapable issues. And even though the poem ends with a touch of dark humor, it is a serious poem about a serious matter.

In reaching an interpretation of this or of any poem, we should be concerned less with finding the *right* answer than with arriving at a satisfying explanation. Some interpretations, nonetheless, will be more satisfying than others. They will be more convincing, largely because they take into account more of the poem's details. Other interpretations, while perhaps not as convincing, may be valuable for the intellectual stimulation they provide. Still others may strain credibility to the breaking point. Because we invariably bring different experiences to our reading of poems, we will each see different things in them. The different things we see and the varying interpretations we make depend largely on our values, on our attitude toward what matters most to us. Through conversation and discussion we can debate the merits of those viewpoints and values while sharpening and enriching our understanding of poetry.

Evaluating   An *evaluation* is essentially a judgment, an opinion about a text formulated as a conclusion. We may agree or disagree with the attitude toward madness and sanity expressed in Dickinson's poem. We may accept or reject the behavior displayed in

Frost's "Dust of Snow." And we may approve or disapprove of the comments made by Carver's speaker in "Photograph of My Father in His Twenty-second Year." However we evaluate these poems, though, we invariably measure their values and attitudes against our own.

Evaluating is partly an unconscious process. We are not always aware, except perhaps in a vaguely general way, why we respond to something as we do. We may know that we like or dislike it without bothering much to think about why. We accept particular ideas, events, experiences, or works of art, and reject others sometimes almost instinctively, even automatically. Even though part of our evaluation of a work is unconscious, we can make it more deliberate and more fully conscious. We simply need to ask ourselves how we respond to the values the work supports and why we respond as we do. By asking these questions, we should be able to consider our own values more clearly and to discuss more fairly and sensibly why we agree or disagree with those displayed in the poem.

When we evaluate a poem, we appraise it according to our own unique combination of cultural, moral, and aesthetic values. Our cultural values derive from our lives as members of families and societies. Our moral values reflect our ethical norms—what we consider to be good or evil, right or wrong. Our aesthetic values concern what we see as beautiful or ugly, well-made or ill-made. Over time, through education and experience, our values change. A poem that we once valued for what it reveals about human experience or for its moral perspective may mean little to us later. Conversely, a work that we once found uninteresting or disappointing we may later find to be powerfully engaging.

Our personal response to any poem's values is closely tied to our interpretation of it. Evaluation depends upon interpretation; our judgment of a poem's values (and perhaps its value as a literary work as well) depends on how well we understand it. Our evaluation, moreover, may be linked to our initial experience of the poem, with our first impressions and pre-critical, pre-analytical reactions. If our reaction is unsympathetic to the poem as a whole or to the values it seems to display, we may be reluctant to change both our interpretation and our evaluation, even when we discover convincing evidence to warrant a reconsideration of both.

Consider "Dust of Snow" from the standpoint of evaluation.

What values seem to animate the poem's speaker? What, for example, is the speaker's attitude toward nature? Does he see nature as malevolent or benevolent? Does he consider nature as being related to his life? In addition, what does the poem suggest about the emotional experience of human beings? Is it good or bad, for example, to experience such rapid changes of mood over such apparently trivial occurrences? Can you think of situations in your own life where you experienced something similar to Frost's speaker—where you underwent a swift change of mood? How did you value that experience, and why? Finally, how do you evaluate the poem as an imaginative rendering of such a possible human experience?

Consider also the implicit values of Dickinson's and Carver's poems. Is Carver's speaker overly concerned with his image as a "man" who can "hold his liquor"? Does he somehow blame his father for passing on to him an inability to drink liquor without showing its effects? Is he too hard on himself for not measuring up to his father's ability to catch fish? Does he blame his father for not teaching him the places to fish? What do you think of the images of manhood that the poem displays overall?

With Dickinson's paradoxes, you might ask whether or not she is right. Is apparent madness sometimes sensible, and is apparent sense sometimes madness? Is Dickinson's speaker correct about majority opinion? Does it usually prevail, and if so, what do you think about that prevalence? What do you think about those who demur, who don't assent to the majority view, and who may thus be labeled thereby as mad? What are the dangers and virtues of going against the grain of conventional wisdom, of majority opinion? How important is it for you to be one of the majority? How important are other perspectives, alternate ways of seeing, thinking, and valuing—perspectives that run counter to the views of the majority?

Of the kinds of evaluations we make when reading poetry, those about a poem's aesthetic qualities are hardest to discuss. Aesthetic responses are difficult to describe because they involve our feelings and perceptions, especially our subjective personal impressions about what we find pleasing. They also involve our expectations about what we think a poem should be, as well as our prior experience in reading poems or having them read to us when we were young. Our aesthetic responses, moreover, are complicated still further by our tendency to react quickly and decisively to what we like and dislike, often without knowing why we respond as we do.

Of the three poems you have read so far—Frost's, Carver's, and Dickinson's—which is the most pleasing from the standpoint of its beauty or its craftsmanship? Why? (Even though you will be in a better position to answer this question after you have studied chapter two, you can give it preliminary consideration now.) Admittedly, without a good deal of experience in reading poetry, judgments about a poem's values and considerations of its aesthetic merit need to be made with caution. But we must begin somewhere, since evaluation is inevitable. We cannot avoid judging the poems we read any more than we can avoid judging the people we meet. The process is natural.

How we develop our aesthetic responses to poetry, moreover, depends partly on letting the informed and sensitive responses of other experienced readers enrich our own perceptions. These other readers may be classmates or teachers. They may also be critics who have written articles and books about the literary works we read. Their understanding of poetry can deepen and enrich our own. Besides learning directly from what critics say about particular poems, we can also learn how to discuss literature. The best literary critics, for example, provide models we can emulate, while the worst can at least show us what to avoid. Our goal in reading, interpreting, and evaluating poetry—and also in listening to the views of other readers—is to develop a sense of literary tact, the kind of balanced judgment that comes with experience in reading and living, coupled with thoughtful reflection on both. There are no shortcuts or simple formulas for developing such evaluative competence and confidence. They come with practice in attentive reading of many literary works, with a patient consideration of their language and details, and with a willingness to reflect on our responses to them. Above all, perhaps, literary understanding and appreciation are achieved by devotion, effort, and repeated acts of loving attentiveness.

Application Although we have isolated the processes of reading, interpreting, and evaluating, the three acts occur simultaneously in an intricate web of thinking and feeling. To derive the fullest pleasure from the poems we read, we should be alert for all three aspects of our experience in reading them. In doing so we will develop our skills as thoughtful, sensitive readers who know what we think, how we feel, and why. As you read the following poem by Adrienne Rich, consider each of these three aspects of literary response. After you have read the poem a few times, write one paragraph about your subjective experience of reading, write a second paragraph about your intellectual understanding or interpretation, and a third on your assessment of the poem's values.

ADRIENNE RICH

[b. 1929]

◆

Aunt Jennifer's Tigers

Aunt Jennifer's tigers prance across a screen,
Bright topaz denizens of a world of green.
They do not fear the men beneath the tree;
They pace in sleek chivalric certainty.

Aunt Jennifer's fingers fluttering through her wool   5
Find even the ivory needle hard to pull.
The massive weight of Uncle's wedding band
Sits heavily upon Aunt Jennifer's hand.

When Aunt is dead, her terrified hands will lie
Still ringed with ordeals she was mastered by.   10
The tigers in the panel that she made
Will go on prancing, proud and unafraid.

Questions

Reading What associations about your own aunts and uncles do you bring to the poem? Can the situation described in this poem apply to your parents rather than to your aunts and uncles? What words in the poem triggered your responses most strongly? Why?

Interpreting   Did you encounter words, phrases, lines, or stanzas that confused or baffled you? What observations can you make about significant details and recurring words or phrases? What words and phrases recur and what details are significant to you? Why? What connections can you make and what inferences can you draw after reading the poem a few times? How, for now at least, would you explain your interpretation of "Aunt Jennifer's Tigers"?

Evaluating   What values are associated with Aunt Jennifer? With the uncle? With the tigers? What is the relationship among the values associated with these three figures? How do your own values, beliefs, and convictions clash with or support those displayed in the poem?

Comments   Whatever our initial impressions of the poem's language and situation, eventually we will ascertain that the speaker is a woman (possibly the poet herself) who values her aunt's needlepoint or embroidered tigers very much. We may or may not feel pity or sympathy for Aunt Jennifer; we may or may not think much about the nameless "Uncle" whose wedding ring is such a burden for his wife. But we certainly must respond to the speaker's celebration of the tigers.

The poem begins and ends with the tigers, and they appear with Aunt Jennifer in the title. The tigers thus are associated with her; they somehow belong to her. The tigers are said to "prance"; they also "pace," and they are unafraid of "the men" (hunters perhaps) depicted beneath the tree on Aunt Jennifer's wool picture. The tigers, moreover, are portrayed in bright colors. They appear as majestic creatures—vibrant, strong, certain, and very much alive. And they seem more interesting and more powerful than the men in the poem. This much we can glean from the opening stanza.

The second stanza shows Aunt Jennifer having difficulty making her stitches. Her heavy wedding band impedes her, inhibiting and slowing her progress. From the way the wedding band is described, we suspect that Rich's speaker means more than the words literally say. We suspect that the wedding band is symbolic, representing the heaviness and oppressiveness of a life married to "Uncle." It is the constraining forces of men and marriage that weigh Aunt Jennifer down, keeping her in her place as she performs her womanly tasks.

How far we may like to go with such an argument depends on our personal experience, our observation of details in the poem, our knowledge of Adrienne Rich's poetry in general, and our own values.

The final stanza leaps forward in time to when Aunt Jennifer has died. Even in death she will lie "ringed" with ordeals that oppressed her in life. The implication here is that there is no escape from the stultifying effects of traditional socio-sexual relationships, even in death. Even the rituals established for death have been sexually stereotyped, and the perceptions of Aunt Jennifer by those who live on will be made in the context of her place as a woman and the wife of "Uncle." This is not to suggest that "Uncle" is somehow the villain of the piece. He is most likely a decent fellow. But he is clearly meant to represent an attitude, a way of living and being, that Rich's speaker considers destructive. And it is that larger social attitude—its implied way of seeing and valuing women—that the poem rebels against.

Even though Aunt Jennifer maintains her place, and even though she remains "Aunt Jennifer" in death, her tigers continue to prance. They go on living, a product of her handiwork, representing an aspect of Aunt Jennifer that she could not herself display—freedom from male domination, freedom from fear. Through her art Aunt Jennifer creates an image of a power and vitality she could possess only in imagination. Thus, in a way, even though Aunt Jennifer is mastered by her fate, she ultimately prevails through the imaginative vision displayed in her art.

In considering the poem's values, we need to address questions about the power of men to control the lives of women. And we need to consider the presumed submission of women along with the reasons for it. We may want to shift perspective and not see submission at all but rather an acceptance of a natural and socially viable order. That is, although we need to consider the values attached to Uncle and to Aunt Jennifer as described by the speaker, we might consider whether or not Aunt Jennifer and Uncle would ever see themselves the way the speaker does. And we certainly need to consider the role and value of art for the speaker, for the poet, and for the lives of people more generally. Such considerations lead us to examine the cultural assumptions, sexual stereotypes, and social dispositions suggested by the poem. They may lead to a consideration of whether Aunt Jennifer's woolwork is truly a form of "art" (and an implicit rebellion) or rather simply another example of how she (and women in general) perform only socially sanctioned acts in socially acceptable ways.

Chapter Two

ૐ

ELEMENTS OF POETRY

In Chapter One we discussed an approach to reading poetry based on three aspects of responding to poetic texts: reading, interpreting, and evaluating. In this chapter we offer a critical vocabulary for discussing poetry. Besides introducing the language of poetry, chapter two explains how to interpret poems by analyzing their elements: speaker and situation; diction and imagery; figures of speech and symbolism; irony and allusion; syntax and structure; rhythm and meter; sound and sense. Although we will discuss these elements individually, this is strictly a matter of convenience. No poetic element exists in isolation. Poems are unified, complex networks of meaning and reference that we analyze piecemeal only to better understand how they work and what they achieve.

Speaker and Situation

When we read a poem the first thing we hear is the voice of its speaker. In listening to the speaker we gain a sense of his or her circumstances and situation. We learn, that is, what the speaker is talking about, and why. So our first concern is to determine whom we are listening to and what is happening in the poem.

Think back to the poems in Chapter One. In "Dust of Snow" a speaker is reflecting on a past experience. The speaker is an older person, mature and thoughtful, who seems to take pleasure in reflecting on this experience. In "Photograph of My Father in His Twenty-second Year" the speaker is a son whose memory of his father is stimulated by a snapshot of the father holding a string of fish and a bottle of beer. The son remembers his father and measures himself against him. "Much Madness is divinest Sense" gives us a confident speaker, one who neither reflects on experience like Frost's speaker, nor questions it as Carver's does. Instead, Dickinson's speaker comments on what she has observed; from her observed experience she generalizes an axiom or truth. And finally, "Aunt Jennifer's Tigers" includes a speaker who thinks about the relationship and values of her aunt and uncle as she contemplates an embroidered pattern of tigers made by her aunt.

Who is the speaker and what is the situation in the following poem?

LANGSTON HUGHES

[1902–1967]

♦

Mother to Son

Well, son, I'll tell you:
Life for me ain't been no crystal stair.
It's had tacks in it,
And splinters,
And boards torn up,   5
And places with no carpet on the floor—
Bare.
But all the time
I'se been a-climbin' on,
And reachin' landin's,   10
And turnin' corners,
And sometimes goin' in the dark
Where there ain't been no light.
So boy, don't you turn back.
Don't you set down on the steps   15
'Cause you finds it's kinder hard.

Don't you fall now—
For I'se still goin', honey,
I'se still climbin',
And life for me ain't been no crystal stair.   20

Even without the title ("Mother to Son") we would clearly see
that the speaker is a parent giving advice to a child. We are not told
the specific occasion. Nor are we provided with particularities of
their circumstances. Those things are left to our imagination. What
we are given, however, is a general sense of their situation. The
mother is encouraging her son to persist in his efforts, not to give
up, not even to slow down, regardless of the difficulties that will
probably come his way. She presents herself, moreover, as a model
for him to imitate. Although she is tired of her struggles in life, she
is still "climbin'," still doing what she believes is necessary.

We hear a different speaker and voice in the next poem. As an
exercise in coming to terms with a poem's speaker and situation,
listen carefully to the language. Identify words and phrases that describe the speaker's situation and attitude.

A. E. HOUSMAN

[1859–1936]

♦

When I was one-and-twenty

When I was one-and-twenty
  I heard a wise man say,
'Give crowns and pounds and guineas
  But not your heart away;
Give pearls away and rubies   5
  But keep your fancy free.'

But I was one-and-twenty,
No use to talk to me.

When I was one-and-twenty
I heard him say again,   10
'The heart out of the bosom
Was never given in vain;
'Tis paid with sighs a plenty
And sold for endless rue.'
And I am two-and-twenty,   15
And oh, 'tis true, 'tis true.

Diction and Imagery

Diction   Diction refers to the words of a poem, specifically to the selection of words the poet employs. We can speak of a poem's diction as being primarily abstract or concrete, formal or informal, general or specific. A word like *shovel,* a general word, is less specific than *garden shovel* or *snow shovel,* yet more specific than *garden tool* or *snow implement.* Shovel is a concrete word in so far as it refers to an object rather than an idea. Words like *fear, love,* and *beauty* are abstract. They refer to concepts, not things. Poets typically, however, will use such words in specific contexts to bring them, so to speak, down to earth and close to home. Instead of fear a poet might describe "a tighter breathing" (Emily Dickinson's "A narrow Fellow in the Grass"); instead of love a poet might describe "two hearts beating each to each" (Robert Browning's "Meeting at Night"); instead of beauty, "a red, red rose" (Robert Burns' "A Red, Red Rose").

Formality and informality refer to the social standing of a word. Some words are more commonly used, more familiar, and hence more informal than others. *Sidewalk,* for example, is more common than its more formal counterpart, *pavement.* It is more likely to be used in everyday conversation and less likely to be reserved for formal situations.

The diction of the following lines from Robert Francis' poem, "Pitcher," is more abstract than concrete, more general than specific, more formal than informal.

His art is eccentricity, his aim
How not to hit the mark he seems to aim at,

His passion how to avoid the obvious,
His technique how to vary the avoidance. . . .

You will notice that a number of Francis' words are polysyllabic (composed of many syllables). Polysyllabic words are often of Latin derivation. The shorter monosyllabic (one syllable) words are more often of Anglo-Saxon derivation and are typically part of the more familiar language of ordinary discourse. (The word *discourse* is itself an "educated" or more formal word for which *speech* would be a less formal equivalent). Notice how the relative formality, generality, and abstract vocabulary of "Pitcher" contrasts with the more informal, concrete, and specific language of another baseball poem, "Cobb Would Have Caught It" by Robert Fitzgerald.

In sunburnt parks where Sunday lies,
Or the wide wastes beyond the cities,
Teams in grey deploy through sunlight.

Talk it up, boys, a little practice.

Coming in stubby and fast, the baseman
Gathers a grounder in fat green grass,
Picks it stinging and clipped as wit
Into the leather: a swinging step
Wings it deadeye down to first.
Smack. Oh, attaboy, attaoldboy.

To read poetry well you need to attend to the poet's words. One way to do this is to listen carefully to the words, perhaps reading them aloud. Another is to become aware of the rich variety of verbal choices poets can make. A dictionary can prove invaluable in understanding such choices by providing not only the primary meaning of a word but secondary and tertiary meanings as well. In addition, a good dictionary will give a word's etymology, or origin, and perhaps indicate its relationship to cognate words (words of similar origin) by revealing its root in another language such as

Latin or French. Beyond that, of course, the dictionary will show you how to pronounce a word, how to spell it, and how to break it into syllables.

But as valuable as a dictionary is for the careful reading of poetry, it does not tell you all you need to know about words in order to understand how they function in poems. A dictionary will provide a denotative definition, or literal meaning, but it will not generally include a word's connotation. *Connotation* refers to the suggestions and implications a word may possess beyond its dictionary or denotative meaning. The word *mother,* for example, means female parent. One dictionary offers as its primary definition, "a female that has borne an offspring." Now this is perfectly correct as far as it goes. But we all know that *mother* means much more. We associate *mother* with all those ideas, attitudes, feelings, impulses, and personal experiences that our own mothers conjure up in our minds and hearts. Our individual personal associations, together with a more public set of shared associations attached to the word, comprise its connotations. For a word such as *mother,* the connotations vastly outweigh in significance its denotative meaning.

If words like *mother* or *vacation* are strongly connotative, words like *tangent* or *sodium bicarbonate* typically are not. Why? Because such mathematical and scientific terms are meant to express one and only one thing. They are deliberately devoid of feeling (as much as this is possible in language) in order to avoid the very personal associations and emotional reverberations that other more connotatively charged words bear. As a general rule, technical terms are often relatively barren of connotation. Their denotative meaning is by far the more important. You can see how different a technical term is in this respect when you compare it with a more commonly used counterpart. Consider the following example. The term *myocardial infarction* refers to a particular kind of heart ailment in which the muscle tissue of the heart dies. *Coronary thrombosis* refers to a different kind of heart ailment in which a blood clot forms in the heart. However, for the nontechnical expert, neither term possesses the imaginative and emotional power of *heart attack.* Why? Primarily because *heart attack* conjures up various images, feelings, or fears—or perhaps memories and personal associations. This more familiar term is part of our linguistic and life experience in ways the more technical terms are not.

It isn't necessary to be an expert in language to appreciate these distinctions between denotative and connotative meaning. Nor is it possible for you to know all about words before you begin reading poetry seriously. One of the pleasures and benefits of studying poetry, in fact, is to enrich your word hoard (an Anglo-Saxon term for vocabulary or stock of words). Another pleasure of reading poetry is seeing how poets play with the various meanings of words—their denotations, their connotations, and their associations with other words and experiences. But these are things you learn in the course of reading poetry attentively. They are not prerequisites.

Consider, for example, the following excerpt from "A narrow Fellow in the Grass" by Emily Dickinson. In these lines, in which a speaker describes a fear of snakes, the poet has selected her words for both their connotative impact and their etymological significance.

> Several of Nature's People
> I know, and they know me—
> I feel for them a transport
> Of cordiality—
>
> But never met this Fellow
> Attended, or alone
> Without a tighter breathing
> And Zero at the Bone—

Look first at the way Dickinson describes the animals as "Nature's People," which suggests intimacy and friendly feeling. The word "feel" conveys literally the emotional character of the speaker's experience. But this feeling is intensified by the words "transport" and "cordiality." The first term (from the Latin *trans* or across and *portare* to carry) suggests a state of being carried across or over something, usually a boundary. The speaker seems to be carried over a boundary that is the normal distance between the human and animal worlds. That distance is bridged by the speaker's feeling of "cordiality," a word that can be defined as *friendliness* or *sincere fellow feeling*. The etymology of "cordiality," however, indicates its derivation from the Latin *cor,* meaning heart, which is similar to cognates or related derivations in Italian (*cuore*), Spanish (*corazón*), and French (*coeur*)—all of which also mean heart. The connotations of "cordiality" further suggest a genuine warmth, a much closer and intimate form of feeling than perhaps would be indicated by *approval* or *respect*. *Cordiality* connotes, then, a sincere warmth of friendly feeling that is especially appropriate in context—appearing, that is, a few lines before the contrasting language that describes the speaker's cold and paralyzing fear of snakes.

One way to practice attending to the words of a poem is to consider alternative possibilities for some of the words the poet uses. Here, for example, is John Updike's "The Mosquito" arranged so that you can choose one word per line. (Updike's choices appear inverted at the end of the poem.) In making your choices be prepared to explain why you chose the words you did.

JOHN UPDIKE

[b. 1932]

♦

The Mosquito

On the fine wire of her (whine, buzz, sound) she walked,
Unseen in the (stagnant, ominous, fearsome) bedroom dark.
A traitor to her (invisibility, smallness, camouflage), she
   talked
A blue streak (clear, distinct, bright) as a spark.

I was to her a (large, fragrant, provident) lake of blood   5
From which she had to (taste, drink, sip) a drop or die.
A reservoir, a lavish field of (food, grain, meat),
I lay awake, (unknowing, unconscious, thinking) of my size.

We seemed fair-matched opponents. (Quietly, Quick, Soft)
   she dropped
Down like an anchor on her (thread, surge, wing) of song.   10
Her nose sank (happily, thankfully, heavily) in; then I slapped
At the sting on my arm, (clever, shrewd, cunning) and strong.

A cunning, strong Gargantua, I (squished, hit, struck)
This lover pinned in the (meat, feast, folds) of my flesh,
(Lulled, sated, pleased) by my blood, relaxed, half-sated,
stuck   15
Engrossed in the (large, big, gross) rivers of myself.

Success! Without a (sound, cry, noise) the creature died,
Became a fleck of (black, dirt, fluff) upon the sheet.
The small (sting, welt, bite) of remorse subsides as side
By side we, murderer and (killed, annihilated, murdered),
sleep.   20

cry, fluff, welt, murdered.
struck, feast, Lulled, gross.
Soft, thread, thankfully, cunning.
fragrant, sip, food, unconscious.
Answers: whine, ominous, camouflage, distinct.

Imagery   We perceive the world through our senses. We see, hear, touch, taste, and smell. When poets use language in ways that stimulate our senses or our imaginative recall of sense experience, they do so by means of images. An image in poetry is a word or phrase that refers to a sense experience—seeing a leaf fall or touching a marble surface. Images appeal to one or more of our senses and may be visual, aural, olfactory, tactile, or gustatory; they refer, that is, to things seen, heard, smelled, touched, or tasted.

Each of the poems in chapter one contained images. Frost's "Dust of Snow" contains the tactile image of snow dusting the speaker. Carver's "Photograph of My Father in His Twenty-second Year" contains visual images that depict the father holding a bottle of beer and a string of fish. Dickinson's "Much Madness is divinest Sense" includes an image that is both tactile and visual—the chain used to handle those considered mad. Adrienne Rich's "Aunt Jennifer's Tigers" contains a similar blend of tactile and visual imagery in Aunt Jennifer's needlework and wedding ring. Many poems, most in fact, employ images. And although we will find that poems generally include more visual images than other kinds, poets are adept at using many types of images, often in rich combinations.

Consider, for example, the following poem in which the poet describes a lover traveling to meet his beloved.

ROBERT BROWNING

[1812–1889]

♦

Meeting at Night

The gray sea and the long black land;
And the yellow half-moon large and low;
And the startled little waves that leap
In fiery ringlets from their sleep,
As I gain the cove with pushing prow,   5
And quench its speed i' the slushy sand.

Then a mile of warm sea-scented beach;
Three fields to cross till a farm appears;
A tap at the pane, the quick sharp scratch
And blue spurt of a lighted match,   10
And a voice less loud, through its joys and fears,
Than the two hearts beating each to each!

Each line includes a specific image. In stanza one, the imagery is
largely visual (lines 1–4) and tactile (lines 5–6). You envision seeing
the sea, land, moon, and waves; you imagine feeling the boat being
slowed as it is dragged across the sand. In stanza two, images of
sound (the tap at the pane, the sharp scratch of the match, the sound
of speaking voice and beating hearts) accumulate to support and
enrich a tactile image (the warm beach), an olfactory image (the
scent of the beach), and visual images of fields, a farm, and the blue
flame of a match. Taken together, the images allow us to imagine
the experience that the poet describes. In addition, they suggest the
speaker's heightened awareness as he approaches his beloved. Ultimately, they convey how strongly the two lovers feel about one
another, particularly in the familiar but fine image of their two
hearts beating together.

Images are not merely decorative. Poets employ them not only to stimulate our imagination but also to convey feeling. Sometimes a poet will use a physical image to suggest an emotional experience. For example, the speaker of the following lines from William Butler Yeats' "The Lake Isle of Innisfree" describes an emotional experience in physical terms as he remembers a sound and associates it with his strong feeling for a place.

> I will arise and go now, for always night and day
> I hear lake water lapping with low sounds by the shore;
> While I stand on the roadway, or on the pavement gray,
> I hear it in the deep heart's core.

The speaker in Ezra Pound's "The River-Merchant's Wife: A Letter" describes things she sees and hears. In the process, she makes us aware of her loneliness as she awaits her husband's return from a long journey. Her thoughts are cast in the form of a letter written to him.

> And you have been gone five months.
> The monkeys make sorrowful noise overhead.
>
> You dragged your feet when you went out.
> By the gate now, the moss is grown, the different mosses,
> Too deep to clear them away!
> The leaves fall early this autumn, in wind.
> The paired butterflies are already yellow with August
> Over the grass in the West garden;
> They hurt me. I grow older.

The poet's selection of images and details reveal the woman's state of mind. In describing the monkeys' noise as "sorrowful," the speaker provides an index of her own sorrow. This sorrow is further exemplified by her inability to clear away the deeply overgrown mosses, and even more poignantly by her description of the yellow butterflies, whose brief lives are nearly over. By noticing that the butterflies are "paired," the speaker is revealing her own lonely fear of growing old without her husband. The poet embellishes and enriches the sense of sadness and loss with the image of leaves falling in autumn, a suggestion of the twilight of life. Rather than making the speaker's feelings explicit, the poet's carefully selected images speak for her.

Images provide clues to a poem's thought and feeling. They concretize ideas and make them memorable; they dramatize feelings and make them vivid. Poetic images convey thought and express feeling by describing the concrete particularities of human experience. One of America's most influential modern poets, Ezra Pound, admonished young followers to "go in fear of abstractions." Another modern American poet, William Carlos Williams, had as his motto, "No ideas but in things." Neither Pound nor Williams believed that poetry should avoid ideas; they believed rather that ideas in poems always be anchored in reality, that ideas be rooted in the particularity of experience. One of Pound's most famous poems, in fact, consists of two images juxtaposed or placed side by side:

EZRA POUND

[1885–1972]

♦

In a Station of the Metro

The apparition of these faces in the crowd;
Petals on a wet, black bough.

That's the entire poem. The first line describes an appearance of faces that the poet saw in a crowd of people at a Paris subway station (the Metro). The second line provides an alternative way of seeing those faces: as flower petals on the bough of a tree with dark, wet bark. For Pound, such combinations of images yield the essence of poetry. They reveal the vividness of the poetic image; they suggest its power of compression; and they imply both an intellectual and emotional charge that brings the two images together for readers to ponder.

In considering a poem's imagery, it is important not only to identify the images and enjoy their vivid descriptive qualities but also to consider what the images imply—what ideas they suggest and what feelings they convey. In addition, it is useful to look for patterns of imagery, that is, for a coherently related series of images by which the poet presents a unified expression of experience. Consider, for example, the relationship among the images in the following poem.

WILLIAM WORDSWORTH

[1770–1850]

♦

I *wandered lonely as a cloud*

I wandered lonely as a cloud
That floats on high o'er vales and hills,
When all at once I saw a crowd,
A host, of golden daffodils;
Beside the lake, beneath the trees,   5
Fluttering and dancing in the breeze.

Continuous as the stars that shine
And twinkle on the milky way,
They stretched in never-ending line
Along the margin of a bay: 10
Ten thousand saw I at a glance,
Tossing their heads in sprightly dance.

The waves beside them danced; but they
Outdid the sparkling waves in glee:
A poet could not but be gay,   15
In such a jocund company:
I gazed—and gazed—but little thought
What wealth the show to me had brought:

For oft, when on my couch I lie
In vacant or in pensive mood,   20
They flash upon that inward eye
Which is the bliss of solitude;
And then my heart with pleasure fills,
And dances with the daffodils.

Although the poem's images are exclusively visual, Wordsworth
is not primarily interested in presenting a pretty picture of a natural
scene. His images serve more than a pictorial purpose. Instead, they
present a belief in nature's power to restore the human spirit. They
also imply an intimacy that exists both within the natural world and
between nature and mankind.

Wordsworth suggests the unity of nature by describing the daffodils, yellow flowers that grow in clusters, fluttering in the breeze
coming from a lake. Nature here appears as wind or air, as water,
and as flower. (Earth is implied since flowers grow in soil.) Another
natural element, fire, is also implied—though much more ten-
uously—in the daffodils' golden color, which can be related to the
shining of the stars described in stanza two. Other connections
among the natural elements include those between the waves and
the flowers (both dance in the wind); between the flowers and the
stars (both are numerous); and between the stars and the waves
(both sparkle and twinkle as they reflect the light of the sun).

The primary concern of the poem, however, is not the unity of
nature but rather the power of nature to move the human spirit to
feelings of joy. This movement occurs in three stages. First is the
direct experience of nature, which the poet/speaker undergoes. Second is the poet/speaker's remembrance of that experience in all its
imagistic particularity. And third is the realization of the importance of the experience, its wealth of meaning, its power to fill the
heart with happiness. Wordsworth underscores the unity of human
and natural worlds in the last line where the speaker indicates that
his heart "dances with the daffodils."

As an exercise in considering imagery in poetry, read the following poem and identify its images. Look for patterns of related images, and consider their implications in both expressing thought

and conveying feeling. Consider not only what the individual images help you to imagine, but also what connections you discern among them, and what those connections might mean.

SYLVIA PLATH

[1932–1963]

♦

Blackberrying

Nobody in the lane, and nothing, nothing but blackberries,
Blackberries on either side, though on the right mainly,
A blackberry alley, going down in hooks, and a sea
Somewhere at the end of it, heaving. Blackberries
Big as the ball of my thumb, and dumb as eyes   5
Ebon in the hedges, fat
With blue-red juices. These they squander on my fingers.
I had not asked for such a blood sisterhood; they must
    love me.
They accommodate themselves to my milkbottle, flattening
    their sides.

Overhead go the choughs in black, cacophonous flocks—   10
Bits of burnt paper wheeling in a blown sky.
Theirs is the only voice, protesting, protesting.
I do not think the sea will appear at all.
The high, green meadows are glowing, as if lit from within.
I come to one bush of berries so ripe it is a bush of flies,   15
Hanging their blue-green bellies and their wing panes in a
    Chinese screen.
The honey-feast of the berries has stunned them; they
    believe in heaven.
One more hook, and the berries and bushes end.

The only thing to come now is the sea.
From between two hills a sudden wind funnels at me,   20
Slapping its phantom laundry in my face.
These hills are too green and sweet to have tasted salt.
I follow the sheep path between them. A last hook brings me
To the hills' northern face, and the face is orange rock
That looks out on nothing, nothing but a great space   25
Of white and pewter lights, and a din like silversmiths
Beating and beating at an intractable metal.

Figures of Speech and Symbolism

Figures of Speech   Language can be conveniently classified as either literal or figurative. When we speak literally, we mean exactly what each word conveys; when we use figurative language, we mean something other than the actual meaning of the words. "Go jump in the lake," for example, if meant literally would be intended as a command to *leave* (go) and *jump* (not dive or wade) into a *lake* (not a pond or a stream). Usually, however, such an expression is not meant literally. In telling someone to go jump in the lake, we are telling them something, to be sure, but what we mean differs from the literal meaning of the words.

Of the more than two-hundred-fifty types of figures of speech, the most important for poetry, perhaps, are *metaphor* and *simile*. The heart of both these figures of speech is comparison—the making of connections between normally unrelated things, seeing one thing in terms of another. More than 2,300 years ago Aristotle defined metaphor as "an intuitive perception of the similarity in dissimilars." And he suggested further that to be a "master of metaphor" is the greatest of a poet's achievement. In our century, Robert Frost has echoed Aristotle by suggesting that metaphor is central to poetry, and that, essentially, poetry is a way of "saying one thing and meaning another, saying one thing in terms of another."

Although both simile and metaphor involve comparisons between unlike things, *simile* establishes the comparison explicitly with the words *like* or *as*. *Metaphor*, on the other hand, employs no such explicit verbal clue. The comparison is implied in such a way that the figurative term is substituted for or identified with the literal. "My son talks like an encyclopedia" is a simile; "my son devours ideas" is a metaphor. The difference involves more than the word *like:* The simile is more restricted in its comparative suggestion than is the metaphor. That is, the son's comparison with the encyclopedia is limited to the way he sounds when he talks. But in the more extensive metaphor of eating ideas, there is a suggestion that his appetite for ideas matches his appetite for food. It is a natural appetite, one essential for survival.

Consider the opening line of Wordsworth's poem about the daffodils: "I wandered lonely as a cloud," which suggests the speaker's isolation. But it does not indicate other ways in which cloud and speaker are related. Later in the poem the speaker uses another simile to compare the daffodils with stars, a simile that accentuates the large number of both flowers and stars. In both examples of simile the poet directs us to the comparative connection. He also restricts their application. In an additional comparison from the same poem, this time a metaphor, Wordsworth writes that the daffodils "flash" upon the "inward eye" of the speaker. The "flash" implies that he sees the flowers in his mind's eye, the inward eye of memory and imagination. Moreover, when he "sees" the daffodils in this "inward eye," the speaker realizes the "wealth" they have brought him. This "wealth" is also a figure of speech: Wordsworth uses "wealth" as a metaphor for joy.

Metaphor is a pervasive element of language. It is so common that we can speak of *dead* metaphors—comparisons that have become so familiar that we hardly notice them as metaphors at all. We speak, for example, of the legs of a table, the eye of a needle, the arms of a chair, the head of an organization. For us, roads *branch,* checks *bounce,* books *talk,* love *grows,* musical instruments *sing.* These metaphorical expressions are based on comparison, which is the heart of metaphor (itself a metaphor, though one that still beats with life).

Good poets handle metaphor and simile with skill and originality. The best poets use these figures of speech to help us see things in previously unrecognized ways. In addition to the examples noted above, John Donne, in "A Valediction: Forbidding Mourning" (p. 106), compares the relationship between a pair of lovers to planetary motion, to two geometrical drawing compasses, and to particular properties of gold. Robert Wallace (p. 357) describes a baseball double play in terms of a dance, and in the process also compares both dance and double play to poetry. Robert Frost compares a woman to a silken tent, describing both of them simultaneously in language that is perfectly suitable for each (p. 237). And in a famous example, Robert Burns employs similes to describe a speaker's love in "A Red, Red Rose."

> O, my luve's like a red, red rose
> That's newly sprung in June;
> O, my luve's like the melodie
> That's sweetly played in tune.

In using such similes, Burns's speaker conveys an impression both of the girl he loves and of his feeling for her. In the following short poem, Emily Dickinson employs metaphor in comparing suffering to a broken heart. What is impressive about Dickinson's handling of this familiar metaphor, however, is the way she gives it a new twist.

EMILY DICKINSON

[1830–1886]

♦

The Bustle in a House

The Bustle in a House
The Morning after Death
Is solemnest of industries
Enacted upon Earth—

The Sweeping up the Heart   5
And putting Love away
We shall not want to use again
Until Eternity.

One way of thinking about metaphor is as an *image with implications*—imagery that conveys implied thought and feeling. Imagery becomes metaphor, as the following poem demonstrates.

WILLIAM SHAKESPEARE

[1564–1616]

♦

That time of year thou may'st in me behold

That time of year thou may'st in me behold
When yellow leaves, or none, or few, do hang
Upon those boughs which shake against the cold,
Bare ruined choirs where late the sweet birds sang.
In me thou see'st the twilight of such day   5
As after sunset fadeth in the west,
Which by-and-by black night doth take away,
Death's second self that seals up all in rest.
In me thou see'st the glowing of such fire
That on the ashes of his youth doth lie,   10
As the deathbed whereon it must expire,
Consumed with that which it was nourished by.
    This thou perceiv'st, which makes thy love more strong,
    To love that well which thou must leave ere long.

Shakespeare's poem includes images that appeal to three senses: sight, touch, and hearing. We see the yellow leaves and the bare branches; we feel the cold that shakes the boughs; we hear the singing birds of summer (in memory). These images, however, also become metaphors, ways of talking of one thing (human mortality) in terms of another (nature—the season of autumn). Autumn, for example, is that time of year when leaves turn yellow and tree branches lose their leaves. But because the speaker says that we can

see autumn in him, we know that he is speaking metaphorically—
of himself in terms of autumn.

The metaphor of autumn is followed by that of twilight (lines 5–
8). The sun is described as fading in the west, and "black" night
takes away the sun's light. Death, moreover, is mentioned explicitly. We sense thus that the images are not merely descriptive or pictorial but are metaphorical. This sense of the poem's metaphorical
language extends into its third set of images (lines 9–12). There the
speaker describes himself on his deathbed and compares himself to
a fire that will inevitably die out. He sees his youth as "ashes" and
his life as a fire whose glow "must expire." These images, coupled
with those in the first eight lines and reinforced by that of the
poem's last two lines, reveal a strongly metaphorical intention.

We have been describing figures of speech in terms of comparison, specifically in terms of metaphor and simile. We should identify, however, some additional types of figurative language used in
poetry. These include personification, synecdoche, and metonymy.

Personification Personification is a type of metaphorical comparison in which abstract concepts or inanimate objects are invested
with human properties or characteristics. Examples include Wordsworth's daffodils "dancing in the breeze"; Aunt Jennifer's tigers
"prancing . . . unafraid"; Updike's mosquito, which walks and
talks to its intended victim. (Updike's poem, in fact, contains numerous examples of simile, metaphor, and personification.)

Consider the following example of personification in "Winter
Trees" by William Carlos Williams.

WILLIAM CARLOS WILLIAMS

[1883–1963]

◆

Winter Trees

All the complicated details
of the attiring and
the disattiring are completed!
A liquid moon
moves gently among   5
the long branches.
Thus having prepared their buds
against a sure winter
the wise trees
stand sleeping in the cold.   10

An even more elaborate use of personification can be found in the odes of John Keats (pp. 168–174). The following excerpt from his "Ode on Melancholy" can serve as illustration. In it, Keats personifies not an aspect of nature, like Williams, but a series of abstractions.

She [Melancholy] dwells with Beauty—Beauty that must die;
　　And Joy, whose hand is ever at his lips
Bidding adieu; and aching Pleasure nigh,
　　Turning to Poison while the bee-mouth sips:

Both Williams and Keats identify a relationship between one thing and another; both make metaphorical connections. Their personifications provide us with a way of envisioning an abstract concept like "Joy" and a way of thinking about the necessity and inevitability of natural processes.

Synecdoche and Metonymy   Two other figures of speech related to metaphor are synecdoche and metonymy. In *synecdoche* a part of something is substituted for the whole, as when we refer to workers as "hands," or to cars as "wheels." In *metonymy* one thing stands for something associated with it, as when we speak of "the oval office" to mean the president or use "the grave" to signify death.

Like other forms of comparison, synecdoche and metonymy approach symbol. It isn't far from associating one thing with another to letting one thing stand for or represent another, which is the essence of symbolism. Although we speak of image, metaphor, and symbol as discrete aspects of poetry, there is really a continuity among them. In discussing Shakespeare's "That time of year thou may'st in me behold," we commented on how its images become metaphors for human experience. We can move one step further and see the poem as a symbol of human feeling. Its patterns of imagery and metaphor combine to produce a symbol of fading life. This symbolism is perhaps most powerfully evident in the image of the dying fire, which represents the speaker's life. The fire, which is burning towards its own extinction, symbolizes the speaker's glowing life, which is being consumed in his very living.

As an exercise in thinking about figures of speech, consider the following poem. Identify the uses of image, metaphor, personification, metonymy, and synecdoche.

JAMES SHIRLEY

[1596–1666]

♦

The glories of our blood and state

The glories of our blood and state
Are shadows, not substantial things;
There is no armor against fate;
Death lays his icy hand on kings.

Scepter and crown   5
Must tumble down
And in the dust be equal made
With the poor crooked scythe and spade.

Some men with swords may reap the field
And plant fresh laurels where they kill,   10
But their strong nerves at last must yield;
They tame but one another still.
  Early or late
  They stoop to fate
And must give up their murmuring breath,   15
When they, pale captives, creep to death.

The garlands wither on your brow,
Then boast no more your mighty deeds;
Upon death's purple altar now
See where the victor-victim bleeds.   20
  Your heads must come
  To the cold tomb;
Only the actions of the just
Smell sweet and blossom in their dust.

Symbolism Like metaphor, symbolism is a way of describing one thing in terms of another. A *symbol* is an object that stands for something beyond itself, a feeling perhaps, or an abstract idea, or an experience. A rose can represent beauty or love or mortality; a lily can stand for purity or innocence. Ashes can represent death; birds can symbolize freedom. Light and darkness can stand for life and death, knowledge and ignorance, joy and sorrow. The possibilities are numerous.

The meaning of a symbol is controlled by its context. Whether fire symbolizes lust, rage, destruction, or purification (or nothing beyond itself) is only determinable within the context of a particular poem. Nor is there any limit to how many symbolic meanings an object, character, or gesture may possess—even within the context of a single poem. In long poems especially, poets have been known to shift the implied meaning of their symbols from beginning to end.

Deciding on the symbolic significance of a poetic detail is not an easy matter. Even when we are fairly confident that something is symbolic, it is not often easy to determine just what it represents. Like any inferential connections we make in interpreting poetry, the decision to view something as symbolic depends partly on our skill in reading and partly on whether the poetic context invites and rewards a symbolic interpretation.

Approaching the symbolic dimension of a poem requires both the impulse to consider what poetic details stand for and the counter-impulse to restrain ourselves from going beyond the bounds of good sense. Interpreting poetry involves developing literary tact, a thoughtful and careful interpretive instinct that relies in part on our experience of reading many literary works and in part on our intuition.

Consider the symbolism of the following poem.

ROBERT FROST

[1874–1963]

♦

Nothing Gold Can Stay

Nature's first green is gold,
Her hardest hue to hold.
Her early leaf's a flower;
But only so an hour.
Then leaf subsides to leaf.   5
So Eden sank to grief,
So dawn goes down to day.
Nothing gold can stay.

Frost employs a series of examples to support the point that whatever gold stands for (the good, the true, the beautiful) does not endure, does not last. Traditionally, however, gold has represented wealth and value; it stands for those things we hold dear. Since poets do not explain their symbols, Frost does not specify precisely what gold symbolizes. Nonetheless, the overall concern of the poem is with transience, with the ephemerality of the precious and valuable. We might, however, also consider it another way: that the most transient things are most valuable *because* they don't last. We value them because we can't retain them forever.

Frost's examples are drawn mostly from nature: "dawn," which begins the day in golden splendor, diminishes to the mere ordinariness of "day." The initial golden green of a tree's first blossom is quickly followed by a greener leaf, with the golden flower lasting only a brief time. And as in nature, so in the story of Eden—a myth of a golden time, a time of perfection, innocence, harmony, and peace. These few carefully selected examples imply that the golden aspects of human experience are equally ephemeral. Frost leaves it to us to decide what these highly valued aspects of life are. But it seems reasonable to assume that "life" itself is one of them, one we treasure all the more for our short hold on it.

As an additional exercise in symbolic reading, consider the following symbolic interpretation of the nursery rhyme "Humpty Dumpty." Decide whether or not you find the interpretation convincing.

> Humpty Dumpty sat on a wall.
> Humpty Dumpty had a great fall.
> All the king's horses and all the king's men
> Couldn't put Humpty Dumpty together again.

Interpretation   Although this poem is familiar as a nursery rhyme, we should not ignore its symbolic significance. For "Humpty Dumpty" is not a children's verse at all. It is, rather, a warning about the dangers of overarching pride. Pride, of course, was the sin of Adam, the first man, who to quote Milton's great epic poem *Paradise Lost,* "brought death into the world and all our woe."

Why is Humpty Dumpty a symbol of pride? Primarily because as an egg sitting on a wall, he is in a very dangerous position, a position in which he should never have placed himself. By sitting on the wall, Humpty Dumpty attempts to go above and beyond his limits as an egg. An egg simply does not belong precariously perched on a wall. In sitting there Humpty Dumpty tries to overreach himself, to be like a man, something he decidedly is not.

This is analogous to the position of Adam, the first man, who wanted to be like God. Like Adam, who attempted to reach beyond the limits of his nature, Humpty Dumpty brings about and deserves his fall. In fact "fall" is the most important word in the poem. Literally, it describes Humpty's precipitous decline and consequent destruction. Symbolically, it represents the *fall* of man from grace into sin. Like Adam, who was cast out of Paradise and who suffered physical hardship resulting from his excessive pride, so Humpty Dumpty, the nursery rhyme Adam, is broken by his fall, never to be made whole again.

Allusion and Irony

Two aspects of poetry that recur with great regularity are allusion and irony. *Allusion* is a reference to historical figures or actions, mythological creatures and happenings, or literary characters and events. *Irony* is a tone—an implied attitude taken by the poet toward his or her subject.

Allusion   Robert Frost's "Nothing Gold Can Stay" contains an allusion or reference to the biblical story of the Garden of Eden. This story of man's fall from God's grace and his banishment from Paradise is found in the book of Genesis. For most readers of Frost's poem, this allusion poses no problem; they know the story and can recognize the allusion. But consider the allusions William Blake employs in the poem on page 46.

WILLIAM BLAKE

[1757–1827]

♦

Mock on, Mock on, Voltaire, Rousseau

Mock on, Mock on, Voltaire, Rousseau;
Mock on, Mock on, 'tis all in vain.
You throw the sand against the wind,
And the wind blows it back again.

And every sand becomes a Gem   5
Reflected in the beams divine;
Blown back, they blind the mocking Eye,
But still in Israel's paths they shine.

The atoms of Democritus
And Newton's Particles of light   10
Are sands upon the Red Sea shore,
Where Israel's tents do shine so bright.

Blake mingles biblical references to the Israelites with allusions to four historical figures: the French writer Voltaire (1694–1778); the French philosopher Jean-Jacques Rousseau (1712–1778); the English physicist and mathematician Sir Isaac Newton (1642–1727); and the Greek philosopher Democritus (ca. 460–ca. 370 B.C.). Without some knowledge of both the biblical allusions and the philosophical and scientific ideas of these historical figures, an interpretation of Blake's poem will be difficult. At the very least, we need to know that Democritus's philosophy centers on the theory that the world and everything in it is composed of atoms, the smallest constituent particles of matter. Democritus was a materialist, for whom spiritual properties simply did not exist. Newton described nature in terms of inanimate particles of light. Like Democritus, his science attempted to explain the mystery of the universe in scientific terms. And Voltaire and Rousseau, though not scientist-philosophers like Democritus and Newton, were thinkers who had little if any use for religious faith and spiritual vision. They both exalted the power and importance of reason.

Blake thus alludes, on one hand, to those who mock religious faith and spiritual vision. On the other hand, he alludes to God's chosen people, the Israelites, who crossed the Red Sea (line 11) when God miraculously parted its waters, a story recounted in the book of Exodus. Knowing what these allusions refer to enables us to begin making the connections necessary for understanding the poem. In simple terms, Blake celebrates the power of God and things spiritual while indicting the inadequacy of human reason.

Allusion in poetry can take many forms and surface in many guises. Some allusions are more explicit than others, which may be camouflaged or only hinted at. Moreover, some poets favor a richly allusive style in which the reader's knowledge of history, mythology, philosophy, religion, art, economics, and other subjects is heavily taxed. Two twentieth-century American poets who consistently make such allusive demands are T. S. Eliot (1888–1965) and Ezra Pound (1885–1972).

Although Eliot's "The Waste Land" is his most consistently and complexly allusive poem, he also includes a number of significant allusions in a more accessible poem, "The Love Song of J. Alfred Prufrock" (p. 267). One of the more noteworthy examples of allusion in that poem occurs in these lines:

> In the room, the women come and go
> Talking of Michelangelo.

Most readers of Eliot's poem know that Michelangelo (1475–1564) was a Florentine painter, architect, and sculptor who is generally recognized as one of the greatest and most influential artists of the Western world. His name is familiar even to many who have never seen originals or reproductions of his works of art. Eliot assumes his readers know who Michelangelo was and what he represents, and he invites us to consider what the women are like who "come and go" through the room talking of him. We can't begin to understand what Eliot might be suggesting without recognizing his allusion.

47

Irony Irony is not so much an element of poetry as a tone of voice and attitude found in it. Irony may appear in poetry in three ways: in a poem's language, in its description of incident, and in its point of view. But in whatever form it appears, irony always involves a contrast or discrepancy between one thing and another. The contrast may be between what is said and what is meant, a form of *verbal irony;* between what happens and what is expected to happen, a form of *situational irony;* between what a character sees and what readers see, a form of *dramatic irony.*

Verbal irony appears in the following poem in which the speaker's words seem to say one thing (that war is kind) but actually mean the opposite (that war is brutal). Crane accentuates the opposition between what the words say literally and what they mean figuratively (ironically) by including numerous details that depict the horrors of war.

STEPHEN CRANE

[1871–1900]

♦

War Is Kind

Do not weep, maiden, for war is kind.
Because your lover threw wild hands toward the sky
And the affrighted steed ran on alone,
Do not weep.
War is kind.   5

      Hoarse, booming drums of the regiment,
      Little souls who thirst for fight,
      These men were born to drill and die.
      The unexplained glory flies above them,
      Great is the battle god, great, and his kingdom   10
      A field where a thousand corpses lie.

Do not weep, babe, for war is kind.
Because your father tumbled in the yellow trenches,
Raged at his breast, gulped and died,
Do not weep.   15
War is kind.

     Swift blazing flag of the regiment,
     Eagle with crest of red and gold,
     These men were born to drill and die.
     Point for them the virtue of slaughter,   20
     Make plain to them the excellence of killing
     And a field where a thousand corpses lie.

Mother whose heart hung humble as a button
On the bright splendid shroud of your son,
Do not weep.   25
War is kind.

Situational irony, also known as irony of circumstance, can be illustrated with A. E. Housman's "Is my team plowing." Housman's speaker has died and speaks from beyond death to ask about events occurring in the world of the living. He wonders, for example, about his fiancée's happiness, imagining her still to be mourning his death. This dead speaker is answered by another living one, his friend, who we discover has been answering each of the first speaker's questions. His answer to the dead speaker's final question, particularly the last two lines, contains a surprising revelation. For there we discover something that the dead speaker certainly never desired and probably never suspected. Moreover, it is not clear whether he fully understands the implications of what the living speaker is telling him. For the reader, however, the implications are unmistakably ironic.

A. E. HOUSMAN

[1859–1936]

◆

Is *my team plowing*

"Is my team plowing,
   That I was used to drive
And hear the harness jingle
   When I was man alive?"

Ay, the horses trample,   5
   The harness jingles now;
No change though you lie under
   The land you used to plow.

"Is football playing
   Along the river shore,
With lads to chase the leather,   10
   Now I stand up no more?"

Ay, the ball is flying,
   The lads play heart and soul;
The goal stands, up, the keeper   15
   Stands up to keep the goal.

"Is my girl happy,
   That I thought hard to leave,
And has she tired of weeping
   As she lies down at eve?"   20

Ay, she lies down lightly,
   She lies not down to weep:
Your girl is well contented.
   Be still, my lad, and sleep.

"Is my friend hearty,   25
    Now I am thin and pine,
And has he found to sleep in
    A better bed than mine?"

Yes, lad, I lie easy,
    I lie as lads would choose;   30
I cheer a dead man's sweetheart,
    Never ask me whose.

Dramatic irony occurs when the perceptions of characters differ from the perception of readers. In dramatic irony characters see and understand things one way while readers see and understand them in a different, often an opposite way. Dramatic irony can be illustrated by Thomas Hardy's "The Ruined Maid," in which two friends meet and discuss their different lives. Hardy lets the reader see 'Melia's situation differently from the way either she sees herself or her companion sees her.

THOMAS HARDY

[1840–1928]

♦

The Ruined Maid

"O 'Melia, my dear, this does everything crown!
Who could have supposed I should meet you in Town?
And whence such fair garments, such prosperi-ty?"
"O didn't you know I'd been ruined?" said she.

"You left us in tatters, without shoes or socks,   5
Tired of digging potatoes, and spudding up docks;
And now you've gay bracelets and bright feathers three!"
"Yes: that's how we dress when we're ruined," said she.

"At home in the barton you said 'thee' and 'thou,'
And 'thik oon,' and 'theäs oon,' and 't'other'; but now   10
Your talking quite fits 'ee for high compa-ny!"
"Some polish is gained with one's ruin," said she.

"Your hands were like paws then, your face blue and bleak
But now I'm bewitched by your delicate cheek,
And your little gloves fit as on any la-dy!"   15
"We never do work when we're ruined," said she.

"You used to call home-life a hag-ridden dream,
And you'd sigh, and you'd sock; but at present you seem
To know not of megrims or melancho-ly!"
"True. One's pretty lively when ruined," said she.   20

"I wish I had feathers, a fine sweeping gown,
And a delicate face, and could strut about Town!"
"My dear—a raw country girl, such as you be,
Cannot quite expect that. You ain't ruined," said she.

As in Housman's "Is my team plowing," Hardy's "The Ruined
Maid" includes two speakers. The first speaker is a poor unnamed
country girl; the second is Amelia, or as the speaker calls her, 'Melia. 'Melia has left her little country village for the splendors of the
larger life of the town. There, according to the perspective of the
first speaker, 'Melia has achieved "prosperity." 'Melia's prosperity,
however, has been achieved by becoming "ruined," by selling her
body in prostitution, perhaps simply by being kept as a rich man's
mistress. Part of the poem's irony resides in the first speaker's lack
of understanding of just what 'Melia gave up to achieve her new
position. The poor country girl wants nothing more than to wear
fine clothes and strut about town like her former country friend,
'Melia. Her last comment in the final stanza suggests as much. But
following this last remark of the country girl, Hardy turns the irony
against the town girl, 'Melia, whose ungrammatical country speech
reveals her as one who is still very much the raw, rustic girl she sees

⁹barton *farm.*
¹⁹megrims *low spirits.*

her old friend as being. Hardy in short sees 'Melia differently from the way she sees herself. And so, ultimately, do we.

When poets consistently display an ironic attitude in their work, we can speak of their *ironic vision,* an overall tone that stresses the incongruity between appearance and reality, expectation and actuality. Thomas Hardy wrote many poems in the ironic mode. You can sample the various forms his ironic vision takes by reading the following poems: "Ah, are you digging on my grave?" (p. 207); "The Voice" (p. 209); "Channel Firing" (p. 206); and "The Man He Killed" (p. 210).

Syntax and Structure

Syntax Syntax is the order or sequence of words in a sentence. Poets occasionally alter the normal syntactic order for purposes such as creating a powerful emotional stimulus, effecting a sense of movement, or imitating the action the words of the poem describe. Poets may invert normal word order, as Robert Frost does in the opening line of "Stopping by Woods on a Snowy Evening": "Whose woods these are I think I know." By reversing the two units of four words (I think I know; whose woods these are), Frost avoids the conventional word order of everyday speech: I think I know whose woods these are. At the same time, however, he doesn't wander too far from the sounds of colloquial speech. The effect is thus to lift the line just a little above the discourse of everyday speech without making it sound unduly "poetic."

In this excerpt from "Tell all the Truth but tell it slant," Emily Dickinson's inversions of normal word order create a different effect, one of compression.

> Tell all the Truth but tell it slant—
> Success in Circuit lies
> Too bright for our infirm Delight
> The Truth's superb surprise

Dickinson inverts normal syntax in the second line after establishing it in line 1. She then alters the word order more dramatically by reversing the order of lines 3–4. You can see and hear the difference simply by reconstructing Dickinson's lines in a more conventional syntactic arrangement:

> Tell all the Truth but tell it slant
> [For] Success lies in Circuit
> The superb surprise [of] Truth's (is)
> Too bright for our infirm Delight.

What we lose most dramatically with the more conventional syntax is the steady rhythm that beats in Dickinson's original lines, which are arranged in alternating units of eight and six syllables. This rhythm and more is lost in the noninverted syntax of the alternative rendering of her lines, which also requires the inclusion of additional words to make sense.

Other forms of syntactic structuring used by poets include balance and symmetry as illustrated by Alexander Pope's *An Essay on Man*. In balanced syntax, words are arranged so that phrases, lines, or parts of lines are set off against one another. Such pairings of phrases and lines may parallel one another so that one line or phrase echoes or repeats the idea of another. Or the pairings may be contrastive so that one line or phrase stands in opposition to another. Lines exhibit symmetry when the syntactic balance is exact, as in lines 5–6 of the following example. Pope employs both parallel and contrastive balances in the following excerpt from "Epistle II" (*An Essay On Man*).

> Know then thyself, presume not God to scan;
> The proper study of mankind is Man.
> Placed on this isthmus of a middle state,
> A being darkly wise, and rudely great:
> With too much knowledge for the skeptic side,
> With too much weakness for the Stoic's pride,
> He hangs between; in doubt to act, or rest,
> In doubt to deem himself a god, or beast;
> In doubt his mind or body to prefer,
> Born but to die, and reasoning but to err; . . .
> Created half to rise, and half to fall;
> Great lord of all things, yet a prey to all;
> Sole judge of truth, in endless error hurled:
> The glory, jest, and riddle of the world!

Pope's balanced syntax neatly captures the two-sided, dual nature of man. On the one hand, man is a great lord of creation, the glory of the world, a rational, wise, godlike creature. On the other hand, he is not great but rude, not possessed of certain knowledge but adrift in uncertainty and ignorance. He is less a master of creation than a victim of it, less the glory of the world than something to be puzzled over and even laughed at. In employing a syntactic structure so well suited to his subject (man's dual nature) and meaning, Pope uses what we can call *mimetic syntax*—an order of words that imitate what they describe.

E. E. Cummings uses mimetic syntax for very different purposes (and in a very different style) in the following poem.

E. E. CUMMINGS

[1894–1962]

♦

Me up at does

Me up at does

out of the floor
quietly Stare

a poisoned mouse   5

still who alive

is asking What
have i done that

You wouldn't have

In order to make sense of this poem we must first rearrange it in conventional syntax. We can begin with the subject of the sentence in something like the following manner: "A poisoned mouse, who, still alive, is asking what have i done that you wouldn't have, does quietly stare out of the floor up at me." By inverting and fracturing syntax the way he does, Cummings surprises us into looking more closely not only at his language, but at the experience it conveys. The emotional and intellectual experience in reading Cummings' original poem and our revision differ significantly. Cummings' redistribution of words on the page and his unusual syntactic arrangement compel us to look more deliberately at his subject. We are made to see much more clearly the mouse's point of view. Instead of a speaker looking down at a dying mouse, Cummings creates a perspective in which the dying mouse is looking up at his executioner. The reversal of perspective is accentuated by the reversal of grammatical subject and predicate and the dispersal of phrases in short poetic lines, each of which focuses on one small aspect of the experience.

Other syntactic patterns of poems include syntax organized around the mental associations of the poem's speaker—as in Eliot's "The Love Song of J. Alfred Prufrock" (p. 267). In such poems, sentences may be interrupted by words and phrases that pierce the speaker's memory of one thing while he is speaking of another. Syntax may also follow patterns of rhetorical persuasiveness as in Tennyson's "Ulysses" (p. 181). In such poems, lines, phrases, and sentences suggest a carefully worded argument, a speech given to persuade an audience to take a particular course of action. Syntax may also be designed either toward a poetic smoothness and continuity as in Robert Frost's "The Silken Tent" (p. 237) or toward the ruptured halting quality of broken speech as in Thomas Hardy's "The Man He Killed" (p. 210). In the first case, Frost spins out one single, smoothly flowing sentence over fourteen lines of a sonnet. In the second instance, Hardy uses interrupted words—included between dashes—to suggest the speaker's confusion. These and other deviations from normal syntax are designed to be expressive. They intensify our experience in reading poetry; they alert us to meanings that go beyond individual words and sentences to include the intellectual and emotional implications of unusual verbal arrangements.

Structure   The structure or form of poetry involves patterned arrangements of language. In addition to the grammatical structure of sentences, or syntax, we can also speak of the structure of sound (pp. 68–78) and the structure of larger poetic units—the stanza, section, and whole poem.

Basically, poetic structures can be either open or closed. Poems written in open forms do not follow a prescribed pattern of rhyme or stanzaic structure. They are freer, looser, and less constrained than poems written in closed or fixed forms, which adhere more closely to prescribed requirements concerning line length, rhyme, and stanzaic structure.

The difference is readily apparent when you look at these two poems by Langston Hughes.

LANGSTON HUGHES

[1902–1967]

♦

My People

The night is beautiful,
So the faces of my people.

The stars are beautiful,
So the eyes of my people.

Beautiful, also, is the sun.   5
Beautiful, also, are the souls of my people.

I, Too

I, too, sing America.

I am the darker brother.
They send me to eat in the kitchen
When company comes,
But I laugh,   5
And eat well,
And grow strong.

Tomorrow,
I'll be at the table
When company comes.   10
Nobody'll dare
Say to me,
"Eat in the kitchen,"
Then.

Besides,   15
They'll see how beautiful I am
And be ashamed—

I, too, am America.

The first poem is written according to a tighter formal structure
than the second. Its three stanzas are *couplets,* or two-line units,
with the second line of each couplet ending with the words "of my
people." This parallel language is supported by many other dou-
blings of language: "The night . . . The stars" . . . "So the faces . . .
So the eyes" . . . "Beautiful, also . . . Beautiful, also." There is,
moreover, a gradual intensification, a kind of crescendo as the poem
moves from night through stars to sun; from faces through eyes to
souls. Hughes' other poem is not formless, however. It is framed by
a nearly exact repetition in its opening and closing lines. Even so,

its remaining sixteen lines are spun out over three stanzas of differing numbers of lines of varying lengths, some with only one word.

In comparison with the strictness of traditional, fixed poetic forms, however, both of Hughes' poems exhibit a comparatively free structure. Neither follows the strict formal constraints of a form such as the *sonnet,* for example, with its fourteen lines arranged according to a carefully controlled pattern of accented and unaccented syllables. The *Shakespearean* or *English sonnet* consists of three quatrains or four-line sections, with the rhyme pattern *abab cdcd efef* followed by a rhymed couplet *gg.* The following poem exemplifies the English, or Shakespearean sonnet form.

EDNA ST. VINCENT MILLAY

[1892–1950]

♦

I *dreamed* I *moved among the Elysian fields*

I dreamed I moved among the Elysian fields,
In converse with sweet women long since dead;
And out of blossoms which that meadow yields
I wove a garland for your living head.
Danae, that was the vessel for a day   5
Of golden Jove, I saw, and at her side,
Whom Jove the Bull desired and bore away,
Europa stood, and the Swan's featherless bride.
All these were mortal women, yet all these
Above the ground had had a god for guest;   10
Freely I walked beside them and at ease,
Addressing them, by them again addressed,
And marvelled nothing, for remembering you,
Wherefore I was among them well I knew.

We can chart the rhyme pattern of the sonnet by designating each rhyming sound with a letter in this manner:

fields	*a*
dead	*b*
yields	*a*
head	*b*
day	*c*
side	*d*
away	*c*
bride	*d*
these	*e*
guest	*f*
ease	*e*
addressed	*f*
you	*g*
knew	*g*

The punctuation of the poem corresponds to its structure of rhyme. And the organization of its sentences approximates its rhyme pattern of three quatrains and a couplet. In the first quatrain, the speaker wanders in the Elysian fields (a mythological paradise) and talks with women who died long before. As she talks, she weaves a garland for her lover's head. The second and third quatrains name three women who were seduced by Jove (Zeus in Greek mythology), the chief god of the Roman pantheon. Jove descended upon Danae, a lovely maiden, as a shower of gold; he carried away Europa after disguising himself as a bull; and in the form of a swan, he raped Leda. The final couplet contains a surprising twist: the speaker feels comfortable talking with these women whom Jove singled out. She feels similarly honored, considering her lover a living god.

The *Italian,* or *Petrarchan sonnet,* is another common sonnet form. It typically falls into two parts: an octave of eight lines and a sestet of six. The octave rhyme pattern is *abba abba;* the rhymes of the sestet are more variable. Some common variations include *cde cde;* or *cde ced;* or *cd cd cd;* or *cde dce.* The following sonnet, again by Edna St. Vincent Millay, exemplifies the Petrarchan, or Italian sonnet form:

What lips my lips have kissed, and where, and why

What lips my lips have kissed, and where, and why,
I have forgotten, and what arms have lain
Under my head till morning; but the rain
Is full of ghosts tonight, that tap and sigh
Upon the glass and listen for reply,   5
And in my heart there stirs a quiet pain
For unremembered lads that not again
Will turn to me at midnight with a cry.
Thus in the winter stands the lonely tree,
Nor knows what birds have vanished one by one,   10
Yet knows its boughs more silent than before:
I cannot say what loves have come and gone,
I only know that summer sang in me
A little while, that in me sings no more.

Composed as two sentences of eight and six lines respectively, this sonnet breaks neatly into syntactic units that parallel the two-part structure of the Italian sonnet. It also adheres to the form's rhyme scheme: *abba abba; cde dce* (with a slight variation in the rhymes of the sestet).

The octave describes the speaker's feelings as she remembers her former lovers. Although she doesn't recall specific details, she feels their loss, as she is presumably now alone. In line 9 the poem turns to an image of a tree in which birds once sang but which is now abandoned. The shift to this image after the personal exposition in lines 1–8 is characteristic of the Petrarchan sonnet, which frequently changes direction in the first line of the sestet. In the second half of the sestet (lines 12–14) the poet explicitly compares the speaker's lonely predicament with that of the birdless tree.

The two sonnet forms offer different possibilities for poets. The English sonnet is particularly well suited to a theme and variations pattern. In such an arrangement an idea is expressed in the first quatrain and is followed by a pair of varied restatements with different examples or images in the second and third quatrains. The sonnet then concludes with a couplet that serves as a summary or ironic commentary on the idea. The Petrarchan form is especially well suited to the statement of a problem in the octet followed by its solution in the sestet. The Petrarchan form also functions well to capture radical shifts of direction, especially contrasts in tone, idea, and feeling. Millay has exploited the possibilities inherent in both forms with her two carefully structured sonnets.

Closed and open forms represent two general strucural possibilities poets may adopt and modify to suit their expressive purposes. In learning to discern form in poetry, you should notice recurring patterns, recognize shifts of emphasis, changes of tone and mood, and consider the relationship of one part of a poem to another. If a poem is arranged in two stanzas, it is important to consider why, and to ask how the two sections are related. Look, for example, at Ben Jonson's "Still to be neat, still to be dressed" (p. 111), Robert Herrick's "Upon Julia's Clothes" (p. 112), and Walt Whitman's "A Noiseless Patient Spider" (p. 190). Identify the focus of each poem's two stanzas. Then consider how each of the poem's second stanzas relates to its opening stanza. Moreover, if a poem is set up as three or more stanzas, it is necessary to consider what happens in each stanza and how the parts are related. Consider whether any significant changes occur from one stanza to another. Consider what each stanza focuses on, and whether the stanzas together suggest a shifting perspective on experience (Donne's "Song," p. 105), a changing set of attitudes (Larkin's "A Study of Reading Habits," p. 329), a movement from description to reflection to feeling (Wordsworth's "The Solitary Reaper," p. 135)—or something else.

Conversely, if a poem displays no discernible large-scale structural units like stanzas or verse paragraphs, it may be useful to create them yourself. Walt Whitman's "When I heard the learn'd astronomer" (p. 73) and Robert Frost's "Birches" (p. 234) are printed without stanza breaks. Yet each contains natural divisions that we can sense as we read them. In reading these poems, decide for yourself where the poem shifts direction, where it turns to something different, where it changes in some significant way. In discerning such internal shifts within a poem, you will experience the poem the way the poet designed it. Experiencing such structural design will help you understand the poem.

Form is necessary for poetic art. It makes poetry expressive. It makes it memorable and meaningful. Ultimately, moreover, it is form that makes it poetry.

Rhythm and Meter

Rhythm is the pulse or beat we feel in a line of prose, poetry, or music. It is a pattern of regularly recurring accents or stresses on the syllables of words in a poem or a song. We are familiar with such rhythmic patterning from patriotic songs such as "America the Beautiful." Note the accented or stressed syllables, which we have capitalized.

> Oh BEAUtiFUL for SPAcious SKIES
> For AMber WAVES of GRAIN
> For PURple MOUNtains' MAjesTY
> aBOVE the FRUIted PLAIN
>
> aMERiCA aMERiCA
> God SHED His GRACE on THEE
> And CROWN thy GOOD with BROtherHOOD
> From SEA to SHIning SEA.

An alternative and more conventional way to represent accented or stressed syllables is with a diagonal slash over the syllable: ´. Unaccented syllables are marked with a short line curving upward: ˘. We can mark the syllables of words to indicate stress in any text, whether poetry or prose. For example, this is the opening sentence of Charles Dickens's *A Tale of Two Cities* with stress markings:

> Ĭt wás thĕ bést ŏf tímes; ĭt wás thĕ wórst ŏf tímes.

And here are portions of two familiar nursery rhymes, also with their accented syllables identified.

> Báa Báa bláck shéep! Háve yŏu ánў wóol?

> Lóndŏn Brídge ĭs Fálliňg Dówn
> Fálliňg Dówn, Fálliňg Dówn
> Lóndŏn Brídge ĭs Fálliňg Dówn
> Mý fáir ládў.

Meter is the measuring of the patterns of accent or stress in poetry. Just as music is divided into measures with accented and unaccented beats, language is also divided into patterns of stressed and
unstressed syllables. The basic unit of meter in poetry is called the
foot. Depending upon where the stresses fall, a poetic foot may be
iambic, trochaic, anapestic or dactylic. An *iambic foot,* or *iamb* (˘ ´)
is a two-syllable foot consisting of an unaccented syllable followed
by an accented one, as in the words *hello* and *goodbye*. If we reverse
the order of accented and unaccented syllables, placing the stress on
the first syllable, we have a *trochaic foot,* or *trochee* (´ ˘), as in the
words *story* and *poem*. Because both iambic and trochaic feet contain two syllables per foot, they are called *duple* (or double) *meters*.
These duple meters are distinguished from the triple meters (three-
syllable feet) of anapestic and dactylic meters. An *anapestic foot,* or
anapest (˘ ˘ ´), consists of two unaccented syllables followed by an
accented one, as in *obsolete* and *interject*. A *dactylic foot,* or *dactyl*
(´ ˘ ˘), reverses the anapest's order of accents, beginning with an accented syllable followed by two unaccented ones, as in *frivolous* and
anxiously.

Three additional points must be noted about poetic meter. First,
two accented syllables together are called a *spondee* (kníck-knáck);
two unaccented syllables together are called a *pyrrhic* (ŏf thĕ).
Spondaic and pyrrhic feet serve as substitutes for iambic and trochaic feet. Neither can serve as the metrical norm for a poem in English. Second, anapestic (˘ ˘ ´) and iambic (˘ ´) meters move from an
unstressed syllable to a stressed one. For this reason they are called
rising meters. (They "rise" to the stressed syllable.) Lines in anapestic or iambic meter almost always end with a stressed syllable.
Trochaic (´ ˘) and dactylic (´ ˘ ˘) meters, on the other hand, are said
to be *falling meters* because they begin with a stressed syllable.
(They "fall" in pitch and emphasis.) Thus syllables at the ends of
trochaic and dactylic lines are generally unstressed. Third, we give
names to lines of poetry based on the number of feet they contain.
An eight-syllable or octosyllabic line composed of four iambic feet
is called *iambic tetrameter*. *Iambic* describes the metrical pattern;
tetrameter indicates the number of feet in each line (from the Greek
word *tetra* for four). Robert Frost's "Stopping by Woods on a
Snowy Evening" (p. 239) is one poem written in iambic tetrameter.
His sonnet, "The Silken Tent" (p. 237), which contains ten-syllable

lines in an iambic meter is described as being in iambic *pentameter* (from the Greek *penta,* meaning five). Sonnets in fact are typically written in iambic pentameter.

The following chart summarizes the various meters and poetic feet.

	Foot	Meter	Example
Rising or Ascending Feet	iamb	iambic	hĕlló
	anapest	anapestic	ŏbsŏléte
Falling or Descending Feet	trochee	trochaic	stórў
	dactyl	dactylic	ańxĭouslУ
Substitute Feet	spondee	spondaic	kník-knáck
	pyrrhic	pyrrhic	[hít] ŏf thc [yćar]

Duple Meters: two syllables per foot; iambic and trochaic
Triple Meters: three syllables per foot: anapestic and dactylic

Number of feet per line

one foot	monometer
two feet	dimeter
thrcc feet	trimeter
four feet	tetrameter
five feet	pentameter
six feet	hexameter
seven feet	heptameter
eight feet	octameter

In determining a poem's prevailing meter, it is important to retain a sense of the logic of its sentences. It is necessary, therefore, to hear the metrical beat while simultaneously accenting words of a line because of their position and importance in a sentence rather than merely as part of a metrical pattern of stressed and unstressed syllables. In reading the poems on pages 66–67, we need to feel the iambic pulse beating in the lines. But we should also hear the sense made by the sentences. Sometimes metrical accent and sentence emphasis will coincide. At other times there will be tension between them. In such cases readers may feel pulled in two directions at once.

We confront a similar problem of emphasis in reading poems with *enjambed* or *run-on lines*. *End-stopped* lines contain a pause or stop at the end of the line, indicated by a punctuation mark. When there is no mark of punctuation, and where the sense of the sentence remains incomplete until the next line, we experience a double commitment. On the one hand, we are inclined to stop at the end of the line (after all, it is a poem with lines and perhaps rhymes clearly indicated). On the other hand, we are also propelled past the end of the line, rhyme or not, since the sense of the sentence demands completion in the line or lines that follow it. Preserving a balance between such competing impulses is one of the challenges of writing poetry and one of the pleasures of reading it.

To practice hearing the rhythm and meter of poems, read the following poems aloud. Identify the accented syllables and the prevailing meter.

COUNTEE CULLEN

[1903–1946]

♦

Incident

Once riding in old Baltimore,
　　Heart-filled, head-filled with glee,
I saw a Baltimorean
　　Keep looking straight at me.

Now I was eight and very small,　　　　　　　　　　5
　　And he was no whit bigger,
And so I smiled, but he poked out
　　His tongue and called me, "Nigger."

I saw the whole of Baltimore
　　From May until December:　　　　　　　　　　10
Of all the things that happened there
　　That's all that I remember.

66

EMILY DICKINSON

[1830–1886]

◆

Because I could not stop for Death

Because I could not stop for Death—
He kindly stopped for me—
The Carriage held but just Ourselves—
And Immortality.

We slowly drove—He knew no haste   5
And I had put away
My labor and my leisure too,
For His Civility—

We passed the School, where Children strove
At Recess—in the Ring—   10
We passed the Fields of Gazing Grain—
We passed the Setting Sun—

Or rather—He passed Us—
The Dews drew quivering and chill—
For only Gossamer, my Gown—   15
My Tippet—only Tulle—

We paused before a House that seemed
A Swelling of the Ground—
The Roof was scarcely visible—
The Cornice—in the Ground—   20

Since then—'tis Centuries—and yet
Feels shorter than the Day
I first surmised the Horses' Heads
Were toward Eternity—

---

[16]**Tippet** *scarf or stole.*

Sound and Sense

Rhyme   The sound of poems is an important ingredient of meaning and a significant conveyor of feeling. Sound, in fact, contributes to sense. Perhaps the most familiar and certainly the most common form of poetic sound effect is *rhyme,* the matching of final vowel and consonant sounds in two or more words. The alternating lines rhyme in the following stanza from Edward Arlington Robinson's "Richard Cory."

> Whenever Richard Cory went downtown,
> We people on the pavement looked at him:
> He was a gentleman from sole to crown,
> Clean favored, and imperially slim.

Although such alternating rhymes are common in poetry, also common is the rhyming of successive lines, as in this concluding couplet from Shakespeare's "When in disgrace with fortune and men's eyes."

> For thy sweet love remembered such wealth brings
> That then I scorn to change my state with kings.

Both of these examples employ what we call *end rhyme,* or rhymes at the ends of lines. On occasion, however, poets will rhyme words within a line with an end-of-line sound, thus producing *internal rhyme,* as in this example from Edgar Allan Poe's "Annabel Lee."

> For the moon never **beams** without bringing me **dreams**
> Of the beautiful Annabel Lee;
> And the stars never **rise** but I see the bright **eyes**
> Of the beautiful Annabel Lee;

Both Poe's internal rhyming and Shakespeare's end rhyming exemplify exact or perfect rhyme. In *perfect rhyme,* the rhymed words share the same number of syllables and stresses while echoing the same vowel and consonant sounds. When this is not the case, when rhymes are imperfect, we call them *slant rhymes* or *approximate rhymes* (because they approximate perfect rhymes.)

Emily Dickinson frequently employs slant rhyme in varying approximations of perfect rhyme. The following poem exemplifies slant rhyme with "Door"/"more"; "Gate"/"Mat";"One"/"Stone"; the last pair comes closest to exact rhyme. In addition, the poem illustrates *feminine rhyme,* which is the rhyming of words ending in unaccented syllables. Feminine rhyme occurs on "nation"/"attention"—really a slant feminine rhyme. *Masculine rhyme,* by contrast, occurs on accented final syllables or on one-syllable words, as in the rhymes on "him"/"slim" from "Richard Cory" and "brings"/"kings" from Shakespeare's "When in disgrace with fortune and men's eyes" (see p. 68).

EMILY DICKINSON

[1830–1886]

♦

The Soul selects her own Society

The Soul selects her own Society—
Then—shuts the Door—
To her divine Majority—
Present no more—

Unmoved—she notes the Chariots—passing—   5
At her low Gate—
Unmoved—an Emperor be kneeling
Upon her Mat—

I've known her—from an ample nation—
Choose One—   10
Then—close the Valves of her attention—
Like Stone—

For readers, rhyme is a pleasure; for poets, a challenge. Part of its pleasure for readers is in anticipating and hearing a poem's echoing sounds. Part of its challenge for poets is in rhyming naturally, without forcing the rhythm, the syntax, or the sense. When the challenge is successfully met, a poem is a pleasure to listen to; it sounds natural to the ear, and its rhyme makes it easier to remember.

Alliteration, Assonance, and Onomatopoeia   In addition to rhyme, poets frequently employ other devices of sound. Three of the more prominent devices are alliteration, assonance, and onomatopoeia. *Onomatopoeia* is the use of words to imitate the sounds they describe. *Clank* and *buzz* are onomatopoetic, since they sound like the noises the words describe. *Assonance* is the repetition of vowel sounds; *alliteration* is the repetition of consonant sounds, especially at the beginning of words. The first stanza of Alfred Tennyson's "The Eagle" exemplifies alliteration.

> He clasps the crag with crooked hands;
> Close to the sun in lonely lands,
> Ringed with the azure world, he stands.

Tennyson's use of the hard *c* sounds that are echoed in the similarly hard *g* and *k* sounds together suggest the strength of the eagle. The softer, more liquid *l* sounds provide a contrast in sound. The repetitions of "the" and the rhyming of "hands," "lands," and "stands" knit the stanza in a tight web of sound.

Assonance appears along with alliteration in the last stanza of Gerard Manley Hopkins' "Inversnaid."

> What would the world be, once bereft
> Of wet and of wildness? Let them be left,
> O let them be left, wildness and wet;
> Long live the weeds and the wilderness yet.

Hopkins makes an even more intense and rich use of sound than Tennyson does in his poem about the eagle. Hopkins uses alliteration with the repeated *l*'s and *w*'s. Both are soft sounds easy on the voice and ear. They harmonize eloquently with the heavy repeated assonantal *i*'s and *e*'s. The long *i* of "wildness" balances the short *i* of "live" and "wilderness"; the long *e* of "be" and "weeds" balances the short *e* of "let," "wet," "left," and "bereft." Hopkins intensifies his musical harmonies by repeating words and rhyming both within and at the ends of lines.

As the eighteenth-century poet Alexander Pope has written, "Sound must seem an echo to the sense." Pope follows his own advice in describing the Greek warrior, Ajax, in his attempt to use a boulder as a weapon.

> When Ajax strives, some rock's vast weight to throw.

Pope clusters consonants together in a line whose sound imitates the struggle it describes. But it must be read aloud for Pope's achievement to be truly discernible. In an even more elaborate use of sound to echo sense, John Dryden (1631–1700) imitates the sound of musical instruments in his "A Song for St. Cecilia's Day." He tailors his language carefully to represent the sounds made by different instruments.

> The trumpet's loud clangor
>   Excites us to arms,
> With shrill notes of anger
>   And mortal alarms.
> The double double double beat
>   Of the thundering drum
> Cries "Hark! the foes come;
> Charge, charge, 'tis too late to retreat!"
>
> The soft complaining flute
> In dying notes discovers
> The woes of hopeless lovers,
> Whose dirge is whispered by the warbling lute.

Dryden employs onomatopoeia in describing the "clangor" of the trumpet, the "thundering" of the drum, and the "whispered" tone of the flute. The uses of onomatopoeia are embellished by alliterative *w*'s in the final lines of stanza three and by the repeated "double" and *d* sounds in stanza two. Assonance enriches the musical harmony, especially in stanza three with its play of long and short *o* sounds in "soft," "notes," "woes," and "hopeless"; "complaining," "discovers," and "lovers." Rhymes in all three stanzas complete the play of sound.

Such a use of sound to echo sense and convey experience is one of the most distinctive features of poetry. It is also one of poetry's loveliest pleasures. In the following poem consider how Helen Chasin exploits assonance, alliteration, and onomatopoeia to convey the feeling of eating a plum. Slowly read the poem aloud a few times. Try to feel the words in your mouth. Taste the words and perhaps you'll also taste Chasin's plum.

HELEN CHASIN

[b. 1938]

♦

The Word Plum

The word *plum* is delicious

pout and push, luxury of
self-love, and savoring murmur

full in the mouth and falling
like fruit   5

taut skin
pierced, bitten, provoked into
juice, and tart flesh

question
and reply, lip and tongue   10
of pleasure.

Application   To show how all the elements of poetry work together to create meaning and convey feeling, we consider the following poem from the standpoint of its poetic elements.

WALT WHITMAN

[1819–1892]

♦

When I heard the learn'd astronomer

When I heard the learn'd astronomer,
When the proofs, the figures, were ranged in columns
    before me,
When I was shown the charts and diagrams, to add,
    divide, and measure them,
When I sitting heard the astronomer where he lectured
    with much applause in the lecture-room,
How soon unaccountable I became tired and sick,   5
Till rising and gliding out I wander'd off by myself,
In the mystical moist night-air, and from time to time,
Look'd up in perfect silence at the stars.

Speaker and Situation   The situation of this poem is clear and
very likely familiar to most readers. The speaker is a student sitting
in a lecture hall listening to a lecture. As the astronomer lectures,
the speaker becomes increasingly discontented. Finally, when he
can no longer stand it, he leaves the lecture hall and walks out into
the starry night. Although the speaker does not give reasons for his
becoming tired and sick, we suspect it has something to do with a
discrepancy between what he needs at the time and what he is experiencing. The lecture, presumably, bores him. Interestingly
enough, others in the audience seem to enjoy it, and applaud the

lecturer approvingly. The speaker's experience, however, is different. He goes off into the night alone.

Diction and Imagery   The language of the poem is simple. Most of its words are familiar. Many are monosyllabic. A few ("When" and "I") are repeated. You will notice a difference between the way Whitman spells "learn'd" and "look'd" and the way we spell those words today. You notice too how "night-air" has been hyphenated to make it a single term rather than a paired adjective and noun. Other than these minor verbal details, the words of the poem should pose no problems for most readers.

There are, however, a few noteworthy features of the poem's language. One, of course, is the preponderance of mathematical words ("proofs," "figures," "columns," "add," and "divide") in lines 2–3. These are supplemented by other words ("charts," "diagrams," and "astronomer") suggesting science. Such mathematical and scientific terms are absent from the last four lines of the poem. In those lines, instead of words suggesting quantification, measurement, and numerical description, we find words that describe feelings ("tired and sick"), sense experience ("moist"), and nature ("stars"). And one word ("mystical") describes something that transcends all these things.

The poem is relatively devoid of imagistic detail. Rather than presenting us with a specific set of details that describe the astronomer's words, actions, gestures, clothing, and so on, we are given a more general picture of an astronomer using various traditional and general charts and diagrams to explain some unidentified astronomical phenomena. This very lack of specific detail is important. For it suggests that it is not the astronomy lecture itself that matters but rather the speaker's reaction to it.

Figures of Speech   Figures of speech are absent from this poem. Their absence is noteworthy because it indicates in yet another way the directness and simplicity of the poem.

Allusion and Irony   There are no allusions in the poem. Nor is there the slightest hint of irony.

Syntax and Structure The poem is cast as a single long sentence. Its structure is readily apparent: Four subordinate clauses, each beginning with "when," are followed by an independent clause that describes the speaker's actions. The only line not completely regular in its word order is line 5. Whitman could have begun the line with "I." And he also could have reversed the words "tired and sick" to read: "sick and tired." By avoiding these more familiar syntactical arrangements, Whitman avoids predictability and cliché. He achieves a poetic freshness that allows the words to resonate more powerfully.

Even though the poem is a single sentence spun out over eight uneven lines, it can be divided into two parts of four lines each. This two-part division accentuates a set of contrasts at the heart of the poem. Most important to the poem's *plot*, or action, is the speaker's passivity as he listens to the lecturer. He sits, he listens, he watches. In the second half of the poem, however, he is shown acting rather than being acted upon. He rises, wanders off, and looks at the stars. This contrast is reflected in the verb tenses in the poem's two parts: Lines 1–4 contain a number of verbs in the passive voice, such as, "were ranged" and "was shown"; lines 5–8 contain verbs in the active voice, such as, "wander'd" and "Look'd." In both cases the speaker is the grammatical subject; in the first instance, however, he is passive and in the second he is active.

Other important distinctions between the poem's two parts include the speaker's actions of sitting and standing and his being part of a group versus his isolation. He wanders off, he tells us, "by myself." There is even a contrast in his manner of going: His gliding out and wandering off suggest a stance more open to experience, less rigidly prescribed than sitting in place listening to someone talk. Still another contrast between the parts includes the noise of the lecture hall comprised of the astronomer's voice and the audience's applause with the "perfect silence" of the speaker looking at the stars.

These contrasts, moreover, serve to accentuate the poem's movement from one kind of learning to another: from passive listening to active observation, from indirect factual knowledge to direct mystical apprehension. Instead of listening to scientific explanations of the stars, the speaker puts himself into a mysterious spiritual communion with them. Whether the poet or speaker actually rejects the first form of knowledge for the second, or whether he suggests that both are necessary, is not directly stated. The emphasis, nonetheless, is on the speaker's need to be alone and to experience nature directly.

Rhythm and Meter Whitman's poem is written in *free verse* or verse without a fixed metrical pattern. "When I heard the learn'd astronomer" is characteristic of much free verse in its varying line lengths and accents per line and in its imitation of the cadences of speech. The last line of the poem, however, differs from the others. It seems to be organized in an iambic pattern of five feet, making it an iambic pentameter line. We can scan it like this:

Lŏok'd úp iň pérfečt sílěnce át thĕ stárs.

This line of strict iambic pentameter carries considerable expressive power since it follows the seemingly casual metrical organization (free verse) of the previous seven lines. To feel its expressive impact fully, you need to reread the line in the context of the whole poem and to read it aloud.

In addition to the expressive use of metrical variation, this poem exhibits additional elements of rhythmic control. Its long lines contain breaks or pauses (*caesuras*) in different places; its short lines contain no caesuras at all; and all its lines regardless of length are consistently end-stopped. Moreover, as we noted earlier, the first four lines all begin with the same word: "When," and three of the four lines begin with "When I." Such repetition and variations in rhythm and meter give the poem great flexibility and naturalness. Reading it, we sense that it is poetry, even though its structure is open, its meter is free, its line lengths are variable, and rhyme is absent.

To gain a greater appreciation of Whitman's rhythmical accomplishment in this poem, read the following alternative abbreviated versions.

> When I heard the learn'd astronomer,
> When the proofs, the figures
> Were ranged in columns before me,

When I was shown the charts and diagrams
To add, divide, and measure them,
When I sitting heard the astronomer
Where he lectured to much applause
In the lecture-room. . . .

Or:

When I heard
The learn'd astronomer,
When the proofs,
The figures were ranged
In columns
Before me,
When I was shown
The charts and diagrams
To add, divide and
Measure them. . . .

Sound and Sense   We have already remarked on the absence of rhyme in "When I heard the learn'd astronomer." But this was an exaggeration. The poem does include a moderate degree of assonance, which is a form of rhyme. Although most of the poem's vowel music is concentrated in the last four lines, the long *i*'s begin in lines 1, 3, and 4, then accumulate and gather force in lines 5–8. The relevant words are these: "*I*," "t*i*red," "r*i*sing," "gl*i*ding," "*I*," "myself," "n*i*ght," "t*i*me to t*i*me," and "s*i*lence." To some extent this assonantal music is hidden in the poem, since most of the words with this lone *i* sound are dispersed rather than congregated in the same place. Nonetheless, the assonance sweetens the sound of the poem as it reaches its conclusion, highlighting its radical shift of action and feeling.

Before leaving the poem, we should note that Whitman's rhythmic effects work together with other devices of sound, structure, and diction. In the same way, for example, that the strict iambic pentameter of the last line varies the prevailing meter expressively, so too does the poem's assonance deviate expressively from the previously established avoidance of vowel music. In addition, the meter of the final line stresses the words "silence" and "stars," both of which the speaker values and celebrates. As in any good poem, rhythm, meter, and sound work together to accentuate the poem's meaning. Sound supports and enlivens sense.

Part Two

꙰

ANTHOLOGY
OF POEMS

SAPPHO

[fl. ca. 610–ca. 580 B.C.]

♦

To me he seems like a god

To me he seems like a god
as he sits facing you and
hears you near as you speak
softly and laugh
in a sweet echo that jolts   5
the heart in my ribs. For now
as I look at you my voice
is empty and

can say nothing as my tongue
cracks and slender fire is quick   10
under my skin. My eyes are dead
to light, my ears

pound, and sweat pours over me.
I convulse, paler than grass,
and feel my mind slip as I   15
go close to death

[but must suffer all, being poor.]

TRANSLATED BY WILLIS BARNSTONE

Anonymous

◆

Western Wind

Westron wynde when wyll thow blow
the smalle rayne downe can rayne
Chryst yf my love were in my armys
and I yn my bed agayne[†]

Western wind, when will thou blow,
  The small rain down can rain?
Christ, if my love were in my arms
  And I in my bed again!

Anonymous

◆

Edward, Edward

I

"Why does your brand sae drap wi' bluid,
  Edward, Edward,
Why does your brand sae drap wi' bluid,
  And why sae sad gang ye, O?"

[†]As the poem appeared in 1500 when it was first written.

[1]**brand** *sword* / **sae** *so* / **bluid** *blood.*
[4]**gang** *go.*

"O I ha'e killed my hawke sae guid, 5
    Mither, mither,
O I ha'e killed my hawke sae guid,
    And I had nae mair but he, O."

II

"Your hawke's bluid was never sae reid, 10
    Edward, Edward,
Your hawke's bluid was never sae reid,
    My dear son I tell thee, O."
"O I ha'e killed my reid-roan steed,
    Mither, mither,
O I ha'e killed my reid-roan steed, 15
    That erst was sae fair and free, O."

III

"Your steed was auld, and ye ha'e got mair,
    Edward, Edward,
Your steed was auld, and ye ha'e got mair,
    Some other dule ye drie, O." 20
"O I ha'e killed my fader dear,
    Mither, mither,
O I ha'e killed my fader dear,
    Alas, and wae is me, O!"

IV

"And whatten penance wul ye drie for that, 25
    Edward, Edward?
And whatten penance wul ye drie for that,
    My dear son, now tell me O?"

---

[5]**guid** *good.*
[10]**reid** *red.*
[20]**dule** *grief* / **drie** *suffer.*
[24]**wae** *woe.*
[25]**whatten** *what kind of.*

"I'll set my feet in yonder boat,
    Mither, mither,   30
I'll set my feet in yonder boat,
    And I'll fare over the sea, O."

V

"And what wul ye do wi' your towers and your ha',
    Edward, Edward?
And what wul ye do wi' your towers and your ha',   35
    That were sae fair to see, O?"
"I'll let them stand tul down they fa',
    Mither, mither,
I'll let them stand tul down they fa',
    For here never mair maun I be, O."   40

VI

"And what wul ye leave to your bairns and your wife,
    Edward, Edward?
And what wul ye leave to your bairns and your wife,
    When ye gang over the sea, O?"
"The warlde's room, let them beg thrae life,   45
    Mither, mither,
The warlde's room, let them beg thrae life,
    For them never mair wul I see, O."

VII

"And what wul ye leave to your ain mither dear,
    Edward, Edward?   50
And what wul ye leave to your ain mither dear,
    My dear son, now tell me, O?"

[40]maun *must.*
[41]bairns *children.*
[45]thrae *through.*

"The curse of hell frae me sall ye bear,
    Mither, mither,
The curse of hell frae me sall ye bear,   55
    Sic counsels ye gave to me, O."

Anonymous

◆

The Twa Corbies

As I was walking all alane,
I heard twa corbies making a mane;
The tane unto the t'other say,
"Where sall we gang and dine today?"

"In behint yon auld fail dyke,   5
I wot there lies a new slain knight;
And naebody kens that he lies there,
But his hawk, his hound, and lady fair.

"His hound is to the hunting gane,
His hawk to fetch the wild-fowl hame,   10
His lady's ta'en another mate,
So we may mak our dinner sweet.

[53]**frae** *from* / **sall** *shall.*
[56]**sic** *such.*

[2]**corbies** *ravens* / **mane** *moan.*
[3]**tane** *one.*
[4]**gang** *go.*
[5]**dyke** *turf wall.*
[6]**wot** *know.*
[7]**kens** *knows.*

"Ye'll sit on his white hause-bane,
And I'll pike out his bonny blue een;
Wi' ae lock o' his gowden hair   15
We'll theek our nest when it grows bare.

"Mony a one for him makes mane,
But nane sall ken where he is gane;
O'er his white banes, when they are bare,
The wind sall blaw for evermair."   20

JOHN SKELTON

[1460–1529]

♦

To Mistress Margaret Hussey

Merry Margaret,
   As midsummer flower,
Gentle as falcon
Or hawk of the tower:
With solace and gladness,   5
Much mirth and no madness,
All good and no badness;
   So joyously,
   So maidenly,
   So womanly   10
Her demeaning
In every thing,
Far, far passing

[13]**hause-bane** *neck bone.*
[14]**een** *eyes.*
[15]**ae** *one.*
[16]**theek** *thatch.*

That I can indite,
　Or suffice to write   15
Of Merry Margaret
　　As midsummer flower,
Gentle as falcon
Or hawk of the tower.
　As patient and still   20
And as full of good will
As fair Isaphill,
Coriander,
Sweet pomander,
Good Cassander,   25
Steadfast of thought,
Well made, well wrought,
Far may be sought
Ere that ye can find
So courteous, so kind   30
As Merry Margaret,
　This midsummer flower,
Gentle as falcon
Or hawk of the tower.

---

[14]indite *say.*
[22]Isaphill *Hypsipyle, queen of an island in the Aegean Sea (Lemnos). Famed for her devotion to her father and children.*
[23]coriander *an aromatic medicinal herb.*
[24]pomander *a perfumed ball.*
[25]Cassander *Cassandra, a steadfast prophet.*

THOMAS WYATT

[1503–1542]

♦

They flee from me

They flee from me, that sometime did me seek,
With naked foot stalking in my chamber.
I have seen them, gentle, tame, and meek,
That now are wild, and do not remember
That sometime they put themselves in danger   5
To take bread at my hand; and now they range,
Busily seeking with a continual change.

Thanked be Fortune it hath been otherwise,
Twenty times better; but once in special,
In thin array, after a pleasant guise,   10
When her loose gown from her shoulders did fall,
And she me caught in her arms long and small,
And therewith all sweetly did me kiss
And softly said, "Dear heart, how like you this?"

It was no dream, I lay broad waking.   15
But all is turned, thorough my gentleness,
Into a strange fashion of forsaking;
And I have leave to go, of her goodness.
And she also to use newfangleness.
But since that I so kindly am served,   20
I fain would know what she hath deserved.

[12]small *thin.*
[16]thorough *through.*

HENRY HOWARD, EARL OF SURREY

[ca. 1517–1547]

◆

My friend, the things that do attain

My friend, the things that do attain
The happy life be these, I find:
The riches left, not got with pain;
The fruitful ground; the quiet mind;

The equal friend; no grudge, no strife;   5
No charge of rule, nor governance;
Without disease, the healthy life;
The household of continuance;

The mean diet, no dainty fare;
Wisdom joined with simpleness;   10
The night dischargéd of all care,
Where wine the wit may not oppress;

The faithful wife, without debate;
Such sleeps as may beguile the night;
Content thyself with thine estate,   15
Neither wish death, nor fear his might.

SIR WALTER RALEGH

[ca. 1552–1618]

♦

The Lie

Go, soul, the body's guest,
Upon a thankless errand;
Fear not to touch the best;
The truth shall be thy warrant.
Go, since I needs must die,   5
And give the world the lie.

Say to the court, it glows
And shines like rotten wood;
Say to the church, it shows
What's good, and doth no good.   10
If church and court reply,
Then give them both the lie.

Tell potentates, they live
Acting by others' action;
Not loved unless they give,   15
Not strong but by a faction.
If potentates reply,
Give potentates the lie.

Tell men of high condition,
That manage the estate,   20
Their purpose is ambition,
Their practice only hate.
And if they once reply,
Then give them all the lie.

Tell them that brave it most,   25
They beg for more by spending,
Who, in their greatest cost,
Seek nothing but commending.
And if they make reply,
Then give them all the lie.   30

Tell zeal it wants devotion;
Tell love it is but lust;
Tell time it is but motion;
Tell flesh it is but dust.
And wish them not reply,   35
For thou must give the lie.

Tell age it daily wasteth;
Tell honor how it alters;
Tell beauty how she blasteth;
Tell favor how it falters.   40
And as they shall reply,
Give every one the lie.

Tell wit how much it wrangles
In tickle points of niceness;
Tell wisdom she entangles   45
Herself in overwiseness.
And when they do reply,
Straight give them both the lie.

Tell physic of her boldness;
Tell skill it is pretension;   50
Tell charity of coldness;
Tell law it is contention.
And as they do reply,
So give them still the lie.

---

⁴⁴**tickle** *delicate.*

Tell fortune of her blindness;   55
Tell nature of decay;
Tell friendship of unkindness;
Tell justice of delay.
And if they will reply,
Then give them all the lie.   60

Tell arts they have no soundness,
But vary by esteeming;
Tell schools they want profoundness,
And stand too much on seeming.
If arts and schools reply,   65
Give arts and schools the lie.

Tell faith it's fled the city;
Tell how the country erreth;
Tell manhood shakes off pity;
Tell virtue least preferreth.   70
And if they do reply,
Spare not to give the lie.

So when thou hast, as I
Commanded thee, done blabbing—
Although to give the lie   75
Deserves no less than stabbing—
Stab at thee he that will,
No stab the soul can kill.

The Nymph's Reply to the Shepherd[†]

If all the world and love were young,
And truth in every shepherd's tongue,
These pretty pleasures might me move
To live with thee and be thy love.

Time drives the flocks from field to fold   5
When rivers rage and rocks grow cold,
And Philomel becometh dumb;
The rest complains of cares to come.

The flowers do fade, and wanton fields
To wayward winter reckoning yields;   10
A honey tongue, a heart of gall,
Is fancy's spring, but sorrow's fall.

Thy gowns, thy shoes, thy beds of roses,
Thy cap, thy kirtle, and thy posies
Soon break, soon wither, soon forgotten—   15
In folly ripe, in reason rotten.

Thy belt of straw and ivy buds,
Thy coral clasps and amber studs,
All these in me no means can move
To come to thee and be thy love.   20

But could youth last and love still breed,
Had joys no date nor age no need,
Then these delights my mind might move
To live with thee and be thy love.

[†]An answer to Christopher Marlowe's "The Passionate Shepherd to His Love," p. 98.

[7]**Philomel** *the nightingale. According to Ovid's* Metamorphoses, *Philomel's brother-in-law Tereus had her tongue cut out to prevent her from revealing that he had raped her.*

[14]**kirtle** *dress or skirt.*

[22]**date** *end.*

SIR PHILIP SIDNEY

[1554–1586]

◆

From *Astrophel and Stella*

I

Loving in truth, and fain in verse my love to show,
That she dear she might take some pleasure of my pain,
Pleasure might cause her read, reading might make her know,
Knowledge might pity win, and pity grace obtain,
I sought fit words to paint the blackest face of woe: 5
Studying inventions fine, her wits to entertain,
Oft turning others' leaves, to see if thence would flow
Some fresh and fruitful showers upon my sunburned brain.
But words came halting forth, wanting Invention's stay;
Invention, Nature's child, fled stepdame Study's blows;   10
And others' feet still seemed but strangers in my way.
Thus, great with child to speak, and helpless in my throes,
Biting my truant pen, beating myself for spite:
"Fool," said my Muse to me, "look in thy heart, and write."

¹fain *eager*.

CHIDIOCK TICHBORNE

[ca. 1558–1586]

♦

Tichborne's Elegy†

WRITTEN WITH HIS OWN HAND
IN THE TOWER BEFORE HIS EXECUTION

My prime of youth is but a frost of cares,
My feast of joy is but a dish of pain,
My crop of corn is but a field of tares,
And all my good is but vain hope of gain;
The day is past, and yet I saw no sun,   5
And now I live, and now my life is done.

My tale was heard and yet it was not told,
My fruit is fallen and yet my leaves are green,
My youth is spent and yet I am not old,
I saw the world and yet I was not seen;   10
My thread is cut and yet it is not spun,
And now I live, and now my life is done.

I sought my death and found it in my womb,
I looked for life and saw it was a shade,
I trod the earth and knew it was my tomb,   15
And now I die, and now I was but made;
My glass is full, and now my glass is run,
And now I live, and now my life is done.

---

†Tichborne was hanged for plotting to kill Queen Elizabeth I.
³**corn** *wheat* / **tares** *weeds.*
¹¹**My thread is cut** *The three fates of Greek mythology spun, measured, and cut the thread of men's lives.*

ROBERT SOUTHWELL

[1561–1595]

♦

The Burning Babe

As I in hoary winter's night stood shivering in the snow,
Surprised I was with sudden heat which made my heart
  to glow;
And lifting up a fearful eye to view what fire was near,
A pretty babe all burning bright did in the air appear;
Who, scorchéd with excessive heat, such floods of tears
  did shed   5
As though his floods should quench his flames which with
  his tears were fed.
"Alas," quoth he, "but newly born in fiery heats I fry,
Yet none approach to warm their hearts or feel my fire but I!
My faultless breast the furnace is, the fuel wounding thorns,
Love is the fire, and sighs the smoke, the ashes shame and
  scorns;   10
The fuel justice layeth on, and mercy blows the coals,
The metal in this furnace wrought are men's defiléd souls,
For which, as now on fire I am to work them to their good,
So will I melt into a bath to wash them in my blood."
With this he vanished out of sight and swiftly shrunk away,   15
And straight I calléd unto mind that it was Christmas day.

MICHAEL DRAYTON

[1563–1631]

♦

Since there's no help,
come let us kiss and part

Since there's no help, come let us kiss and part;
Nay, I have done, you get no more of me,
And I am glad, yea glad with all my heart
That thus so cleanly I myself can free;
Shake hands forever, cancel all our vows,   5
And when we meet at any time again,
Be it not seen in either of our brows
That we one jot of former love retain.
Now at the last gasp of love's latest breath,
When, his pulse failing, passion speechless lies,   10
When faith is kneeling by his bed of death,
And innocence is closing up his eyes,
    Now if thou wouldst, when all have given him over,
    From death to life thou mightst him yet recover.

CHRISTOPHER MARLOWE

[1564–1593]

♦

The Passionate Shepherd to His Love†

Come live with me and be my love,
And we will all the pleasures prove
That valleys, groves, hills, and fields,
Woods, or steepy mountain yields.

And we will sit upon the rocks,   5
Seeing the shepherds feed their flocks,
By shallow rivers to whose falls
Melodious birds sing madrigals.

And I will make thee beds of roses
And a thousand fragrant posies,   10
A cap of flowers, and a kirtle
Embroidered all with leaves of myrtle;

A gown made of the finest wool
Which from our pretty lambs we pull;
Fair lined slippers for the cold,   15
With buckles of the purest gold;

A belt of straw and ivy buds,
With coral clasps and amber studs:
And if these pleasures may thee move,
Come live with me, and be my love.   20

---

†See Ralegh's "The Nymph's Reply to the Shepherd," p. 93.
²prove *try.*
¹¹kirtle *dress or skirt.*

The shepherds' swains shall dance and sing
For thy delight each May morning:
If these delights thy mind may move,
Then live with me and be my love.

WILLIAM SHAKESPEARE

[1564–1616]

◆

When in disgrace with fortune and men's eyes

When, in disgrace with fortune and men's eyes,
I all alone beweep my outcast state,
And trouble deaf heaven with my bootless cries,
And look upon myself, and curse my fate,
Wishing me like to one more rich in hope,   5
Featured like him, like him with friends possessed,
Desiring this man's art and that man's scope,
With what I most enjoy contented least;
Yet in these thoughts myself almost despising,
Haply I think on thee—and then my state,   10
Like to the lark at break of day arising
From sullen earth, sings hymns at heaven's gate;
For thy sweet love remembered such wealth brings
That then I scorn to change my state with kings.

³bootless *useless.*

Let me not to the marriage of true minds

Let me not to the marriage of true minds
Admit impediments. Love is not love
Which alters when it alteration finds,
Or bends with the remover to remove:
Oh, no! it is an ever-fixéd mark,   5
That looks on tempests and is never shaken;
It is the star to every wandering bark,
Whose worth's unknown, although his height be taken.
Love's not Time's fool, though rosy lips and cheeks
Within his bending sickle's compass come;   10
Love alters not with his brief hours and weeks,
But bears it out even to the edge of doom.
If this be error and upon me proved,
I never writ, nor no man ever loved.

Th' expense of spirit in a waste of shame

Th' expense of spirit in a waste of shame
Is lust in action; and till action, lust
Is perjured, murderous, bloody, full of blame,
Savage, extreme, rude, cruel, not to trust;
Enjoyed no sooner but despiséd straight: 5
Past reason hunted; and no sooner had,
Past reason hated, as a swallowed bait,
On purpose laid to make the taker mad:
Mad in pursuit, and in possession so;
Had, having, and in quest to have, extreme;   10

²impediments *hindrances*.
⁷bark *ship*.
⁸height be taken *its elevation be measured*.
¹²bears *lasts* / doom *judgment day*.

A bliss in proof, and proved, a very woe;
Before, a joy proposed; behind, a dream.
All this the world well knows; yet none knows well
To shun the heaven that leads men to this hell.

My mistress' eyes are nothing like the sun

My mistress' eyes are nothing like the sun;
Coral is far more red than her lips' red;
If snow be white, why then her breasts are dun;
If hairs be wires, black wires grow on her head.
I have seen roses damasked, red and white,   5
But no such roses see I in her cheeks;
And in some perfumes is there more delight
Than in the breath that from my mistress reeks.
I love to hear her speak, yet well I know
That music hath a far more pleasing sound;   10
I grant I never saw a goddess go,
My mistress, when she walks, treads on the ground.
And yet, by heaven, I think my love as rare
As any she belied with false compare.

---

[11]**in proof** *in the experience.*

[5]**damasked** *variegated.*
[11]**go** *walk.*

THOMAS CAMPION

[1567–1620]

♦

There is a garden in her face

There is a garden in her face,
Where roses and white lilies grow,
A heavenly paradise is that place,
Wherein all pleasant fruits do flow.
There cherries grow, which none may buy   5
Till "Cherry ripe!" themselves do cry.

Those cherries fairly do enclose
Of orient pearl a double row,
Which when her lovely laughter shows,
They look like rosebuds filled with snow.   10
Yet them nor peer nor prince can buy,
Till "Cherry ripe!" themselves do cry.

Her eyes like angels watch them still;
Her brows like bended bows do stand,
Threatening with piercing frowns to kill   15
All that attempt with eye or hand
Those sacred cherries come to nigh,
Till "Cherry ripe!" themselves do cry.

THOMAS NASHE

[1567–1601]

♦

A Litany in Time of Plague

Adieu, farewell, earth's bliss;
This world uncertain is;
Fond are life's lustful joys;
Death proves them all but toys;
None from his darts can fly;   5
I am sick, I must die.
    Lord, have mercy on us!

Rich men, trust not in wealth,
Gold cannot buy you health;
Physic himself must fade.   10
All things to end are made,
The plague full swift goes by;
I am sick, I must die.
    Lord, have mercy on us!

Beauty is but a flower   15
Which wrinkles will devour;
Brightness falls from the air;
Queens have died young and fair;
Dust hath closed Helen's eye.
I am sick, I must die.   20
    Lord, have mercy on us!

[3]**fond** *foolish.*
[4]**toys** *trifles.*

Strength stoops unto the grave,
Worms feed on Hector brave;
Swords may not fight with fate,
Earth still holds ope her gate.   25
"Come, come!" the bells do cry.
I am sick, I must die.
    Lord, have mercy on us!

Wit with his wantonness
Tasteth death's bitterness;   30
Hell's executioner
Hath no ears for to hear
What vain art can reply.
I am sick, I must die.
    Lord, have mercy on us!   35

Haste, therefore, each degree,
To welcome destiny;
Heaven is our heritage,
Earth but a player's stage;
Mount we unto the sky.   40
I am sick, I must die.
    Lord, have mercy on us!

JOHN DONNE

[1572–1631]

♦

Song

Go, and catch a falling star,
  Get with child a mandrake root,
Tell me where all past years are,
  Or who cleft the devil's foot,
Teach me to hear mermaids singing   5
Or to keep off envy's stinging,
    And find
    What wind
Serves to advance an honest mind.

If thou beest born to strange sights,   10
  Things invisible to see,
Ride ten thousand days and nights,
  Till age snow white hairs on thee;
Thou, when thou return'st, wilt tell me
All strange wonders that befell thee,   15
    And swear,
    No where
Lives a woman true, and fair.

If thou find'st one, let me know:
  Such a pilgrimage were sweet.   20
Yet do not, I would not go,
  Though at next door we might meet:
Though she were true when you met her,

---

[2]**mandrake root** *Resembling a human body, the forked root of the mandrake was used as a medicine to induce conception.*

And last till you write your letter,
  Yet she   25
  Will be
False, ere I come, to two, or three.

A Valediction: Forbidding Mourning

As virtuous men pass mildly away,
  And whisper to their souls to go,
Whilst some of their sad friends do say,
  "The breath goes now," and some say, "No,"

So let us melt, and make no noise,   5
  No tear-floods, nor sigh-tempests move;
'Twere profanation of our joys
  To tell the laity our love.

Moving of the earth brings harms and fears,
  Men reckon what it did and meant;   10
But trepidation of the spheres,
  Though greater far, is innocent.

Dull sublunary lovers' love
  (Whose soul is sense) cannot admit
Absence, because it doth remove   15
  Those things which elemented it.

But we, by a love so much refined
  That our selves know not what it is;
Inter-assured of the mind,
  Care less, eyes, lips, and hands to miss.   20

---

[9]**moving of the earth** *earthquakes.*
[13]**sublunary** *earthly.*
[16]**elemented** *composed.*

Our two souls therefore, which are one,
    Though I must go, endure not yet
A breach, but an expansion,
    Like gold to airy thinness beat.

If they be two, they are two so   25
    As stiff twin compasses are two:
Thy soul, the fixed foot, makes no show
    To move, but doth, if the other do;

And though it in the center sit,
    Yet when the other far doth roam,   30
It leans, and hearkens after it,
    And grows erect, as that comes home.

Such wilt thou be to me, who must,
    Like the other foot, obliquely run;
Thy firmness makes my circle just,   35
    And makes me end where I begun.

The Good-Morrow

I wonder, by my troth, what thou and I
Did, till we loved? were we not weaned till then?
But sucked on country pleasures, childishly?
Or snorted we in the Seven Sleepers' den?
'Twas so; but this, all pleasures fancies be.   5
If ever any beauty I did see,
Which I desired, and got, 'twas but a dream of thee.

---

⁵**but** *except for.*

And now good-morrow to our waking souls,
Which watch not one another out of fear;
For love, all love of other sights controls,   10
And makes one little room an everywhere.
Let sea-discoverers to new worlds have gone,
Let maps to others, worlds on worlds have shown,
Let us possess one world, each hath one, and is one.

My face in thine eye, thine in mine appears,   15
And true plain hearts do in the faces rest;
Where can we find two better hemispheres,
Without sharp north, without declining west?
Whatever dies was not mixed equally;
If our two loves be one, or, thou and I   20
Love so alike that none do slacken, none can die.

Death, be not proud

Death, be not proud, though some have called thee
Mighty and dreadful, for thou are not so;
For those whom thou think'st thou dost overthrow
Die not, poor Death, nor yet canst thou kill me.
From rest and sleep, which but thy pictures be,   5
Much pleasure; then from thee much more must flow,
And soonest our best men with thee do go,
Rest of their bones, and soul's delivery.
Thou art slave to fate, chance, kings, and desperate men,
And dost with poison, war, and sickness dwell,   10
And poppy or charms can make us sleep as well
And better than thy stroke; why swell'st thou then?
One short sleep past, we wake eternally
And death shall be no more; Death, thou shalt die.

[13]**maps** *sky charts.*

Batter my heart, three-personed God

Batter my heart, three-personed God; for You
As yet but knock, breathe, shine, and seek to mend;
That I may rise and stand, o'erthrow me, and bend
Your force to break, blow, burn, and make me new.
I, like an usurped town, to another due,   5
Labor to admit You, but O, to no end;
Reason, Your viceroy in me, me should defend,
But is captived, and proves weak or untrue.
Yet dearly I love You, and would be loved fain,
But am betrothed unto Your enemy,   10
Divorce me, untie or break that knot again;
Take me to You, imprison me, for I,
Except You enthrall me, never shall be free,
Nor ever chaste, except You ravish me.

Hymn to God the Father

I

Wilt thou forgive that sin where I begun,
    Which was my sin though it were done before?
Wilt thou forgive that sin through which I run,
    And do run still, though still I do deplore?
        When thou hast done, thou hast not done,   5
        For I have more.

II

Wilt thou forgive that sin by which I've won
    Others to sin, and made my sin their door?
Wilt thou forgive that sin which I did shun
    A year or two, but wallowed in a score?   10

⁹**fain** *gladly.*

109

When thou hast done, thou hast not done,
    For I have more.

III

I have a sin of fear, that when I've spun
    My last thread, I shall perish on the shore;
But swear by thyself that at my death thy son   15
    Shall shine as he shines now, and heretofore;
        And having done that, Thou hast done;
        I fear no more.

BEN JONSON

[1573–1637]

♦

On My First Daughter

Here lies, to each her parents' ruth,
Mary, the daughter of their youth;
Yet all heaven's gifts being heaven's due,
It makes the father less to rue.
At six months' end she parted hence   5
With safety of her innocence;
Whose soul heaven's queen, whose name she bears,
In comfort of her mother's tears,
Hath placed amongst her virgin-train:
Where, while that severed doth remain,   10
This grave partakes the fleshly birth;
Which cover lightly, gentle earth!

---

[1]**ruth** *sorrow.*

On My First Son

Farewell, thou child of my right hand, and joy;
My sin was too much hope of thee, loved boy:
Seven years thou wert lent to me, and I thee pay,
Exacted by thy fate, on the just day.
O could I lose all father now! for why   5
Will man lament the state he should envy,
To have so soon 'scaped world's and flesh's rage,
And, if no other misery, yet age?
Rest in soft peace, and asked, say, "Here doth lie
Ben Jonson his best piece of poetry."   10
For whose sake henceforth all his vows be such
As what he loves may never like too much.

Still to be neat, still to be dressed

Still to be neat, still to be dressed,
As you were going to a feast:
Still to be powdered, still perfumed:
Lady, it is to be presumed,
Though art's hid causes are not found,   5
All is not sweet, all is not sound.

Give me a look, give me a face,
That makes simplicity a grace;
Robes loosely flowing, hair as free:
Such sweet neglect more taketh me   10
Than all the adulteries of art;
They strike mine eyes, but not my heart.

---

[1]child of my right hand *the literal meaning, in Hebrew, of Benjamin, the boy's name.*
[4]the just day *Jonson's son died on his 7th birthday.*

ROBERT HERRICK

[1591–1674]

♦

Delight in Disorder

A sweet disorder in the dress
Kindles in clothes a wantonness.
A lawn about the shoulders thrown
Into a fine distraction;
An erring lace, which here and there   5
Enthralls the crimson stomacher;
A cuff neglectful, and thereby
Ribbons to flow confusedly;
A winning wave, deserving note,
In the tempestuous petticoat;   10
A careless shoestring, in whose tie
I see a wild civility;
Do more bewitch me than when art
Is too precise in every part.

Upon Julia's Clothes

Whenas in silks my Julia goes,
Then, then, methinks, how sweetly flows
That liquefaction of her clothes.

Next, when I cast mine eyes and see
That brave vibration each way free,   5
O how that glittering taketh me!

To the Virgins, to Make Much of Time

Gather ye rosebuds while ye may:
   Old Time is still a-flying;
And this same flower that smiles today,
   Tomorrow will be dying.

The glorious lamp of heaven, the sun,   5
   The higher he's a-getting,
The sooner will his race be run,
   And nearer he's to setting.

That age is best which is the first,
   When youth and blood are warmer;   10
But being spent, the worse, and worst
   Times, still succeed the former.

Then be not coy, but use your time;
   And while ye may, go marry:
For, having lost but once your prime,   15
   You may for ever tarry.

GEORGE HERBERT

[1593–1633]

♦

Easter Wings

Lord, who createdst man in wealth and store,¹
   Though foolishly he lost the same,
      Decaying   more   and   more
         Till   he   became
           Most   poor: 5
           With   thee
         O   let   me   rise
    As   larks,   harmoniously,
  And   sing   this   day   thy   victories:
Then shall the fall further the flight in me.   10

My   tender   age   in   sorrow   did   begin;
   And still   with   sicknesses   and   shame
      Thou   didst   so   punish   sin,
         That   I   became
           Most   thin.   15
           With   thee
         Let   me   combine,
    And feel this day thy victory;
  For,   if   I   imp   my   wing   on   thine,
Affliction   shall   advance   the   flight   in   me.   20

¹**store** *abundance.*

Denial

When my devotions could not pierce
Thy silent ears,
Then was my heart broken, as was my verse;
My breast was full of fears
And disorder. 5

My bent thoughts, like a brittle bow,
Did fly asunder:
Each took his way; some would to pleasures go,
Some to the wars and thunder
Of alarms. 10

As good go anywhere, they say,
As to benumb
Both knees and heart, in crying night and day,
Come, come, my God, O come!
But no hearing. 15

O that thou shouldst give dust a tongue
To cry to thee,
And then not hear it crying! All day long
My heart was in my knee,
But no hearing. 20

Therefore my soul lay out of sight,
Untuned, unstrung:
My feeble spirit, unable to look right,
Like a nipped blossom, hung
Discontented. 25

O cheer and tune my heartless breast,
Defer no time;
That so thy favors granting my request,
They and my mind may chime,
And mend my rhyme. 30

The Pulley

When God at first made man,
Having a glass of blessings standing by,
   "Let us," said he, "pour on him all we can:
Let the world's riches, which dispersed lie,
   Contract into a span."   5

   So Strength first made a way;
Then Beauty flowed; then Wisdom, Honor, Pleasure.
   When almost all was out, God made a stay,
Perceiving that alone of all his treasure
   Rest in the bottom lay.   10

   "For if I should," said he,
"Bestow this jewel also on my creature,
   He would adore my gifts instead of me,
And rest in Nature, not the God of Nature;
   So both should losers be.   15

   "Yet let him keep the rest,
But keep them with repining restlessness:
   Let him be rich and weary, that at least,
If goodness lead him not, yet weariness
   May toss him to my breast."   20

Love (III)

Love bade me welcome: yet my soul drew back,
   Guilty of dust and sin.
But quick-eyed Love, observing me grow slack
   From my first entrance in,
Drew nearer to me, sweetly questioning   5
   If I lacked anything.

"A guest," I answered, "worthy to be here":
    Love said, "You shall be he."
"I, the unkind, ungrateful? Ah, my dear,
    I cannot look on thee."   10
Love took my hand, and smiling did reply,
    "Who made the eyes but I?"

"Truth, Lord; but I have marred them; let my shame
    Go where it doth deserve."
"And know you not," says Love, "who bore the blame?"   15
    "My dear, then I will serve."
"You must sit down," says Love, "and taste my meat."
    So I did sit and eat.

JOHN MILTON

[1608–1674]

◆

When I consider how my light is spent[†]

When I consider how my light is spent
    Ere half my days, in this dark world and wide,
    And that one talent which is death to hide
    Lodged with me useless, though my soul more bent
To serve therewith my Maker and present   5
    My true account, lest he returning chide;
    "Doth God exact day-labor, light denied?"
    I fondly ask; but Patience to prevent

[†]Milton went blind in 1651.
[3]**one talent** *An allusion to Jesus's parable of the talents, in which the servant who buried the talent, or coin, given him by his master was cast into the darkness (Matthew 25:14–30).*
[8]**fondly** *foolishly.*

That murmur, soon replies, "God doth not need
   Either man's work or his own gifts; who best   10
   Bear his mild yoke, they serve him best. His state
Is kingly. Thousands at his bidding speed
   And post o'er land and ocean without rest:
   They also serve who only stand and wait."

On the Late Massacre in Piedmont†

Avenge, O Lord, thy slaughtered saints, whose bones
   Lie scattered on the Alpine mountains cold,
   Even them who kept thy truth so pure of old
   When all our fathers worshipped stocks and stones
Forget not: in thy book record their groans   5
   Who were thy sheep and in their ancient fold
   Slain by the bloody Piedmontese that rolled
   Mother with infant down the rocks. Their moans
The vales redoubled to the hills, and they
   To Heaven. Their martyred blood and ashes sow   10
   O'er all th' Italian fields where still doth sway
The triple tyrant: that from these may grow
   A hundredfold, who having learnt thy way
   Early may fly the Babylonian woe.

†The Duke of Savoy in 1655 massacred 1700 Waldensians, members of a Protestant sect.
⁴**stocks** *idols.*
¹²**The triple tyrant** *The pope, whose tiara contains three crowns.*

ANNE BRADSTREET

[1612–1672]

♦

In Memory of My Dear Grandchild Anne Bradstreet Who Deceased June 20, 1669, Being Three Years and Seven Months Old

With troubled heart and trembling hand I write,
The heavens have changed to sorrow my delight.
How oft with disappointment have I met,
When I on fading things my hopes have set?
Experience might 'fore this have made me wise,   5
To value things according to their price.
Was ever stable joy yet found below?
Or perfect bliss without mixture of woe?
I knew she was but as a withering flower,
That's here today, perhaps gone in an hour;   10
Like as a bubble, or the brittle glass,
Or like a shadow turning as it was.
More fool then I to look on that was lent
As if mine own, when thus impermanent.
Farewell dear child, thou ne'er shall come to me,   15
But yet a while, and I shall go to thee;
Mean time my throbbing heart's cheered up with this:
Thou with thy Saviour art in endless bliss.

RICHARD LOVELACE

[1618–1658]

◆

To Althea, from Prison

When Love with unconfinéd wings
Hovers within my gates,
And my divine Althea brings
To whisper at the grates;
When I lie tangled in her hair   5
And fettered to her eye,
The birds that wanton in the air
Know no such liberty.

When flowing cups run swiftly round,
With no allaying Thames,   10
Our careless heads with roses bound,
Our hearts with loyal flames;
When thirsty grief in wine we steep,
When healths and draughts go free,
Fishes, that tipple in the deep,   15
Know no such liberty.

When, like committed linnets, I
With shriller throat shall sing
The sweetness, mercy, majesty,
And glories of my King;   20
When I shall voice aloud how good
He is, how great should be,
Enlargéd winds, that curl the flood,
Know no such liberty.

[17]committed *caged.*

Stone walls do not a prison make,   25
Nor iron bars a cage;
Minds innocent and quiet take
That for an hermitage.
If I have freedom in my love,
And in my soul am free,   30
Angels alone, that soar above,
Enjoy such liberty.

To Lucasta, Going to the Wars

Tell me not, sweet, I am unkind
That from the nunnery
Of thy chaste breast and quiet mind,
To war and arms I fly.

True, a new mistress now I chase,   5
The first foe in the field;
And with a stronger faith embrace
A sword, a horse, a shield.

Yet this inconstancy is such
As you too shall adore;   10
I could not love thee, dear, so much,
Loved I not honor more.

ANDREW MARVELL

[1621–1678]

♦

To His Coy Mistress

Had we but world enough, and time,
This coyness, lady, were no crime.
We would sit down, and think which way
To walk, and pass our long love's day.
Thou by the Indian Ganges' side   5
Shoudst rubies find; I by the tide
Of Humber would complain. I would
Love you ten years before the flood,
And you should, if you please, refuse
Till the conversion of the Jews.   10
My vegetable love should grow
Vaster than empires and more slow;
An hundred years should go to praise
Thine eyes, and on thy forehead gaze;
Two hundred to adore each breast,   15
But thirty thousand to the rest;
An age at least to every part,
And the last age should show your heart.
For, lady, you deserve this state,
Nor would I love at lower rate.   20
　But at my back I always hear
Time's wingéd chariot hurrying near;
And yonder all before us lie
Deserts of vast eternity.
Thy beauty shall no more be found;   25
Nor, in thy marble vault, shall sound
My echoing song; then worms shall try
That long-preserved virginity,

And your quaint honor turn to dust,
And into ashes all my lust: 30
The grave's a fine and private place,
But none, I think, do there embrace.
  Now therefore, while the youthful hue
Sits on thy skin like morning dew
And while thy willing soul transpires   35
At every pore with instant fires,
Now let us sport us while we may,
And now, like amorous birds of prey,
Rather at once our time devour
Than languish in his slow-chapped power.   40
Let us roll all our strength and all
Our sweetness up into one ball,
And tear our pleasures with rough strife
Thorough the iron gates of life:
Thus, though we cannot make our sun   45
Stand still, yet we will make him run.

THOMAS GRAY

[1716–1771]

♦

Elegy Written in a Country Churchyard

The curfew tolls the knell of parting day,
  The lowing herd wind slowly o'er the lea,
The plowman homeward plods his weary way,
  And leaves the world to darkness and to me.

---

[29]quaint *overscrupulous.*
[35]transpires *breathes forth.*
[40]slow-chapped *slow-jawed.*

Now fades the glimmering landscape on the sight,   5
    And all the air a solemn stillness holds,
Save where the beetle wheels his droning flight,
    And drowsy tinklings lull the distant folds;

Save that from yonder ivy-mantled tower
    The moping owl does to the moon complain   10
Of such, as wandering near her secret bower,
    Molest her ancient solitary reign.

Beneath those rugged elms, that yew tree's shade,
    Where heaves the turf in many a moldering heap,
Each in his narrow cell forever laid,   15
    The rude forefathers of the hamlet sleep.

The breezy call of incense-breathing morn,
    The swallow twittering from the straw-built shed,
The cock's shrill clarion, or the echoing horn,
    No more shall rouse them from their lowly bed.   20

For them no more the blazing hearth shall burn,
    Or busy housewife ply her evening care;
No children run to lisp their sire's return,
    Or climb his knees the envied kiss to share.

Oft did the harvest to their sickle yield,   25
    Their furrow oft the stubborn glebe has broke;
How jocund did they drive their team afield!
    How bowed the woods beneath their sturdy stroke!

Let not Ambition mock their useful toil,
    Their homely joys, and destiny obscure;   30
Nor Grandeur hear with a disdainful smile
    The short and simple annals of the poor.

---

[16]**rude** *rustic.*
[19]**echoing horn** *hunter's horn.*
[26]**glebe** *soil.*

The boast of heraldry, the pomp of power,
　And all that beauty, all that wealth e'er gave,
Awaits alike the inevitable hour.　　　　　　　　35
　The paths of glory lead but to the grave.

Nor you, ye proud, impute to these the fault,
　If Memory o'er their tomb no trophies raise,
Where through the long-drawn aisle and fretted vault
　The pealing anthem swells the note of praise.　　40

Can storied urn or animated bust
　Back to its mansion call the fleeting breath?
Can Honor's voice provoke the silent dust,
　Or Flattery soothe the dull cold ear of Death?

Perhaps in this neglected spot is laid　　　　　　45
　Some heart once pregnant with celestial fire;
Hands that the rod of empire might have swayed,
　Or waked to ecstasy the living lyre.

But Knowledge to their eyes her ample page
　Rich with the spoils of time did ne'er unroll;　　50
Chill Penury repressed their noble rage,
　And froze the genial current of the soul.

Full many a gem of purest ray serene,
　The dark unfathomed caves of ocean bear:
Full many a flower is born to blush unseen,　　　55
　And waste its sweetness on the desert air.

Some village Hampden, that with dauntless breast
　The little tyrant of his fields withstood;
Some mute inglorious Milton here may rest,
　Some Cromwell guiltless of his country's blood.　60

³⁹**fretted** *ornamented.*
⁴¹**animated** *lifelike*
⁴³**provoke** *call forth.*
⁵¹**noble rage** *ardor.*

The applause of listening senates to command,
　　The threats of pain and ruin to despise,
To scatter plenty o'er a smiling land,
　　And read their history in a nation's eyes,

Their lot forbade: nor circumscribed alone　　　65
　　Their growing virtues, but their crimes confined;
Forbade to wade through slaughter to a throne,
　　And shut the gates of mercy on mankind,

The struggling pangs of conscious truth to hide,
　　To quench the blushes of ingenuous shame,　　70
Or heap the shrine of Luxury and Pride
　　With incense kindled at the Muse's flame.

Far from the madding crowd's ignoble strife,
　　Their sober wishes never learned to stray;
Along the cool sequestered vale of life　　　75
　　They kept the noiseless tenor of their way.

Yet even these bones from insult to protect
　　Some frail memorial still erected nigh,
With uncouth rhymes and shapeless sculpture decked,
　　Implores the passing tribute of a sigh.　　80

Their name, their years, spelt by the unlettered Muse,
　　The place of fame and elegy supply:
And many a holy text around she strews,
　　That teach the rustic moralist to die.

For who to dumb Forgetfulness a prey,　　　85
　　This pleasing anxious being e'er resigned,
Left the warm precincts of the cheerful day,
　　Nor cast one longing lingering look behind?

---

[73]madding *milling.*

On some fond breast the parting soul relies,
   Some pious drops the closing eye requires;   90
Even from the tomb the voice of Nature cries,
   Even in our ashes live their wonted fires.

For thee, who mindful of the unhonored dead
   Dost in these lines their artless tale relate;
If chance, by lonely contemplation led,   95
   Some kindred spirit shall inquire thy fate.

Haply some hoary-headed swain may say,
   "Oft have we seen him at the peep of dawn
Brushing with hasty steps the dews away
   To meet the sun upon the upland lawn.   100

"There at the foot of yonder nodding beech
   That wreathes its old fantastic roots so high,
His listless length at noontide would he stretch,
   And pore upon the brook that babbles by.

"Hard by yon wood, now smiling as in scorn,   105
   Muttering his wayward fancies he would rove,
Now drooping, woeful wan, like one forlorn,
   Or crazed with care, or crossed in hopeless love.

"One morn I missed him on the customed hill,
   Along the heath and near his favorite tree;   110
Another came; nor yet beside the rill,
   Nor up the lawn, nor at the wood was he;

"The next with dirges due in sad array
   Slow through the churchway path we saw him borne.
Approach and read (for thou canst read) the lay,   115
   Graved on the stone beneath yon aged thorn."

The Epitaph

Here rests his head upon the lap of Earth
A youth to Fortune and to Fame unknown.
Fair Science frowned not on his humble birth,
And Melancholy marked him for her own.   120

Large was his bounty, and his soul sincere,
Heaven did a recompense as largely send:
He gave to Misery all he had, a tear,
He gained from Heaven ('twas all he wished) a friend.

No farther seek his merits to disclose,   125
Or draw his frailties from their dread abode
There they alike in trembling hope reposed,
The bosom of his Father and his God.

WILLIAM BLAKE

[1757–1827]

♦

The Lamb

Little Lamb, who made thee?
　Dost thou know who made thee?
Gave thee life & bid thee feed,
By the stream & o'er the mead;
Gave thee clothing of delight,   5
Softest clothing wooly bright;
Gave thee such a tender voice,
Making all the vales rejoice!
　Little Lamb who made thee?
　Dost thou know who made thee?   10

---

[119]Science *Learning.*

Little Lamb I'll tell thee,
Little Lamb I'll tell thee!
He is calléd by thy name,
For he calls himself a Lamb:
He is meek & he is mild,   15
He became a little child:
I a child & thou a lamb,
We are calléd by his name.
   Little Lamb God bless thee.
   Little Lamb God bless thee.   20

The Tyger

Tyger! Tyger! burning bright
In the forests of the night,
What immortal hand or eye
Could frame thy fearful symmetry?

In what distant deeps or skies   5
Burnt the fire of thine eyes?
On what wings dare he aspire?
What the hand, dare seize the fire?

And what shoulder, & what art,
Could twist the sinews of thy heart?   10
And when thy heart began to beat,
What dread hand? & what dread feet?

What the hammer? what the chain?
In what furnace was thy brain?
What the anvil? what dread grasp   15
Dare its deadly terrors clasp?

When the stars threw down their spears,
And water'd heaven with their tears,
Did he smile his work to see?
Did he who made the Lamb make thee?   20

Tyger! Tyger! burning bright
In the forests of the night,
What immortal hand or eye
Dare frame thy fearful symmetry?

The Garden of Love

I went to the Garden of Love,
And saw what I never had seen:
A Chapel was built in the midst,
Where I used to play on the green.

And the gates of this Chapel were shut,   5
And "Thou shalt not" writ over the door;
So I turn'd to the Garden of Love,
That so many sweet flowers bore,

And I saw it was filled with graves,
And tomb-stones where flowers should be: 10
And Priests in black gowns were walking their rounds,
And binding with briars my joys & desires.

The Sick Rose

O Rose, thou art sick.
The invisible worm
That flies in the night
In the howling storm

Has found out thy bed   5
Of crimson joy,
And his dark secret love
Does thy life destroy.

The Clod & the Pebble

"Love seeketh not Itself to please,
Nor for itself hath any care;
But for another gives its ease,
And builds a Heaven in Hell's despair."

So sang a little Clod of Clay,   5
Trodden with the cattle's feet;
But a Pebble of the brook,
Warbled out these metres meet:

"Love seeketh only Self to please,
To bind another to its delight,   10
Joys in another's loss of ease,
And builds a Hell in Heaven's despite."

London

I wander thro' each charter'd street,
Near where the charter'd Thames does flow,
And mark in every face I meet
Marks of weakness, marks of woe.

In every cry of every man,   5
In every Infant's cry of fear,
In every voice, in every ban,
The mind-forg'd manacles I hear.

How the Chimney-sweeper's cry
Every blackning Church appalls;   10
And the hapless Soldier's sigh
Runs in blood down Palace walls.

But most thro' midnight streets I hear
How the youthful Harlot's curse
Blasts the new-born Infant's tear,   15
And blights with plagues the Marriage hearse.

ROBERT BURNS

[1759–1796]

♦

A Red, Red Rose

O my luve's like a red, red rose,
    That's newly sprung in June;
O my luve's like the melodie
    That's sweetly played in tune.

As fair art thou, my bonnie lass,   5
  So deep in luve am I;
And I will luve thee still, my dear,
  Till a' the seas gang dry.

Till a' the seas gang dry, my dear,
  And the rocks melt wi' the sun: 10
O I will love thee still, my dear,
  While the sands o' life shall run.

And fare thee weel, my only luve,
  And fare thee weel awhile!
And I will come again, my luve,   15
  Though it were ten thousand mile.

WILLIAM WORDSWORTH

[1770–1850]

♦

She dwelt among the untrodden ways

She dwelt among the untrodden ways
  Beside the springs of Dove.
A Maid whom there were none to praise
  And very few to love;

A violet by a mossy stone   5
  Half hidden from the eye!
—Fair as a star, when only one
  Is shining in the sky.

She lived unknown, and few could know
  When Lucy ceased to be;   10
But she is in her grave, and, oh,
  The difference to me!

My *heart leaps up*

My heart leaps up when I behold
   A rainbow in the sky:
So was it when my life began;
So is it now I am a man;
So be it when I shall grow old,   5
   Or let me die!
The Child is father of the Man;
And I could wish my days to be
Bound each to each by natural piety.

It *is a beauteous evening*

It is a beauteous evening, calm and free,
The holy time is quiet as a Nun
Breathless with adoration; the broad sun
Is sinking down in its tranquility;
The gentleness of heaven broods o'er the Sea: 5
Listen! the mighty Being is awake,
And doth with his eternal motion make
A sound like thunder—everlastingly.
Dear Child! dear Girl! that walkest with me here,
If thou appear untouched by solemn thought,   10
Thy nature is not therefore less divine:
Thou liest in Abraham's bosom all the year,
And worship'st at the Temple's inner shrine,
God being with thee when we know it not.

The world is too much with us

The world is too much with us; late and soon,
Getting and spending, we lay waste our powers;
Little we see in Nature that is ours;
We have given our hearts away, a sordid boon!
This Sea that bares her bosom to the moon,   5
The winds that will be howling at all hours,
And are up-gathered now like sleeping flowers,
For this, for everything, we are out of tune;
It moves us not.—Great God! I'd rather be
A Pagan suckled in a creed outworn;   10
So might I, standing on this pleasant lea,
Have glimpses that would make me less forlorn;
Have sight of Proteus rising from the sea;
Or hear old Triton blow his wreathéd horn.

The Solitary Reaper

Behold her, single in the field,
Yon solitary Highland Lass!
Reaping and singing by herself;
Stop here, or gently pass!
Alone she cuts and binds the grain,   5
And sings a melancholy strain;
O listen! for the Vale profound
Is overflowing with the sound.

No Nightingale did ever chaunt
More welcome notes to weary bands   10
Of travellers in some shady haunt,
Among Arabian sands;

A voice so thrilling ne'er was heard
In springtime from the Cuckoo bird,
Breaking the silence of the seas   15
Among the farthest Hebrides.

Will no one tell me what she sings?—
Perhaps the plaintive numbers flow
For old, unhappy, far-off things,
And battles long ago;   20
Or is it some more humble lay,
Familiar matter of today?
Some natural sorrow, loss, or pain,
That has been, and may be again?

Whate'er the theme, the Maiden sang   25
As if her song could have no ending;
I saw her singing at her work,
And o'er the sickle bending—
I listened, motionless and still;
And, as I mounted up the hill,   30
The music in my heart I bore,
Long after it was heard no more.

SAMUEL TAYLOR COLERIDGE

[1772–1834]

♦

Kubla Khan

OR A VISION IN A DREAM. A FRAGMENT

In Xanadu did Kubla Khan
A stately pleasure dome decree:
Where Alph, the sacred river, ran
Through caverns measureless to man
   Down to a sunless sea.   5
So twice five miles of fertile ground
With walls and towers were girdled round:
And there were gardens bright with sinuous rills,
Where blossomed many an incense-bearing tree;
And here were forests ancient as the hills,   10
Enfolding sunny spots of greenery.

But oh! that deep romantic chasm which slanted
Down the green hill athwart a cedarn cover!
A savage place! as holy and enchanted
As e'er beneath a waning moon was haunted   15
By woman wailing for her demon lover!
And from this chasm, with ceaseless turmoil seething,
As if this earth in fast thick pants were breathing,
A mighty fountain momently was forced:
Amid whose swift half-intermitted burst   20
Huge fragments vaulted like rebounding hail,
Or chaffy grain beneath the thresher's flail:
And 'mid these dancing rocks at once and ever
It flung up momently the sacred river.
Five miles meandering with a mazy motion   25
Through wood and dale the sacred river ran,
Then reached the caverns measureless to man,

And sank in tumult to a lifeless ocean:
And 'mid this tumult Kubla heard from far
Ancestral voices prophesying war!   30
   The shadow of the dome of pleasure
   Floated midway on the waves;
   Where was heard the mingled measure
   From the fountain and the caves.
It was a miracle of rare device,   35
A sunny pleasure dome with caves of ice!

   A damsel with a dulcimer
   In a vision once I saw:
   It was an Abyssinian maid,
   And on her dulcimer she played,   40
   Singing of Mount Abora.
   Could I revive within me
   Her symphony and song,
   To such a deep delight 'twould win me,
That with music loud and long,   45
I would build that dome in air,
That sunny dome! those caves of ice!
And all who heard should see them there,
And all should cry, Beware! Beware!
His flashing eyes, his floating hair!   50
Weave a circle round him thrice,
And close your eyes with holy dread,
For he on honey-dew hath fed,
And drunk the milk of Paradise.

The Rime of the Ancient Mariner

IN SEVEN PARTS

Facile credo, plures esse Naturas invisibles quam visibiles in rerum universitate. Sed horum [sic] omnium familiam quis nobis enarrabit? et gradus et cognationes et discrimina et singulorum munera? Quid agunt? quae loca habitant? Harum rerum notitiam semper ambivit ingenium humanum, nunquam attigit. Juvat, interea, non diffiteor, quandoque in animo, in tabulâ, majoris et melioris mundi imaginem contemplari: ne mens assuefacta hodiernae vitae minutiis se contrahat nimis, et tota subsidat in pusillas cogitationes. Sed veritati interea invigilandum est, modusque servandus, ut certa ab incertis, diem a nocte, distinguamus.

—T. BURNET[†]

ARGUMENT

How a Ship having past the Line was driven by storms to the cold Country towards the South Pole; and how from thence she made her course to the tropical Latitude of the Great Pacific Ocean; and of the strange things that befell; and in what manner the Ancyent Marinere came back to his own Country.

PART I

An ancient Mariner meeteth three Gallants bidden to a wedding feast, and detaineth one.

It is an ancient Mariner
And he stoppeth one of three.
—"By thy long gray beard and glittering eye,
Now wherefore stopp'st thou me?

[†]From *Archaeologiae Philosophiae*, p. 68. "I can easily believe that there are more invisible than visible beings in the universe. But of their families, degrees, connections, distinctions, and functions, who shall tell us? How do they act? Where are they found? About such matters the human mind has always circled without attaining knowledge. Yet I do not doubt that sometimes it is well for the soul to contemplate as in a picture the image of a larger and better world, lest the mind, habituated to the small concerns of daily life, limit itself too much and sink entirely into trivial thinking. But meanwhile we must be on watch for the truth, avoiding extremes, so that we may distinguish certain from uncertain, day from night." Burnet was a 17th-century English theologian.

The Bridegroom's doors are opened wide,   5
And I am next of kin;
The guests are met, the feast is set:
May'st hear the merry din."

He holds him with his skinny hand,
"There was a ship," quoth he.   10
"Hold off! unhand me, graybeard loon!"
Eftsoons his hand dropped he.

*The Wedding
Guest is spellbound
by the eye of the
old seafaring man,
and constrained to
hear his tale.*

He holds him with his glittering eye—
The Wedding Guest stood still,
And listens like a three years' child: 15
The Mariner hath his will.

The Wedding Guest sat on a stone:
He cannot choose but hear;
And thus spake on that ancient man,
The bright-eyed Mariner.   20

"The ship was cheered, the harbor cleared,
Merrily did we drop
Below the kirk, below the hill,
Below the lighthouse top.

*The Mariner tells
how the ship sailed
southward with a
good wind and fair
weather, till it
reached the line.*

The Sun came up upon the left,   25
Out of the sea came he!
And he shone bright, and on the right
Went down into the sea.

Higher and higher every day,
Till over the mast at noon—"   30
The Wedding Guest here beat his breast,
For he heard the loud bassoon.

[12]**Eftsoons** *straightway.*
[23]**kirk** *church.*

*The Wedding
Guest heareth the
bridal music; but
the Mariner contin-
ueth his tale.*

The bride hath paced into the hall,
Red as a rose is she;
Nodding their heads before her goes   35
The merry minstrelsy.

The Wedding Guest he beat his breast,
Yet he cannot choose but hear;
And thus spake on that ancient man,
The bright-eyed Mariner.   40

*The ship driven by
a storm toward the
South Pole.*

"And now the STORM-BLAST came, and he
Was tyrannous and strong;
He struck with his o'ertaking wings,
And chased us south along.

With sloping masts and dipping prow,   45
As who pursued with yell and blow
Still treads the shadow of his foe,
And forward bends his head,
The ship drove fast, loud roared the blast,
And southward aye we fled.   50

And now there came both mist and snow,
And it grew wondrous cold:
And ice, mast-high, came floating by,
As green as emerald.

*The land of ice,
and of fearful
sounds where no
living thing was to
be seen.*

And through the drifts the snowy clifts   55
Did send a dismal sheen:
Nor shapes of men nor beasts we ken—
The ice was all between.

The ice was here, the ice was there,
The ice was all around: 60
It cracked and growled, and roared and howled,
Like noises in a swound!

⁵⁵**clifts** *cliffs.*
⁶²**swound** *swoon.*

Till a great sea bird, called the Albatross, came through the snow-fog, and was received with great joy and hospitality.

At length did cross an Albatross,
Thorough the fog it came;
As if it had been a Christian soul,   65
We hailed it in God's name.

It ate the food it ne'er had eat,
And round and round it flew.
The ice did split with a thunder-fit;
The helmsman steered us through!   70

And lo! the Albatross proveth a bird of good omen, and followeth the ship as it returned northward through fog and floating ice.

And a good south wind sprung up behind;
The Albatross did follow,
And every day, for food or play,
Came to the mariners' hollo!

In mist or cloud, on mast or shroud,   75
It perched for vespers nine;
Whiles all the night, through fog-smoke white,
Glimmered the white Moon-shine."

The ancient Mariner inhospitably killeth the pious bird of good omen.

"God save thee, ancient Mariner!
From the fiends, that plague thee thus!—   80
Why look'st thou so?"—With my crossbow
I shot the ALBATROSS.

PART II

The Sun now rose upon the right:
Out of the sea came he,
Still hid in mist, and on the left   85
Went down into the sea.

And the good south wind still blew behind,
But no sweet bird did follow,
Nor any day for food or play
Came to the mariners' hollo!   90

And I had done a hellish thing,
And it would work 'em woe:
For all averred, I had killed the bird
That made the breeze to blow.
Ah wretch! said they, the bird to slay,   95
That made the breeze to blow!

Nor dim nor red, like God's own head,
The glorious Sun uprist:
Then all averred, I had killed the bird
That brought the fog and mist.   100
'Twas right, said they, such birds to slay,
That bring the fog and mist.

The fair breeze blew, the white foam flew,
The furrow followed free;
We were the first that ever burst   105
Into that silent sea.

Down dropped the breeze, the sails dropped
    down,
'Twas sad as sad could be;
And we did speak only to break
The silence of the sea!   110

All in a hot and copper sky,
The bloody Sun, at noon,
Right up above the mast did stand,
No bigger than the Moon.

Day after day, day after day,   115
We stuck, nor breath nor motion;
As idle as a painted ship
Upon a painted ocean.

[98]**uprist** *arose.*

And the Albatross
begins to be
avenged.

Water, water, everywhere,
And all the boards did shrink;   120
Water, water, everywhere,
Nor any drop to drink.

The very deep did rot: O Christ!
That ever this should be!
Yea, slimy things did crawl with legs   125
Upon the slimy sea.

About, about, in reel and rout
The death-fires danced at night;
The water, like a witch's oils,
Burnt green, and blue and white.   130

And some in dreams assuréd were
Of the Spirit that plagued us so;
Nine fathom deep he had followed us
From the land of mist and snow.

A Spirit had fol-
lowed them; one of
the invisible inhab-
itants of this
planet, neither de-
parted souls nor
angels; concerning
whom the learned
Jew, Josephus, and
the Platonic Con-
stantinopolitan,
Michael Psellus,
may be consulted.
They are very nu-
merous, and there
is no climate or ele-
ment without one
or more.

And every tongue, through utter drought,   135
Was withered at the root;
We could not speak, no more than if
We had been choked with soot.

The shipmates, in
their sore distress,
would fain throw
the whole guilt on
the ancient Mari-
ner: in sign
whereof they hang
the dead sea bird
round his neck.

Ah! well-a-day! what evil looks
Had I from old and young!   140
Instead of the cross, the Albatross
About my neck was hung.

PART III

There passed a weary time. Each throat
Was parched, and glazed each eye.
A weary time! a weary time!   145
How glazed each weary eye,
The ancient Mari- When looking westward, I beheld
ner beholdeth a A something in the sky.
sign in the element
afar off.

At first it seemed a little speck,
And then it seemed a mist;   150
It moved and moved, and took at last
A certain shape, I wist.

A speck, a mist, a shape, I wist!
And still it neared and neared:
As if it dodged a water sprite,   155
It plunged and tacked and veered.

At its nearer ap- With throats unslaked, with black lips baked,
proach, it seemeth We could nor laugh nor wail;
him to be a ship; Through utter drought all dumb we stood!
and at a dear ran-
som he freeth his I bit my arm, I sucked the blood,   160
speech from the And cried, A sail! a sail!
bonds of thirst.

With throats unslaked, with black lips baked,
Agape they heard me call:
A flash of joy; Gramercy! they for joy did grin,
And all at once their breath drew in,   165
As they were drinking all.

And horror fol- See! see! (I cried) she tacks no more!
lows. For can it be Hither to work us weal;
a ship that comes
onward without Without a breeze, without a tide,
wind or tide? She steadies with upright keel!   170

---

[152]**wist** *knew.*
[164]**Gramercy!** *Thank heavens!*
[168]**weal** *benefit.*

The western wave was all aflame.
The day was well nigh done!
Almost upon the western wave
Rested the broad bright Sun;
When that strange shape drove suddenly   175
Betwixt us and the Sun.

It seemeth him but the skeleton of a ship.

And straight the Sun was flecked with bars,
(Heaven's Mother send us grace!)
As if through a dungeon grate he peered
With broad and burning face.   180

And its ribs are seen as bars on the face of the setting Sun.

Alas! (thought I, and my heart beat loud)
How fast she nears and nears!
Are those *her* sails that glance in the Sun,
Like restless gossameres?

The Specter-Woman and her Deathmate, and no other on board the skeleton ship.

Are those *her* ribs through which the Sun   185
Did peer, as through a grate?
And is that Woman all her crew?
Is that a DEATH? and are there two?
Is DEATH that woman's mate?

Like vessel, like crew!

Her lips were red, *her* looks were free,   190
Her locks were yellow as gold:
Her skin was as white as leprosy,
The Nightmare LIFE-IN-DEATH was she,
Who thicks man's blood with cold.

Death and Life-in-Death have diced for the ship's crew, and she (the latter) winneth the ancient Mariner.

The naked hulk alongside came,   195
And the twain were casting dice;
"The game is done! I've won! I've won!"
Quoth she, and whistles thrice.

No twilight within the courts of the Sun.

The Sun's rim dips; the stars rush out:
At one stride comes the dark;
With far-heard whisper, o'er the sea,   200
Off shot the specter-bark.

At the rising of the Moon,
We listened and looked sideways up!
Fear at my heart, as at a cup,
My lifeblood seemed to sip!   205
The stars were dim, and thick the night,
The steersman's face by his lamp gleamed white;
From the sails the dew did drip—
Till clomb above the eastern bar
The hornéd Moon, with one bright star   210
Within the nether tip.

One after another,
One after one, by the star-dogged Moon,
Too quick for groan or sigh,
Each turned his face with ghastly pang,
And cursed me with his eye.   215

His shipmates drop down dead.
Four times fifty living men,
(And I heard nor sigh nor groan)
With heavy thump, a lifeless lump,
They dropped down one by one.

But Life-in-Death begins her work on the ancient Mariner.
The souls did from their bodies fly—   220
They fled to bliss or woe!
And every soul, it passed me by,
Like the whizz of my cross-bow!

PART IV

The Wedding Guest feareth that a Spirit is talking to him;
"I fear thee, ancient Mariner!
I fear thy skinny hand!   225
And thou art long, and lank, and brown,
As is the ribbed sea-sand.

But the ancient Mariner assureth him of his bodily life, and proceedeth to relate his horrible penance.
I fear thee and thy glittering eye,
And thy skinny hand, so brown."—
Fear not, fear not, thou Wedding Guest!   230
This body dropped not down.

Alone, alone, all, all alone,
Alone on a wide wide sea!
And never a saint took pity on
My soul in agony.   235

*He despiseth the
creatures of the
calm,*

The many men, so beautiful!
And they all dead did lie:
And a thousand thousand slimy things
Lived on; and so did I.

*And envieth that
they should live,
and so many lie
dead.*

I looked upon the rotting sea,   240
And drew my eyes away;
I looked upon the rotting deck,
And there the dead men lay.

I looked to heaven, and tried to pray;
But or ever a prayer had gushed,   245
A wicked whisper came, and made
My heart as dry as dust.

I closed my lids, and kept them close,
And the balls like pulses beat,
For the sky and the sea, and the sea and
    the sky
Lay like a load on my weary eye,   250
And the dead were at my feet.

*But the curse liveth
for him in the eye
of the dead men.*

The cold sweat melted from their limbs,
Nor rot nor reek did they:
The look with which they looked on me   255
Had never passed away.

An orphan's curse would drag to hell
A spirit from on high;
But oh! more horrible than that
Is the curse in a dead man's eye!   260
Seven days, seven nights, I saw that curse,
And yet I could not die.

The moving Moon went up the sky,
And nowhere did abide:
Softly she was going up,   265
And a star or two beside—

Her beams bemocked the sultry main,
Like April hoar-frost spread;
But where the ship's huge shadow lay,
The charméd water burnt alway   270
A still and awful red.

Beyond the shadow of the ship,
I watched the water snakes:
They moved in tracks of shining white,
And when they reared, the elfish light   275
Fell off in hoary flakes.

Within the shadow of the ship
I watched their rich attire:
Blue, glossy green, and velvet black,
They coiled and swam; and every track   280
Was a flash of golden fire.

O happy living things! no tongue
Their beauty might declare:
A spring of love gushed from my heart,
And I blessed them unaware: 285
Sure my kind saint took pity on me,
And I blessed them unaware.

In his loneliness and fixedness he yearneth towards the journeying Moon, and the stars that still sojourn, yet still move onward; and everywhere the blue sky belongs to them, and is their appointed rest, and their native country and their own natural homes, which they enter unannounced, as lords that are certainly expected and yet there is a silent joy at their arrival.

By the light of the Moon he beholdeth God's creatures of the great calm.

Their beauty and their happiness.

He blesseth them in his heart.

[276]**hoary** *gray or white.*

The spell begins to break.

The self-same moment I could pray;
And from my neck so free
The Albatross fell off, and sank   290
Like lead into the sea.

PART·V

Oh sleep! it is a gentle thing,
Beloved from pole to pole!
To Mary Queen the praise be given!
She sent the gentle sleep from Heaven,   295
That slid into my soul.

By grace of the holy Mother, the ancient Mariner is refreshed with rain.

The silly buckets on the deck,
That had so long remained,
I dreamt that they were filled with dew;
And when I awoke, it rained.   300

My lips were wet, my throat was cold,
My garments all were dank;
Sure I had drunken in my dreams,
And still my body drank.

I moved, and could not feel my limbs: 305
I was so light—almost
I thought that I had died in sleep,
And was a blessèd ghost.

He heareth sounds and seeth strange sights and commotions in the sky and the element.

And soon I heard a roaring wind:
It did not come anear;   310
But with its sound it shook the sails,
That were so thin and sere.

²⁹⁷**silly** *lowly, harmless.*

The upper air burst into life!
And a hundred fire-flags sheen,
To and fro they were hurried about!   315
And to and fro, and in and out,
The wan stars danced between.

And the coming wind did roar more loud,
And the sails did sigh like sedge;
And the rain poured down from one black
    cloud;   320
The Moon was at its edge.

The thick black cloud was cleft, and still
The Moon was at its side:
Like waters shot from some high crag,
The lightning fell with never a jag,   325
A river steep and wide.

The bodies of the
ship's crew are in-
spirited, and the
ship moves on;

The loud wind never reached the ship,
Yet now the ship moved on!
Beneath the lightning and the Moon
The dead men gave a groan.   330

They groaned, they stirred, they all uprose,
Nor spake, nor moved their eyes;
It had been strange, even in a dream,
To have seen those dead men rise.

The helmsman steered, the ship moved on;   335
Yet never a breeze up-blew;
The mariners all'gan work the ropes,
Where they were wont to do;
They raised their limbs like lifeless tools—
We were a ghastly crew.   340

[314]**sheen** *shone.*
[319]**sedge** *rushlike plants bordering streams and lakes.*

The body of my brother's son
Stood by me, knee to knee:
The body and I pulled at one rope,
But he said nought to me.

*But not by the
souls of the men,
nor by demons of
earth or middle air,
but by a blesséd
troop of angelic
spirits, sent down
by the invocation
of the guardian
saint.*

"I fear thee, ancient Mariner!"   345
Be calm, thou Wedding Guest!
'Twas not those souls that fled in pain,
Which to their corses came again,
But a troop of spirits blest:

For when it dawned—they dropped their arms, 350
And clustered round the mast;
Sweet sounds rose slowly through their mouths,
And from their bodies passed.

Around, around, flew each sweet sound,
Then darted to the Sun;   355
Slowly the sounds came back again,
Now mixed, now one by one.

Sometimes a-dropping from the sky
I heard the sky-lark sing;
Sometimes all little birds that are,   360
How they seemed to fill the sea and air
With their sweet jargoning!

And now 'twas like all instruments,
Now like a lonely flute;
And now it is an angel's song,   365
That makes the heavens be mute.

It ceased; yet still the sails made on
A pleasant noise till noon,
A noise like of a hidden brook
In the leafy month of June,   370

[348]**corses** *corpses.*
[62]**jargoning** *warbling.*

That to the sleeping woods all night
Singeth a quiet tune.

Till noon we quietly sailed on,
Yet never a breeze did breathe:
Slowly and smoothly went the ship, 375
Moved onward from beneath.

The lonesome Spirit from the South Pole carries on the ship as far as the Line, in obedience to the angelic troop, but still requireth vengeance.

Under the keel nine fathom deep,
From the land of mist and snow,
The spirit slid: and it was he
That made the ship to go. 380
The sails at noon left off their tune,
And the ship stood still also.

The Sun, right up above the mast,
Had fixed her to the ocean:
But in a minute she 'gan stir, 385
With a short uneasy motion—
Backwards and forwards half her length
With a short uneasy motion.

Then like a pawing horse let go,
She made a sudden bound: 390
It flung the blood into my head,
And I fell down in a swound.

The Polar Spirit's fellow demons, the invisible inhabitants of the element, take part in his wrong; and two of them relate, one to the other, that penance long and heavy for the ancient Mariner hath been accorded to the Polar Spirit, who returneth southward.

How long in that same fit I lay,
I have not to declare;
But ere my living life returned, 395
I heard and in my soul discerned
Two voices in the air.

"Is it he?" quoth one, "Is this the man?
By him who died on cross,
With his cruel bow he laid full low 400
The harmless Albatross.

394**have not** *cannot.*

The spirit who bideth by himself
In the land of mist and snow,
He loved the bird that loved the man
Who shot him with his bow."   405

The other was a softer voice,
As soft as honey-dew:
Quoth he, "The man hath penance done,
And penance more will do."

PART VI

FIRST VOICE

"But tell me, tell me! speak again,   410
Thy soft response renewing—
What makes that ship drive on so fast?
What is the ocean doing?"

SECOND VOICE

"Still as a slave before his lord,
The ocean hath no blast;   415
His great bright eye most silently
Up to the Moon is cast—

If he may know which way to go;
For she guides him smooth or grim.
See, brother, see! how graciously   420
She looketh down on him."

FIRST VOICE

The Mariner hath   "But why drives on that ship so fast,
been cast into a   Without or wave or wind?"
trance; for the an-
gelic power causeth
the vessel to drive   SECOND VOICE
northward faster
than human life   "The air is cut away before,
could endure.   And closes from behind.   425

Fly, brother, fly! more high, more high!
Or we shall be belated:
For slow and slow that ship will go,
When the Mariner's trance is abated."

The supernatural
motion is retarded;
the Mariner
awakes, and his
penance begins
anew.

I woke, and we were sailing on   430
As in a gentle weather:
'Twas night, calm night, the moon was high;
The dead men stood together.

All stood together on the deck,
For a charnel-dungeon fitter: 435
All fixed on me their stony eyes,
That in the Moon did glitter.

The pang, the curse, with which they died,
Had never passed away:
I could not draw my eyes from theirs,   440
Nor turn them up to pray.

The curse is finally
expiated.

And now this spell was snapped: once more
I viewed the ocean green,
And looked far forth, yet little saw
Of what had else been seen—   445

Like one, that on a lonesome road
Doth walk in fear and dread,
And having once turned round walks on,
And turns no more his head;
Because he knows, a frightful fiend   450
Doth close behind him tread.

But soon there breathed a wind on me,
Nor sound nor motion made:
Its path was not upon the sea,
In ripple or in shade.   455

It raised my hair, it fanned my cheek
Like a meadow-gale of spring—
It mingled strangely with my fears,
Yet it felt like a welcoming.

Swiftly, swiftly flew the ship,   460
Yet she sailed softly too:
Sweetly, sweetly blew the breeze—
On me alone it blew.

And the ancient
Mariner beholdeth
his native country.

Oh! dream of joy! is this indeed
The lighthouse top I see?   465
Is this the hill? is this the kirk?
Is this mine own countree?

We drifted o'er the harbor-bar,
And I with sobs did pray—
O let me be awake, my God!   470
Or let me sleep alway.

The harbor-bay was clear as glass,
So smoothly it was strewn!
And on the bay the moonlight lay,
And the shadow of the Moon.   475

The rock shone bright, the kirk no less,
That stands above the rock:
The moonlight steeped in silentness
The steady weathercock.

And the bay was white with silent light,   480
Till rising from the same,

The angelic spirits
leave the dead
bodies,

Full many shapes, that shadows were,
In crimson colors came.

A little distance from the prow
Those crimson shadows were: 485

And appear in their
own forms of light.

I turned my eyes upon the deck—
Oh, Christ! what saw I there!

Each corse lay flat, lifeless and flat,
And, by the holy rood!
A man all light, a seraph-man,   490
On every corse there stood.

This seraph-band, each waved his hand:
It was a heavenly sight!
They stood as signals to the land,
Each one a lovely light;   495

This seraph-band, each waved his hand,
No voice did they impart—
No voice; but oh! the silence sank
Like music on my heart.

But soon I heard the dash of oars,   500
I heard the Pilot's cheer;
My head was turned perforce away
And I saw a boat appear.

The Pilot and the Pilot's boy,
I heard them coming fast: 505
Dear Lord in Heaven! it was a joy
The dead men could not blast.

I saw a third—I heard his voice:
It is the Hermit good!
He singeth loud his godly hymns   510
That he makes in the wood.
He'll shrieve my soul, he'll wash away
The Albatross's blood.

489holy rood *cross of Christ.*
490seraph *angel-like.*
512shrieve *set free from sin.*

157

PART VII

This Hermit good lives in that wood
Which slopes down to the sea.   515
How loudly his sweet voice he rears!
He loves to talk with marineres
That come from a far countree.

He kneels at morn, and noon, and eve—
He hath a cushion plump: 520
It is the moss that wholly hides
The rotted old oak stump.

The skiff-boat neared: I heard them talk,
"Why, this is strange, I trow!
Where are those lights so many and fair,   525
That signal made but now?"

"Strange, by my faith!" the Hermit said—
"And they answered not our cheer!
The planks looked warped! and see those sails,
How thin they are and sere!   530
I never saw aught like to them,
Unless perchance it were

Brown skeletons of leaves that lag
My forest-brook along;
When the ivy tod is heavy with snow,   535
And the owlet whoops to the wolf below,
That eats the she-wolf's young."

"Dear Lord! it hath a fiendish look,"
The Pilot made reply,
"I am a-feared"—"Push on, push on!"   540
Said the Hermit cheerily.

---

[535]**ivy tod** *bushy clump.*

The boat came closer to the ship,
But I nor spake nor stirred;
The boat came close beneath the ship,
And straight a sound was heard.   545

The ship suddenly sinketh.

Under the water it rumbled on,
Still louder and more dread:
It reached the ship, it split the bay;
The ship went down like lead.

The ancient Mariner is saved in the Pilot's boat.

Stunned by that loud and dreadful sound,   550
Which sky and ocean smote,
Like one that hath been seven days drowned
My body lay afloat;
But swift as dreams, myself I found
Within the Pilot's boat.   555

Upon the whirl, where sank the ship,
The boat spun round and round;
And all was still, save that the hill
Was telling of the sound.

I moved my lips—the Pilot shrieked   560
And fell down in a fit;
The holy Hermit raised his eyes,
And prayed where he did sit.

I took the oars: the Pilot's boy,
Who now doth crazy go,   565
Laughed loud and long, and all the while
His eyes went to and fro.
"Ha! ha!" quoth he, "full plain I see,
The Devil knows how to row."

And now, all in my own countree,   570
I stood on the firm land!
The Hermit stepped forth from the boat,
And scarcely he could stand.

The ancient Mariner earnestly entreateth the Hermit to shrieve him; and the penance of life falls on him.

"O shrieve me, shrieve me, holy man!"
The Hermit crossed his brow.   575
"Say quick," quoth he, "I bid thee say—
What manner of man art thou?"

Forthwith this frame of mine was wrenched
With a woeful agony,
Which forced me to begin my tale;   580
And then it left me free.

And ever and anon throughout his future life an agony constraineth him to travel from land to land;

Since then, at an uncertain hour,
That agony returns:
And till my ghastly tale is told,
This heart within me burns.   585

I pass, like night, from land to land;
I have strange power of speech;
That moment that his face I see,
I know the man that must hear me:
To him my tale I teach.   590

What loud uproar bursts from that door!
The wedding guests are there:
But in the garden-bower the bride
And bridemaids singing are:
And hark the little vesper bell,   595
Which biddeth me to prayer!

O Wedding Guest! this soul hath been
Alone on a wide wide sea:
So lonely 'twas, that God himself
Scarce seeméd there to be.   600

O sweeter than the marriage feast,
'Tis sweeter far to me,
To walk together to the kirk
With a goodly company!

---

[575]**crossed** *made the sign of the cross upon.*

To walk together to the kirk,   605
And all together pray,
While each to his great Father bends,
Old men, and babes, and loving friends
And youths and maidens gay!

*And to teach, by
his own example,
love and reverence
to all things that
God made and
loveth.*

Farewell, farewell! but this I tell   610
To thee, thou Wedding Guest!
He prayeth well, who loveth well
Both man and bird and beast.

He prayeth best, who loveth best
All things both great and small;   615
For the dear God who loveth us,
He made and loveth all.

The Mariner, whose eye is bright,
Whose beard with age is hoar,
Is gone: and now the Wedding Guest   620
Turned from the bridegroom's door.

He went like one that hath been stunned,
And is of sense forlorn:
A sadder and a wiser man,
He rose the morrow morn.   625

623**forlorn** *deprived.*

GEORGE GORDON, LORD BYRON

[1788–1824]

◆

She walks in beauty

I

She walks in beauty, like the night
  Of cloudless climes and starry skies;
And all that's best of dark and bright
  Meet in her aspect and her eyes:
Thus mellowed to that tender light   5
  Which heaven to gaudy day denies.

II

One shade the more, one ray the less,
  Had half impaired the nameless grace
Which waves in every raven tress,
  Or softly lightens o'er her face;   10
Where thoughts serenely sweet express
  How pure, how dear their dwelling place.

III

And on that cheek, and o'er that brow,
  So soft, so calm, yet eloquent,
The smiles that win, the tints that glow,   15
  But tell of days in goodness spent,
A mind at peace with all below,
  A heart whose love is innocent!

PERCY BYSSHE SHELLEY

[1792–1822]

♦

Ozymandias†

I met a traveler from an antique land
Who said: Two vast and trunkless legs of stone
Stand in the desert . . . Near them, on the sand,
Half sunk, a shattered visage lies, whose frown,
And wrinkled lip, and sneer of cold command,   5
Tell that its sculptor well those passions read
Which yet survive, stamped on these lifeless things,
The hand that mocked them, and the heart that fed:
And on the pedestal these words appear:
"My name is Ozymandias, king of kings: 10
Look on my works, ye Mighty, and despair!"
Nothing beside remains. Round the decay
Of that colossal wreck, boundless and bare
The lone and level sands stretch far away.

†Greek name for the Egyptian ruler Rameses II, who erected a huge statue in his own likeness.

Ode to the West Wind

I

O wild West Wind, thou breath of Autumn's being,
Thou, from whose unseen presence the leaves dead
Are driven, like ghosts from an enchanter fleeing,

Yellow, and black, and pale, and hectic red,
Pestilence-stricken multitudes: O thou,   5
Who chariotest to their dark wintry bed

The wingéd seeds, where they lie cold and low,
Each like a corpse within its grave, until
Thine azure sister of the Spring shall blow

Her clarion o'er the dreaming earth, and fill   10
(Driving sweet buds like flocks to feed in air)
With living hues and odors plain and hill:

Wild Spirit, which art moving everywhere;
Destroyer and preserver; hear, oh, hear!

II

Thou on whose stream, mid the steep sky's commotion,   15
Loose clouds like earth's decaying leaves are shed,
Shook from the tangled boughs of Heaven and Ocean,

Angels of rain and lightning: there are spread
On the blue surface of thine aery surge,
Like the bright hair uplifted from the head   20

Of some fierce Maenad, even from the dim verge
Of the horizon to the zenith's height,
The locks of the approaching storm. Thou dirge

[10]**clarion** *trumpet call.*
[18]**angels** *messengers.*
[21]**Maenad** *frenzied female worshipper of Dionysus, god of wine and fertility.*

Of the dying year, to which this closing night
Will be the dome of a vast sepulcher,   25
Vaulted with all thy congregated might

Of vapors, from whose solid atmosphere
Black rain, and fire, and hail will burst: oh, hear!

III

Thou who didst waken from his summer dreams
The blue Mediterranean, where he lay,   30
Lulled by the coil of his crystálline streams,

Beside a pumice isle in Baiae's bay
And saw in sleep old palaces and towers
Quivering within the wave's intenser day,

All overgrown with azure moss and flowers   35
So sweet, the sense faints picturing them! Thou
For whose path the Atlantic's level powers

Cleave themselves into chasms, while far below
The sea-blooms and the oozy woods which wear
The sapless foliage of the ocean, know   40

Thy voice, and suddenly grow gray with fear,
And tremble and despoil themselves: oh, hear!

IV

If I were a dead leaf thou mightest bear;
If I were a swift cloud to fly with thee;
A wave to pant beneath thy power, and share   45

The impulse of thy strength, only less free
Than thou, O uncontrollable! If even
I were as in my boyhood, and could be

The comrade of thy wanderings over Heaven,
As then, when to outstrip thy skyey speed   50
Scarce seemed a vision; I would ne'er have striven

As thus with thee in prayer in my sore need.
Oh, lift me as a wave, a leaf, a cloud!
I fall upon the thorns of life! I bleed!

A heavy weight of hours has chained and bowed   55
One too like thee: tameless, and swift, and proud.

V

Make me thy lyre, even as the forest is:
What if my leaves are falling like its own!
The tumult of thy mighty harmonies

Will take from both a deep, autumnal tone,   60
Sweet though in sadness. Be thou, Spirit fierce,
My spirit! Be thou me, impetuous one!

Drive my dead thoughts over the universe
Like withered leaves to quicken a new birth!
And, by the incantation of this verse,   65

Scatter, as from an unextinguished hearth
Ashes and sparks, my words among mankind!
Be through my lips to unawakened earth

The trumpet of a prophecy! O Wind,
If Winter comes, can Spring be far behind?   70

---

⁵⁷**lyre** *small harp.*

JOHN KEATS

[1795–1821]

♦

On First Looking into Chapman's Homer

Much have I traveled in the realms of gold,
  And many goodly states and kingdoms seen;
  Round many western islands have I been
Which bards in fealty to Apollo hold.
Oft of one wide expanse had I been told   5
  That deep-browed Homer ruled as his demesne;
  Yet did I never breathe its pure serene
Till I heard Chapman speak out loud and bold:
Then felt I like some watcher of the skies
  When a new planet swims into his ken;   10
Or like stout Cortez when with eagle eyes
  He stared at the Pacific—and all his men
Looked at each other with a wild surmise—
  Silent, upon a peak in Darien.

[4]**fealty** *allegiance.*
[6]**demesne** *domain.*
[7]**serene** *atmosphere.*
[11]**Cortez** *Spanish conquistador. In fact, it was Balboa, not Cortez, who first sighted the Pacific Ocean from Darien in Panama.*

Ode to a Nightingale

I

My heart aches, and a drowsy numbness pains
  My sense, as though of hemlock I had drunk,
Or emptied some dull opiate to the drains
  One minute past, and Lethe-wards had sunk:
'Tis not through envy of thy happy lot,   5
  But being too happy in thine happiness—
    That thou, light-winged Dryad of the trees,
      In some melodious plot
Of beechen green, and shadows numberless,
  Singest of summer in full-throated ease.   10

II

O, for a draught of vintage! that hath been
  Cool'd a long age in the deep-delved earth,
Tasting of Flora and the country green,
  Dance, and Provençal song, and sunburnt mirth!
O for a beaker full of the warm South,   15
  Full of the true, the blushful Hippocrene,
    With beaded bubbles winking at the brim,
      And purple-stained mouth;
That I might drink, and leave the world unseen,
  And with thee fade away into the forest dim: 20

²**hemlock** *opiate; poisonous in large quantities.*
³**drains** *dregs.*
⁴**Lethe-wards** *toward Lethe, the river of forgetfulness.*
⁷**Dryad** *tree nymph.*
¹³**Flora** *goddess of the flowers.*
¹⁴**Provençal song** *Provence, in southern France, home of the troubadours.*
¹⁶**true . . . Hippocrene** *wine; a fountain on Mt. Helicon in Greece, the waters of which stimulated poetic imagination.*

III

Fade far away, dissolve, and quite forget
　What thou among the leaves hast never known,
The weariness, the fever, and the fret
　Here, where men sit and hear each other groan;
Where palsy shakes a few, sad, last gray hairs,　25
　Where youth grows pale, and specter-thin, and dies;
　　Where but to think is to be full of sorrow
　　　And leaden-eyed despairs,
　Where Beauty cannot keep her lustrous eyes,
　　Or new Love pine at them beyond tomorrow.　30

IV

Away! away! for I will fly to thee,
　Not charioted by Bacchus and his pards,
But on the viewless wings of Poesy,
　Though the dull brain perplexes and retards:
Already with thee! tender is the night,　35
　And haply the Queen-Moon is on her throne,
　　Cluster'd around by all her starry Fays;
　　　But here there is no light,
　Save what from heaven is with the breezes blown
　　Through verdurous glooms and winding mossy ways.　40

V

I cannot see what flowers are at my feet,
　Nor what soft incense hangs upon the boughs,
But, in embalmed darkness, guess each sweet
　Wherewith the seasonable month endows
The grass, the thicket, and the fruit-tree wild;　45
　White hawthorn, and the pastoral eglantine;

[32]Bacchus . . . pards *the god of wine and revelry and the leopards that drew his chariot.*
[33]viewless *invisible.*
[36]haply *perhaps.*
[37]Fays *fairies.*
[43]embalmed *scented.*
[46]eglantine *sweetbriar or honeysuckle.*

Fast fading violets cover'd up in leaves;
  And mid-May's eldest child,
The coming musk-rose, full of dewy wine,
  The murmurous haunt of flies on summer eves.   50

VI

Darkling I listen; and for many a time
  I have been half in love with easeful Death,
Call'd him soft names in many a mused rhyme,
  To take into the air my quiet breath;
Now more than ever seems it rich to die,   55
  To cease upon the midnight with no pain,
    While thou art pouring forth thy soul abroad
      In such an ecstasy!
  Still wouldst thou sing, and I have ears in vain—
    To thy high requiem become a sod.   60

VII

Thou wast not born for death, immortal Bird!
  No hungry generations tread thee down;
The voice I hear this passing night was heard
  In ancient days by emperor and clown:
Perhaps the self-same song that found a path   65
  Through the sad heart of Ruth, when, sick for home,
    She stood in tears amid the alien corn;
      The same that oft-times hath
  Charm'd magic casements, opening on the foam
    Of perilous seas, in faery lands forlorn.   70

VIII

Forlorn! the very word is like a bell
  To toll me back from thee to my sole self!
Adieu! the fancy cannot cheat so well
  As she is fam'd to do, deceiving elf.

[51]**Darkling** *in darkness.*
[66-67]**Ruth . . . corn** *a biblical heroine who worked in the harvest fields in a foreign land.*

Adieu! adieu! thy plaintive anthem fades 75
    Past the near meadows, over the still stream,
    Up the hill-side; and now 'tis buried deep
      In the next valley-glades:
    Was it a vision, or a waking dream?
    Fled is that music:—Do I wake or sleep? 80

Ode on Melancholy

I

No, no, go not to Lethe, neither twist
    Wolf's-bane, tight-rooted, for its poisonous wine;
Nor suffer thy pale forehead to be kiss'd
    By nightshade, ruby grape of Proserpine;
Make not your rosary of yew-berries, 5
    Nor let the beetle, nor the death-moth be
      Your mournful Psyche, nor the downy owl
A partner in your sorrow's mysteries;
    For shade to shade will come too drowsily,
      And drown the wakeful anguish of the soul. 10

II

But when the melancholy fit shall fall
    Sudden from heaven like a weeping cloud,
That fosters the droop-headed flowers all,
    And hides the green hill in an April shroud;

---

[4]nightshade *like wolfsbane, a poisonous herb from which sedatives and opiates were extracted* / **Proserpine** *Queen of Hades.*
[5]yew-berries *symbols of mourning, often growing in cemeteries.*
[7]Psyche *soul, sometimes symbolized by a moth that escapes the mouth in sleep or at death* / owl *beetles, moths, and owls have been traditionally associated with darkness, death, and burial.*

Then glut thy sorrow on a morning rose, 15
  Or on the rainbow of the salt sand-wave,
  Or on the wealth of globed peonies;
Or if thy mistress some rich anger shows,
  Imprison her soft hand, and let her rave,
    And feed deep, deep upon her peerless eyes. 20

III

She dwells with Beauty—Beauty that must die;
  And Joy, whose hand is ever at his lips
Bidding adieu; and aching Pleasure nigh,
  Turning to Poison while the bee-mouth sips:
Ay, in the very temple of Delight 25
  Veil'd Melancholy has her sovran shrine,
    Though seen of none save him whose strenuous tongue
Can burst Joy's grape against his palate fine;
His soul shall taste the sadness of her might,
    And be among her cloudy trophies hung. 30

Ode on a Grecian Urn

I

Thou still unravish'd bride of quietness,
  Thou foster-child of silence and slow time,
Sylvan historian, who canst thus express
  A flowery tale more sweetly than our rhyme:
What leaf-fring'd legend haunts about thy shape 5
  Of deities or mortals, or of both,
    In Tempe or the dales of Arcady?

[21]**She** *the goddess Melancholy.*
[28]**fine** *keen, subtle.*
[30]**trophies** *symbols of victory, such as banners, hung in religious shrines.*

[3]**Sylvan** *woodland.*
[7]**Tempe . . . Arcady** *in Greece, beautiful rural regions.*

What men or gods are these? What maidens loath?
What mad pursuit? What struggle to escape?
    What pipes and timbrels? What wild ecstasy?   10

II

Heard melodies are sweet, but those unheard
  Are sweeter; therefore, ye soft pipes, play on;
Not to the sensual ear, but, more endear'd,
  Pipe to the spirit ditties of no tone:
Fair youth, beneath the trees, thou canst not leave   15
  Thy song, nor ever can those trees be bare;
    Bold Lover, never, never canst thou kiss,
Though winning near the goal—yet, do not grieve;
    She cannot fade, though thou hast not thy bliss,
  Forever wilt thou love, and she be fair!   20

III

Ah, happy, happy boughs! that cannot shed
  Your leaves, nor ever bid the Spring adieu;
And, happy melodist, unwearied,
  Forever piping songs forever new;
More happy love! more happy, happy love!   25
  Forever warm and still to be enjoy'd,
    Forever panting, and forever young;
All breathing human passion far above,
  That leaves a heart high-sorrowful and cloy'd,
    A burning forehead, and a parching tongue.   30

IV

Who are these coming to the sacrifice?
  To what green altar, O mysterious priest,
Lead'st thou that heifer lowing at the skies,
  And all her silken flanks with garlands drest?
What little town by river or sea shore,   35
  Or mountain-built with peaceful citadel,
    Is emptied of this folk, this pious morn?

And, little town, thy streets forevermore
   Will silent be; and not a soul to tell
   Why thou art desolate, can e'er return.   40

                                 V

O Attic shape! Fair attitude! with brede
   Of marble men and maidens overwrought,
With forest branches and the trodden weed;
   Thou, silent form, dost tease us out of thought
As doth eternity: Cold Pastoral!   45
   When old age shall this generation waste,
      Thou shalt remain, in midst of other woe
      Than ours, a friend to man, to whom thou say'st,
"Beauty is truth, truth beauty,"—that is all
   Ye know on earth, and all ye need to know.   50

RALPH WALDO EMERSON

[1803–1882]

◆

Concord Hymn

SUNG AT THE COMPLETION OF THE BATTLE MONUMENT,
JULY 4, 1837[†]

By the rude bridge that arched the flood,
   Their flag to April's breeze unfurled,
Here once the embattled farmers stood
   And fired the shot heard round the world.

---

[41]brede *woven pattern.*
[42]overwrought *ornamented.*

[†]The Battle Monument commemorated the battles of Lexington and Concord in 1775.

The foe long since in silence slept;   5
   Alike the conqueror silent sleeps;
And Time the ruined bridge has swept
   Down the dark stream which seaward creeps.

On this green bank, by this soft stream,
   We set to-day a votive stone;   10
That memory may their deed redeem,
   When, like our sires, our sons are gone.

Spirit, that made those heroes dare
   To die, and leave their children free,
Bid Time and Nature gently spare   15
   The shaft we raise to them and thee.

ELIZABETH BARRETT BROWNING

[1806–1861]

♦

How do I love thee? (Sonnet 43)

How do I love thee? Let me count the ways.
I love thee to the depth and breadth and height
My soul can reach, when feeling out of sight
For the ends of Being and ideal Grace.
I love thee to the level of everyday's   5
Most quiet need, by sun and candle-light.
I love thee freely, as men strive for Right;
I love thee purely, as they turn from Praise.
I love thee with the passion put to use
In my old griefs, and with my childhood's faith.   10
I love thee with a love I seemed to lose
With my lost saints—I love thee with the breath,
Smiles, tears, of all my life!—and, if God choose,
I shall but love thee better after death.

HENRY WADSWORTH LONGFELLOW

[1807–1882]

♦

Snowflakes

Out of the bosom of the Air,
　Out of the cloud-folds of her garments shaken,
Over the woodlands brown and bare,
　Over the harvest-fields forsaken,
　　Silent, and soft, and slow 　　　　　　5
　　Descends the snow.

Even as our cloudy fancies take
　Suddenly shape in some divine expression,
Even as the troubled heart doth make
　In the white countenance confession, 　　10
　　The troubled sky reveals
　　The grief it feels.

This is the poem of the air,
　Slowly in silent syllables recorded;
This is the secret of despair, 　　　　　15
　Long in its cloudy bosom hoarded,
　　Now whispered and revealed
　　To wood and field.

OLIVER WENDELL HOLMES

[1809–1894]

♦

The Chambered Nautilus†

This is the ship of pearl, which, poets feign,
    Sails the unshadowed main,
    The venturous bark that flings
On the sweet summer wind its purpled wings
In gulfs enchanted, where the Siren sings,   5
    And coral reefs lie bare,
Where the cold sea-maids rise to sun their streaming hair.

Its webs of living gauze no more unfurl;
    Wrecked is the ship of pearl!
    And every chambered cell,   10
Where its dim dreaming life was wont to dwell,
As the frail tenant shaped his growing shell,
    Before thee lies revealed,
Its irised ceiling rent, its sunless crypt unsealed!

Year after year beheld the silent toil   15
    That spread his lustrous coil;
    Still, as the spiral grew,
He left the past year's dwelling for the new,
Stole with soft step its shining archway through,
    Built up its idle door,   20
Stretched in his last-found home, and knew the old no more.

---

†A small sea animal, the female of which is protected by a very thin spiral shell, pearly
on the inside (lines 1, 9), and whose webbed arms on its back were once thought to function as sails.

Thanks for the heavenly message brought by thee,
  Child of the wandering sea,
  Cast from her lap, forlorn!
From thy dead lips a clearer note is born   25
Than ever Triton blew from wreathéd horn!
  While on mine ear it rings,
Through the deep caves of thought I hear a voice that sings:

Build thee more stately mansions, O my soul,
  As the swift seasons roll!   30
  Leave thy low-vaulted past!
Let each new temple, nobler than the last,
Shut thee from heaven with a dome more vast,
  Till thou at length art free,
Leaving thine outgrown shell by life's unresting sea! 35

EDGAR ALLAN POE

[1809–1849]

♦

To *Helen*

  Helen, thy beauty is to me
   Like those Nicean barks of yore,
 That gently, o'er a perfumed sea,
   The weary, way-worn wanderer bore
   To his own native shore.   5

²**barks** *ships.*

178

On desperate seas long wont to roam,
    Thy hyacinth hair, thy classic face,
Thy Naiad airs have brought me home
    To the glory that was Greece
And the grandeur that was Rome.   10

Lo! in yon brilliant window-niche
    How statue-like I see thee stand!
    The agate lamp within thy hand,
Ah! Psyche from the regions which
    Are Holy Land!   15

Annabel Lee

It was many and many a year ago,
    In a kingdom by the sea,
That a maiden there lived whom you may know
    By the name of Annabel Lee;
And this maiden she lived with no other thought   5
    Than to love and be loved by me.

She was a child and I was a child,
    In this kingdom by the sea,
But we loved with a love that was more than love—
    I and my Annabel Lee—   10
With a love that the wingéd seraphs of Heaven
    Coveted her and me.

---

[7]**hyacinth hair** *allusion to the curled hair of the slain youth Hyacinthus, beloved of Apollo.*
[8]**Naiad** *water nymph.*

And this was the reason that, long ago,
 In this kingdom by the sea,
A wind blew out of a cloud by night   15
 Chilling my Annabel Lee;
So that her highborn kinsmen came
 And bore her away from me,
To shut her up in a sepulchre
 In this kingdom by the sea.   20

The angels, not half so happy in Heaven,
 Went envying her and me:
Yes! that was the reason (as all men know,
 In this kingdom by the sea)
That the wind came out of the cloud, chilling 25
 And killing my Annabel Lee.

But our love it was stronger by far than the love
 Of those who were older than we—
 Of many far wiser than we—
And neither the angels in Heaven above   30
 Nor the demons down under the sea,
Can ever dissever my soul from the soul
 Of the beautiful Annabel Lee:

For the moon never beams without bringing me dreams
 Of the beautiful Annabel Lee;   35
And the stars never rise but I see the bright eyes
 Of the beautiful Annabel Lee;
And so, all the night-tide, I lie down by the side
Of my darling, my darling, my life and my bride,
 In her sepulchre there by the sea—   40
 In her tomb by the side of the sea.

ALFRED, LORD TENNYSON

[1809–1892]

♦

Ulysses†

It little profits that an idle king,
By this still hearth, among these barren crags,
Matched with an aged wife, I mete and dole
Unequal laws unto a savage race,
That hoard, and sleep, and feed, and know not me.   5
I cannot rest from travel; I will drink
Life to the lees. All times I have enjoyed
Greatly, have suffered greatly, both with those
That loved me, and alone; on shore, and when
Through scudding drifts the rainy Hyades   10
Vext the dim sea. I am become a name;
For always roaming with a hungry heart
Much have I seen and known—cities of men
And manners, climates, councils, governments,
Myself not least, but honored of them all,—   15
And drunk delight of battle with my peers,
Far on the ringing plains of windy Troy.
I am a part of all that I have met;
Yet all experience is an arch wherethrough
Gleams that untraveled world whose margin fades   20
For ever and for ever when I move.
How dull it is to pause, to make an end,
To rust unburnished, not to shine in use!

---

†According to Dante (in *The Inferno*, canto 26), Ulysses, having been away for ten years during the Trojan War, is restless upon returning to his island Kingdom of Ithaca, and he persuades a band of followers to accompany him on a journey.
[10]**Hyades** *a constellation of stars whose rising with the sun forecast rain.*
[14]**manners** *customs.*

As though to breathe were life! Life piled on life
Were all too little, and of one to me   25
Little remains; but every hour is saved
From that eternal silence, something more,
A bringer of new things; and vile it were
For some three suns to store and hoard myself,
And this gray spirit yearning in desire   30
To follow knowledge like a sinking star,
Beyond the utmost bound of human thought.
    This is my son, mine own Telemachus,
To whom I leave the scepter and the isle,
Well-loved of me, discerning to fulfill   35
This labor, by slow prudence to make mild
A rugged people, and through soft degrees
Subdue them to the useful and the good.
Most blameless is he, centered in the sphere
Of common duties, decent not to fail   40
In offices of tenderness, and pay
Meet adoration to my household gods,
When I am gone. He works his work, I mine.
    There lies the port; the vessel puffs her sail;
There gloom the dark, broad seas. My mariners,   45
Souls that have toiled, and wrought, and thought with me,
That ever with a frolic welcome took
The thunder and the sunshine, and opposed
Free hearts, free foreheads—you and I are old;
Old age hath yet his honor and his toil.   50
Death closes all; but something ere the end,
Some work of noble note, may yet be done,
Not unbecoming men that strove with gods.
The lights begin to twinkle from the rocks;
The long day wanes; the slow moon climbs; the deep   55
Moans round with many voices. Come, my friends,
'Tis not too late to seek a newer world.
Push off, and sitting well in order smite

---

[40]decent *proper.*
[41]offices *duties.*
[42]Meet *appropriate.*

The sounding furrows; for my purpose holds
To sail beyond the sunset, and the baths   60
Of all the western stars, until I die.
It may be that the gulfs will wash us down;
It may be we shall touch the Happy Isles,
And see the great Achilles, whom we knew.
Though much is taken, much abides; and though   65
We are not now that strength which in old days
Moved earth and heaven, that which we are, we are,
One equal temper of heroic hearts,
Made weak by time and fate, but strong in will
To strive, to seek, to find, and not to yield.   70

Crossing the Bar

Sunset and evening star,
    And one clear call for me!
And may there be no moaning of the bar,
    When I put out to sea,

But such a tide as moving seems asleep,   5
    Too full for sound and foam,
When that which drew from out the boundless deep
    Turns again home.

Twilight and evening bell,
    And after that the dark!   10
And may there be no sadness of farewell,
    When I embark;

For though from out our bourne of Time and Place
    The flood may bear me far,
I hope to see my Pilot face to face   15
    When I have crossed the bar.

[63]**Happy Isles** *the abode after death of those favored by the gods.*

ROBERT BROWNING

[1812–1889]

♦

My Last Duchess

FERRARA

That's my last duchess painted on the wall,
Looking as if she were alive. I call
That piece a wonder, now: Frà Pandolf's hands
Worked busily a day, and there she stands.
Will't please you sit and look at her? I said   5
"Frà Pandolf" by design, for never read
Strangers like you that pictured countenance,
The depth and passion of its earnest glance,
But to myself they turned (since none puts by
The curtain I have drawn for you, but I)   10
And seemed as they would ask me, if they durst,
How such a glance came there; so, not the first
Are you to turn and ask thus. Sir, 'twas not
Her husband's presence only, called that spot
Of joy into the Duchess' cheek: perhaps   15
Frà Pandolf chanced to say "Her mantle laps
Over my lady's wrist too much," or "Paint
Must never hope to reproduce the faint
Half-flush that dies along her throat": such stuff
Was courtesy, she thought, and cause enough   20
For calling up that spot of joy. She had
A heart—how shall I say?—too soon made glad,
Too easily impressed; she liked whate'er
She looked on, and her looks went everywhere.
Sir, 'twas all one! My favor at her breast,   25
The dropping of the daylight in the West,
The bough of cherries some officious fool
Broke in the orchard for her, the white mule

She rode with round the terrace—all and each
Would draw from her alike the approving speech, 30
Or blush, at least. She thanked men—good! but thanked
Somehow—I know not how—as if she ranked
My gift of a nine-hundred-years-old name
With anybody's gift. Who'd stoop to blame
This sort of trifling? Even had you skill 35
In speech—which I have not—to make your will
Quite clear to such an one, and say, "Just this
Or that in you disgusts me; here you miss,
Or there exceed the mark"—and if she let
Herself be lessoned so, nor plainly set 40
Her wits to yours, forsooth, and made excuse,
—E'en then would be some stooping; and I choose
Never to stoop. Oh sir, she smiled, no doubt,
Whene'er I passed her; but who passed without
Much the same smile? This grew; I gave commands; 45
Then all smiles stopped together. There she stands
As if alive. Will 't please you rise? We'll meet
The company below, then. I repeat,
The Count your master's known munificence
Is ample warrant that no just pretense 50
Of mine for dowry will be disallowed;
Though his fair daughter's self, as I avowed
At starting, is my object. Nay, we'll go
Together down, sir. Notice Neptune, though,
Taming a sea-horse, thought a rarity, 55
Which Claus of Innsbruck cast in bronze for me!

EDWARD LEAR

[1812–1888]

◆

The Owl and the Pussy-cat

I

The Owl and the Pussy-cat went to sea
  In a beautiful pea-green boat,
They took some honey, and plenty of money,
  Wrapped up in a five-pound note.
The Owl looked up to the stars above,   5
  And sang to a small guitar,
"O lovely Pussy! O Pussy, my love,
  What a beautiful Pussy you are,
      You are,
      You are!   10
  What a beautiful Pussy you are!"

II

Pussy said to the Owl, "You elegant fowl!
  How charmingly sweet you sing!
O let us be married! too long we have tarried:
  But what shall we do for a ring?"   15
They sailed away, for a year and a day,
  To the land where the Bong-tree grows
And there in a wood a Piggy-wig stood
  With a ring at the end of his nose,
      His nose,
      His nose,   20
  With a ring at the end of his nose.

III

"Dear Pig, are you willing to sell for one shilling
    Your ring?" Said the Piggy, "I will."
So they took it away, and were married next day   25
    By the Turkey who lives on the hill.
They dined on mince, and slices of quince,
    Which they ate with a runcible spoon,
And hand in hand, on the edge of the sand,
    They danced by the light of the moon,   30
        The moon,
        The moon,
They danced by the light of the moon.

EMILY BRONTË

[1818–1848]

♦

Remembrance

Cold in the earth—and the deep snow piled above thee,
Far, far removed, cold in the dreary grave!
Have I forgot, my only Love, to love thee,
Severed at last by Time's all-severing wave?

Now, when alone, do my thoughts no longer hover   5
Over the mountains, on that northern shore,
Resting their wings where health and fern leaves cover
Thy noble heart forever, ever more?

Cold in the earth—and fifteen wild Decembers,
From those brown hills, have melted into spring;   10
Faithful, indeed, is the spirit that remembers
After such years of change and suffering!

Sweet Love of youth, forgive, if I forget thee,
While the world's tide is bearing me along;
Other desires and other hopes beset me,   15
Hopes which obscure, but cannot do thee wrong!

No later light has lightened up my heaven,
No second morn has ever shone for me;
All my life's bliss from thy dear life was given,
All my life's bliss is in the grave with thee.   20

But, when the days of golden dreams had perished,
And even Despair was powerless to destroy,
Then did I learn how existence could be cherished,
Strengthened, and fed without the aid of joy.

Then did I check the tears of useless passion—   25
Weaned my young soul from yearning after thine;
Sternly denied its burning wish to hasten
Down to that tomb already more than mine.

And, even yet, I dare not let it languish,
Dare not indulge in memory's rapturous pain;   30
Once drinking deep of that divinest anguish,
How could I seek the empty world again?

WALT WHITMAN

[1819–1892]

♦

Beat! Beat! Drums!

Beat! beat! drums! blow! bugles! blow!
Through the windows—through doors—burst like a
    ruthless force,
Into the solemn church, and scatter the congregation,

Into the school where the scholar is studying;
Leave not the bridegroom quiet—no happiness must he
    have now with his bride, 5
Nor the peaceful farmer any peace, ploughing his field or
    gathering his grain,
So fierce you whirr and pound you drums—so shrill you
    bugles blow.

Beat! beat! drums!—blow! bugles! blow!
Over the traffic of cities—over the rumble of wheels in
    the streets;
Are beds prepared for sleepers at night in the houses? no
    sleepers must sleep in those beds, 10
No bargainers' bargains by day—no brokers or speculators—
    would they continue?
Would the talkers be talking? would the singer attempt to
    sing?
Would the lawyer rise in the court to state his case before
    the judge?
Then rattle quicker, heavier drums—you bugles wilder blow.

Beat! beat! drums!—blow! bugles! blow! 15
Make no parley—stop for no expostulation,
Mind not the timid—mind not the weeper or prayer,
Mind not the old man beseeching the young man,
Let not the child's voice be heard, nor the mother's
    entreaties,
Make even the trestles to shake the dead where they lie
    awaiting the hearses, 20
So strong you thump O terrible drums—so loud you
    bugles blow.

Cavalry Crossing a Ford

A line in long array where they wind betwixt green islands,
They take a serpentine course, their arms flash in the sun—
    hark to the musical clank,
Behold the silvery river, in it the splashing horses loitering
    stop to drink,
Behold the brown-faced men, each group, each person a
    picture, the negligent rest on the saddles,
Some emerge on the opposite bank, others are just entering
    the ford—while,   5
Scarlet and blue and snowy white,
The guidon flags flutter gayly in the wind.

A Noiseless Patient Spider

A noiseless patient spider,
I mark'd where on a little promontory it stood isolated,
Mark'd how to explore the vacant vast surrounding,
It launch'd forth filament, filament, filament, out of itself,
Ever unreeling them, ever tirelessly speeding them.   5
And you O my soul where you stand,
Surrounded, detached, in measureless oceans of space,
Ceaselessly musing, venturing, throwing, seeking the
    spheres to connect them,
Till the bridge you will need be form'd, till the ductile
    anchor hold,
Till the gossamer thread you fling catch somewhere,
    O my soul.   10

To a Locomotive in Winter

Thee for my recitative,
Thee in the driving storm even as now, the snow, the winter-
    day declining,
Thee in thy panoply, thy measur'd dual throbbing and thy
    beat convulsive,
Thy black cylindric body, golden brass and silvery steel,
Thy ponderous side-bars, parallel and connecting rods,
    gyrating, shuttling at thy sides,   5
Thy metrical, now swelling pant and roar, now tapering in
    the distance,
Thy great protruding head-light fix'd in front,
Thy long, pale, floating vapor-pennants, tinged with delicate
    purple,
The dense and murky clouds out-belching from thy smoke-
    stack,
Thy knitted frame, thy springs and valves, the tremulous
    twinkle of thy wheels,   10
Thy train of cars behind, obedient, merrily following,
Through gale or calm, now swift, now slack, yet steadily
    careering;
Type of the modern—emblem of motion and power—pulse
    of the continent,
For once come serve the Muse and merge in verse, even as
    here I see thee,
With storm and buffeting gusts of wind and falling snow,   15
By day thy warning ringing bell to sound its notes,
By night thy silent signal lamps to swing.

Fierce-throated beauty!
Roll through my chant with all thy lawless music, thy
    swinging lamps at night,
Thy madly-whistled laughter, echoing, rumbling like an
    earthquake, rousing all,   20

Law of thyself complete, thine own track firmly holding,
(No sweetness debonair of tearful harp or glib piano thine,)
Thy trills of shrieks by rocks and hills return'd,
Launch'd o'er the prairies wide, across the lakes,
To the free skies unpent and glad and strong.   25

MATTHEW ARNOLD

[1822–1888]

♦

Dover Beach

The sea is calm tonight.
The tide is full, the moon lies fair
Upon the straits; on the French coast the light
Gleams and is gone; the cliffs of England stand,
Glimmering and vast, out in the tranquil bay.   5
Come to the window, sweet is the night-air!
Only, from the long line of spray
Where the sea meets the moon-blanched land,
Listen! you hear the grating roar
Of pebbles which the waves draw back, and fling,   10
At their return, up the high strand,
Begin, and cease, and then again begin,
With tremulous cadence slow, and bring
The eternal note of sadness in.

Sophocles long ago   15
Heard it on the Aegean, and it brought
Into his mind the turbid ebb and flow
Of human misery; we
Find also in the sound a thought,
Hearing it by this distant northern sea.   20

The Sea of Faith
Was once, too, at the full, and round earth's shore
Lay like the folds of a bright girdle furled.
But now I only hear
Its melancholy, long, withdrawing roar,   25
Retreating, to the breath
Of the night-wind, down the vast edges drear
And naked shingles of the world.

Ah, love, let us be true
To one another! for the world, which seems   30
To lie before us like a land of dreams,
So various, so beautiful, so new,
Hath really neither joy, nor love, nor light,
Nor certitude, nor peace, nor help for pain;
And we are here as on a darkling plain   35
Swept with confused alarms of struggle and flight,
Where ignorant armies clash by night.

EMILY DICKINSON

[1830–1886]

♦

Success is counted sweetest

Success is counted sweetest
By those who ne'er succeed.
To comprehend a nectar
Requires sorest need.

Not one of all the purple Host   5
Who took the Flag today
Can tell the definition
So clear of Victory

As he defeated—dying—
On whose forbidden ear 10
The distant strains of triumph
Burst agonized and clear!

I'm "wife"—I've finished that

I'm "wife"—I've finished that—
That other state—
I'm Czar—I'm "Woman" now—
It's safer so—

How odd the Girl's life looks 5
Behind this soft Eclipse—
I think that Earth feels so
To folks in Heaven—now—

This being comfort—then
That other kind—was pain— 10
But why compare?
I'm "Wife"! Stop there!

I like a look of Agony

I like a look of Agony,
Because I know it's true—
Men do not sham Convulsion,
Nor simulate, a Throe—

The Eyes glaze once—and that is Death— 5
Impossible to feign
The Beads upon the Forehead
By homely Anguish strung.

There's a certain Slant of light

There's a certain Slant of light,
Winter Afternoons—
That oppresses, like the Heft
Of Cathedral Tunes—

Heavenly Hurt, it gives us—   5
We can find no scar,
But internal difference,
Where the Meanings, are—

None may teach it—Any—
'Tis the Sea Despair—   10
An imperial affliction
Sent us of the Air—

When it comes, the Landscape listens—
Shadows—hold their breath—
When it goes, 'tis like the Distance   15
On the look of Death—

I felt a Funeral, in my Brain

I felt a Funeral, in my Brain,
And Mourners to and fro
Kept treading—treading—till it seemed
That Sense was breaking through—

And when they all were seated,   5
A Service, like a Drum—
Kept beating—beating—till I thought
My Mind was going numb—

And I heard them lift a Box
And creak across my Soul
With those same Boots of Lead, again,
The Space—began to toll,   10

As all the Heavens were a Bell,
And Being, but an Ear,
And I, and Silence, some strange Race   15
Wrecked, solitary, here—

And then a Plank in Reason, broke,
And I dropped down, and down—
And hit a World, at every plunge,
And Finished knowing—then—   20

Some keep the Sabbath going to Church

Some keep the Sabbath going to Church—
I keep it, staying at Home—
With a Bobolink for a Chorister—
And an Orchard, for a Dome—

Some keep the Sabbath in Surplice—   5
I just wear my Wings—
And instead of tolling the Bell, for Church,
Our little Sexton—sings.

God preaches, a noted Clergyman—
And the sermon is never long,   10
So instead of getting to Heaven, at last—
I'm going, all along.

After great pain, a formal feeling comes

After great pain, a formal feeling comes—
The Nerves sit ceremonious, like Tombs—
The stiff Heart questions was it He, that bore,
And Yesterday, or Centuries before?

The Feet, mechanical, go round—   5
Of Ground, or Air, or Ought—
A Wooden way
Regardless grown,
A Quartz contentment, like a stone—

This is the Hour of Lead—   10
Remembered, if outlived,
As Freezing persons, recollect the Snow—
First—Chill—then Stupor—then the letting go—

This was a Poet—It is That

This was a Poet—It is That
Distills amazing sense
From ordinary Meanings—
And Attar so immense

From the familiar species   5
That perished by the Door—
We wonder it was not Ourselves
Arrested it—before—

Of Pictures, the Discloser—
The Poet—it is He—   10
Entitles Us—by Contrast—
To ceaseless Poverty—

Of Portion—so unconscious—
The Robbing—could not harm—
Himself—to Him—a Fortune—   15
Exterior—to Time—

I *died for Beauty—but was scarce*

I died for Beauty—but was scarce
Adjusted in the Tomb
When One who died for Truth, was lain
In an adjoining Room—

He questioned softly "Why I failed"?   5
"For Beauty", I replied—
"And I—for Truth—Themself are One—
We Brethren, are", He said—

And so, as Kinsmen, met a Night—
We talked between the Rooms—   10
Until the Moss had reached our lips—
And covered up—our names—

I *heard a Fly buzz—when I died*

I heard a Fly buzz—when I died—
The Stillness in the Room
Was like the Stillness in the Air—
Between the Heaves of Storm—

The Eyes around—had wrung them dry—   5
And Breaths were gathering firm
For the last Onset—when the King
Be witnessed—in the Room—

I willed my Keepsakes—Signed away
What portion of me be   10
Assignable—and then it was
There interposed a Fly—

With Blue—uncertain stumbling Buzz—
Between the light—and me—
And then the Windows failed—and then   15
I could not see to see—

The Heart asks Pleasure—first

The Heart asks Pleasure—first—
And then—Excuse from Pain—
And then—those little Anodynes
That deaden suffering—

And then—to go to sleep—   5
And then—if it should be
The will of its Inquisitor
The privilege to die—

There is a pain—so utter

There is a pain—so utter—
It swallows substance up—
Then covers the Abyss with Trance—
So Memory can step
Around—across—upon it—   5
As one within a Swoon—
Goes safely—where an open eye—
Would drop Him—Bone by Bone.

Pain—has an Element of Blank

Pain—has an Element of Blank—
It cannot recollect
When it begun—or if there were
A time when it was not—

It has no Future—but itself—   5
Its Infinite contain
Its Past—enlightened to perceive
New Periods—of Pain.

"Nature" is what we see

"Nature" is what we see—
The Hill—the Afternoon—
Squirrel—Eclipse—the Bumble bee—
Nay—Nature is Heaven—
Nature is what we hear—   5
The Bobolink—the Sea—
Thunder—the Cricket—
Nay—Nature is Harmony—
Nature is what we know—
Yet have no art to say—   10
So impotent Our Wisdom is
To her Simplicity.

My Life has stood—a Loaded Gun

My Life has stood—a Loaded Gun—
In Corners—till a Day
The Owner passed—identified—
And carried Me away—

And now We roam in Sovereign Woods—   5
And now We hunt the Doe—
And every time I speak for Him—
The Mountains straight reply—

And do I smile, such cordial light
Upon the Valley glow—   10
It is as a Vesuvian face
Had let its pleasure through—

And when at Night—Our good Day done—
I guard My Master's Head—
'Tis better than the Eider-Duck's   15
Deep Pillow—to have shared—

To foe of His—I'm deadly foe—
None stir the second time—
On whom I lay a Yellow Eye—
Or an emphatic Thumb—   20

Though I than He—may longer live
He longer must—than I—
For I have but the power to kill,
Without—the power to die—

A *narrow* Fellow in the Grass

A narrow Fellow in the Grass
Occasionally rides—
You may have met Him—did you not
His notice sudden is—

The Grass divides as with a Comb—   5
A spotted shaft is seen—
And then it closes at your feet
And opens further on—

He likes a Boggy Acre
A floor too cool for Corn— 10
Yet when a Boy, and Barefoot—
I more than once at Noon
Have passed, I thought, a Whip lash
Unbraiding in the Sun
When stooping to secure it 15
It wrinkled, and was gone—

Several of Nature's People
I know, and they know me—
I feel for them a transport
Of cordiality— 20

But never met this Fellow
Attended, or alone
Without a tighter breathing
And Zero at the Bone—

Title divine—is mine!

Title divine—is mine!
The Wife—without the Sign!
Acute Degree—conferred on me—
Empress of Calvary!
Royal—all but the Crown! 5
Betrothed—without the swoon
God sends us Women—
When you—hold—Garnet to Garnet—
Gold—to Gold—
Born—Bridalled—Shrouded— 10
In a Day—

Tri Victory
"My Husband"—women say—
Stroking the Melody—
Is *this*—the way?   15

Tell all the Truth but tell it slant

Tell all the Truth but tell it slant—
Success in Circuit lies
Too bright for our infirm Delight
The Truth's superb surprise

As Lightning to the Children eased   5
With explanation kind
The Truth must dazzle gradually
Or every man be blind—

My life closed twice before its close

My life closed twice before its close—
It yet remains to see
If Immortality unveil
A third event to me

So huge, so hopeless to conceive   5
As these that twice befell.
Parting is all we know of heaven,
And all we need of hell.

CHRISTINA ROSSETTI

[1830–1894]

♦

Remember

Remember me when I am gone away,
   Gone far away into the silent land;
   When you can no more hold me by the hand,
Nor I half turn to go yet turning stay.
Remember me when no more day by day   5
   You tell me of our future that you planned:
   Only remember me; you understand
It will be late to counsel then or pray.
Yet if you should forget me for a while
   And afterwards remember, do not grieve: 10
   For if the darkness and corruption leave
   A vestige of the thoughts that once I had,
Better by far you should forget and smile
   Than that you should remember and be sad.

LEWIS CARROLL
(Charles Lutwidge Dodgson)

[1832–1898]

♦

Jabberwocky

'Twas brillig, and the slithy toves
   Did gyre and gimble in the wabe:
All mimsy were the borogoves,
   And the mome raths outgrabe.

"Beware the Jabberwock, my son!   5
    The jaws that bite, the claws that catch!
Beware the Jubjub bird, and shun
    The frumious Bandersnatch!"

He took his vorpal sword in hand:
    Long time the manxome foe he sought—   10
So rested he by the Tumtum tree,
    And stood awhile in thought.

And, as in uffish thought he stood,
    The Jabberwock, with eyes of flame,
Came whiffling through the tulgey wood,   15
    And burbled as it came!

One, two! One, two! And through and through
    The vorpal blade went snicker-snack!
He left it dead, and with its head
    He went galumphing back.   20

"And hast thou slain the Jabberwock?
    Come to my arms, my beamish boy!
O frabjous day! Callooh! Callay!"
    He chortled in his joy.

'Twas brillig, and the slithy toves   25
    Did gyre and gimble in the wabe:
All mimsy were the borogoves,
    And the mome raths outgrabe.

THOMAS HARDY

[1840–1928]

◆

Channel Firing

That night your great guns, unawares,
Shook all our coffins as we lay,
And broke the chancel window-squares,
We thought it was the Judgment-day

And sat upright. While drearisome   5
Arose the howl of wakened hounds:
The mouse let fall the altar-crumb,
The worms drew back into the mounds,

The glebe cow drooled. Till God called, "No;
It's gunnery practice out at sea   10
Just as before you went below;
The world is as it used to be:

"All nations striving strong to make
Red war yet redder. Mad as hatters
They do no more for Christés sake   15
Than you who are helpless in such matters.

"That this is not the judgment-hour
For some of them's a blessed thing,
For if it were they'd have to scour
Hell's floor for so much threatening. . . .   20

⁹**glebe** *small field.*

"Ha, ha. It will be warmer when
I blow the trumpet (if indeed
I ever do; for you are men,
And rest eternal sorely need)."

So down we lay again. "I wonder, 25
Will the world ever saner be,"
Said one, "than when He sent us under
In our indifferent century!"

And many a skeleton shook his head.
"Instead of preaching forty year," 30
My neighbor Parson Thirdly said,
"I wish I had stuck to pipes and beer."

Again the guns disturbed the hour,
Roaring their readiness to avenge,
As far inland as Stourton Tower, 35
And Camelot, and starlit Stonehenge.

Ah, are you digging on my grave?

"Ah, are you digging on my grave,
　　My loved one?—planting rue?"
—"No: yesterday he went to wed
One of the brightest wealth has bred.
'It cannot hurt her now,' he said, 5
　　'That I should not be true.'"

[36]**Stonehenge** *a circular grouping of stone monuments dating back to the Bronze Age.*

"Then who is digging on my grave?
    My nearest dearest kin?"
—"Ah, no: they sit and think, 'What use!
What good will planting flowers produce?   10
No tendance of her mound can loose
    Her spirit from Death's gin.' "

"But some one digs upon my grave?
    My enemy?—prodding sly?"
—"Nay: When she heard you had passed the Gate   15
That shuts on all flesh soon or late,
She thought you no more worth her hate,
    And cares not where you lie."

"Then, who is digging on my grave?
    Say—since I have not guessed!"   20
—"O it is I, my mistress dear,
Your little dog, who still lives near,
And much I hope my movements here
    Have not disturbed your rest?"

"Ah, yes! *You* dig upon my grave . . .   25
    Why flashed it not on me
That one true heart was left behind!
What feeling do we ever find
To equal among human kind
    A dog's fidelity!"   30

"Mistress, I dug upon your grave
    To bury a bone, in case
I should be hungry near this spot
When passing on my daily trot.
I am sorry, but I quite forgot   35
    It was your resting-place."

The Voice

Woman much missed, how you call to me, call to me,
Saying that now you are not as you were
When you had changed from the one who was all to me,
But as at first, when our day was fair.

Can it be you that I hear? Let me view you, then,   5
Standing as when I drew near to the town
Where you would wait for me: yes, as I knew you then,
Even to the original air-blue gown!

Or is it only the breeze, in its listlessness
Traveling across the wet mead to me here,   10
You being ever dissolved to wan wistlessness,
Heard no more again far or near?

　　Thus I; faltering forward,
　　Leaves around me falling,
Wind oozing thin through the thorn from norward.   15
　　And the woman calling.

Neutral Tones

We stood by a pond that winter day,
And the sun was white, as though chidden of God,
And a few leaves lay on the starving sod;
　　—They had fallen from an ash, and were gray.

Your eyes on me were as eyes that rove   5
Over tedious riddles of years ago;
And some words played between us to and fro
　　On which lost the more by our love.

The smile on your mouth was the deadest thing
Alive enough to have strength to die;   10
And a grin of bitterness swept thereby
　　Like an ominous bird a-wing. . . .

Since then, keen lessons that love deceives,
And wrings with wrong, have shaped to me
Your face, and the God-curst sun, and a tree,   15
　　And a pond edged with grayish leaves.

The Man He Killed

"Had he and I but met
　　By some old ancient inn,
We should have sat us down to wet
　　Right many a nipperkin!

"But ranged as infantry,   5
　　And staring face to face,
I shot at him as he at me,
　　And killed him in his place.

"I shot him dead because—
　　Because he was my foe,   10
Just so: my foe of course he was;
　　That's clear enough; although

"He thought he'd 'list, perhaps,
　　Off-hand like—just as I—
Was out of work—had sold his traps—   15
　　No other reason why.

"Yes; quaint and curious war is!
　　You shoot a fellow down
You'd treat if met where any bar is,
　　Or help to half-a-crown."   20

GERARD MANLEY HOPKINS

[1844–1889]

♦

God's Grandeur

The world is charged with the grandeur of God.
  It will flame out, like shining from shook foil;
  It gathers to a greatness, like the ooze of oil
Crushed. Why do men then now not reck his rod?
Generations have trod, have trod, have trod;   5
  And all is seared with trade; bleared, smeared with toil;
  And wears man's smudge and shares man's smell: the soil
Is bare now, nor can foot feel, being shod.

And for all this, nature is never spent;
  There lives the dearest freshness deep down things;   10
And though the last lights off the black West went
  Oh, morning, at the brown brink eastward, springs—
Because the Holy Ghost over the bent
  World broods with warm breast and with ah! bright wings.

---

²**foil** *gold or tinsel foil.*
⁴**crushed** *as when olives are crushed for their oil.*

Pied Beauty[†]

Glory be to God for dappled things—
  For skies of couple-colour as a brinded cow;
    For rose-moles all in stipple upon trout that swim;
Fresh-firecoal chestnut-falls; finches' wings;
  Landscape plotted and pieced—fold, fallow, and plough;   5
    And all trades, their gear and tackle and trim.
All things counter, original, spare, strange;
  Whatever is fickle, freckled (who knows how?)
    With swift, slow; sweet, sour; adazzle, dim;
He fathers-forth whose beauty is past change: 10
               Praise him.

Spring and Fall

To a Young Child

Márgarét, áre you gríeving
Over Goldengrove unleaving?
Leáves, líke the things of man, you
With your fresh thoughts care for, can you?
Áh! ás the heart grows older   5
It will come to such sights colder
By and by, nor spare a sigh
Though worlds of wanwood leafmeal lie;
And yet you *will* weep and know why.

[†]Variegated beauty.
[2]**brinded** *brindled, streaked.*
[4]**chestnut-falls** *roasted chestnuts stripped of their husks.*
[6]**trim** *equipment.*
[7]**spare** *unusual.*

[8]**wanwood** *pale or dim—the groves are pale because of their light-colored autumn foliage, or dim because of the filtered light* / **leafmeal** *a word coined by Hopkins by analogy with piecemeal: leaf by leaf or leaf mold—in the first sense, the foliage lies about the grove, having fallen leaf by leaf; in the second, foliage gradually decays to leaf mold.*

Now no matter, child, the name: 10
Sórrow's spríngs áre the same.
Nor mouth had, no nor mind expressed
What heart heard of, ghost guessed:
It ís the blight man was born for,
It is Margaret you mourn for.   15

Inversnaid[†]

This darksome burn, horseback brown,
His rollrock highroad roaring down,
In coop and in comb the fleece of his foam
Flutes and low to the lake falls home.

A windpuff-bonnet of fáwn-fróth   5
Turns and twindles over the broth
Of a pool so pitchblack, féll-frówning,
It rounds and rounds Despair to drowning.

Degged with dew, dappled with dew
Are the groins of the braes that the brook treads through,   10
Wiry heathpacks, flitches of fern,
And the beadbonny ash that sits over the burn.

[13]**ghost** *spirit, soul.*

[†]Town in Scottish Highlands.
[1]**burn** *stream.*
[3]**coop** *hollow* / **comb** *crest.*
[6]**Turns and twindles** The editors of The Poems of Gerard Manley Hopkins, 4th ed., *say that twindles "seems to be a portmanteau coinage inscaping 'twists,' 'twitches,' and 'dwindles' . . . but possibly verbal use of obs. 'twindle' (twin) is intended to suggest the splitting of a whirlpool into two."*
[9]**degged** *sprinkled.*
[10]**braes** *steep banks.*
[11]**heathpacks** *heather* / **flitches** *the editors of the 4th edition say "ragged, russet flakes, tufts or clumps."*
[12]**beadbonny** *with clusters of bright beadlike berries.*

What would the world be, once bereft
Of wet and of wildness? Let them be left.
O let them be left, wildness and wet;   15
Long live the weeds and the wilderness yet.

Thou art indeed just, Lord

Justus quidem tu es, Domine, si disputem tecum:
verumtamen justa loquar ad te:
Quare via impiorum prosperatur?[†]

Thou art indeed just, Lord, if I contend
With thee; but, sir, so what I plead is just.
Why do sinners' ways prosper? and why must
Disappointment all I endeavour end?
Wert thou my enemy, O thou my friend,   5
How wouldst thou worse, I wonder, than thou dost
Defeat, thwart me? Oh, the sots and thralls of lust
Do in spare hours more thrive than I that spend,

Sir, life upon thy cause. See, banks and brakes
Now, leavèd how thick! lacèd they are again   10
With fretty chervil, look, and fresh wind shakes

Them; birds build—but not I build; no, but strain,
Time's eunuch, and not breed one work that wakes.
Mine, O thou lord of life, send my roots rain.

[†]These lines are translated in the first two and one-half lines of the poem.

A. E. HOUSMAN

[1859–1936]

◆

To an Athlete Dying Young

The time you won your town the race
We chaired you through the market-place;
Man and boy stood cheering by,
And home we brought you shoulder-high.

To-day, the road all runners come, 5
Shoulder-high we bring you home,
And set you at your threshold down,
Townsman of a stiller town.

Smart lad, to slip betimes away
From fields where glory does not stay 10
And early though the laurel grows
It withers quicker than the rose.

Eyes the shady night has shut
Cannot see the record cut,
And silence sounds no worse than cheers 15
After earth has stopped the ears:

Now you will not swell the rout
Of lads that wore their honours out,
Runners whom renown outran
And the name died before the man. 20

So set, before its echoes fade,
The fleet foot on the sill of shade,
And hold to the low lintel up
The still-defended challenge-cup.

And round that early-laurelled head   25
Will flock to gaze the strengthless dead
And find unwithered on its curls
The garland briefer than a girl's.

With rue my heart is laden

With rue my heart is laden
　　For golden friends I had,
For many a rose-lipt maiden
　　And many a lightfoot lad.

By brooks too broad for leaping   5
　　The lightfoot boys are laid;
The rose-lipt girls are sleeping
　　In fields where roses fade.

WILLIAM BUTLER YEATS

[1865–1939]

◆

The Lake Isle of Innisfree

I will arise and go now, and go to Innisfree,
And a small cabin build there, of clay and wattles made:
Nine bean-rows will I have there, a hive for the honey-bee,
And live alone in the bee-loud glade.

And I shall have some peace there, for peace comes
   dropping slow   5
Dropping from the veils of the morning to where the
   cricket sings;
There midnight's all a glimmer, and noon a purple glow,
And evening full of the linnet's wings.

I will arise and go now, for always night and day
I hear lake water lapping with low sounds by the shore;   10
While I stand on the roadway, or on the pavements grey,
I hear it in the deep heart's core.

The Wild Swans at Coole

The trees are in their autumn beauty,
The woodland paths are dry,
Under the October twilight the water
Mirrors a still sky;
Upon the brimming water among the stones   5
Are nine-and-fifty swans.

The nineteenth autumn has come upon me
Since I first made my count;
I saw, before I had well finished,
All suddenly mount   10
And scatter wheeling in great broken rings
Upon their clamorous wings.

I have looked upon those brilliant creatures,
And now my heart is sore.
All's changed since I, hearing at twilight,   15
The first time on this shore,
The bell-beat of their wings above my head,
Trod with a lighter tread.

Unwearied still, lover by lover,
They paddle in the cold   20
Companionable streams or climb the air;
Their hearts have not grown old;
Passion or conquest, wander where they will,
Attend upon them still.

But now they drift on the still water,   25
Mysterious, beautiful;
Among what rushes will they build,
By what lake's edge or pool
Delight men's eyes when I awake some day
To find they have flown away?   30

An Irish Airman Foresees His Death

I know that I shall meet my fate
Somewhere among the clouds above;
Those that I fight I do not hate,
Those that I guard I do not love;
My country is Kiltartan Cross   5
My countrymen Kiltartan's poor,
No likely end could bring them loss
Or leave them happier than before.
Nor law, nor duty bade me fight,
Nor public men, nor cheering crowds,   10
A lonely impulse of delight
Drove to this tumult in the clouds;
I balanced all, brought all to mind,
The years to come seemed waste of breath,
A waste of breath the years behind   15
In balance with this life, this death.

The Scholars

Bald heads forgetful of their sins,
Old, learned, respectable bald heads
Edit and annotate the lines
That young men, tossing on their beds,
Rhymed out in love's despair   5
To flatter beauty's ignorant ear.

All shuffle there; all cough in ink;
All wear the carpet with their shoes;
All think what other people think;
All know the man their neighbor knows.   10
Lord, what would they say
Did their Catullus walk that way?

The Second Coming[†]

Turning and turning in the widening gyre
The falcon cannot hear the falconer;
Things fall apart; the center cannot hold;
Mere anarchy is loosed upon the world,
The blood-dimmed tide is loosed, and everywhere   5
The ceremony of innocence is drowned;
The best lack all conviction, while the worst
Are full of passionate intensity.

[12] **Catullus** *Roman poet (ca. 84–54 B.C.) known especially for his love poems.*

[†]The title alludes to the prophesied return of Jesus Christ and also to the beast of the Apocalypse. See Matthew 24 and Revelation.

[1] **gyre** *spiral.*

Surely some revelation is at hand;
Surely the Second Coming is at hand;   10
The Second Coming! Hardly are those words out
When a vast image out of *Spiritus Mundi*
Troubles my sight: somewhere in sands of the desert
A shape with lion body and the head of a man,
A gaze blank and pitiless as the sun,   15
Is moving its slow thighs, while all about it
Reel shadows of the indignant desert birds.
The darkness drops again; but now I know
That twenty centuries of stony sleep
Were vexed to nightmare by a rocking cradle,   20
And what rough beast, its hour come round at last,
Slouches towards Bethlehem to be born?

Leda and the Swan[†]

A sudden blow: the great wings beating still
Above the staggering girl, her thighs caressed
By the dark webs, her nape caught in his bill,
He holds her helpless breast upon his breast.

How can those terrified vague fingers push   5
The feathered glory from her loosening thighs?
And how can body, laid in that white rush,
But feel the strange heart beating where it lies?

---

[12]*Spiritus Mundi for Yeats, a common storehouse of images, a communal human memory.*

[†]According to Greek mythology, Zeus, in the guise of a swan, raped Leda, queen of Sparta. Helen, their daughter, married Menelaus, King of Sparta, but ran off with Paris, son of Priam, King of Troy. A ten-year seige of Troy by the Greeks ensued to bring Helen back.

A shudder in the loins engenders there
The broken wall, the burning roof and tower   10
And Agamemnon dead.
                        Being so caught up,
So mastered by the brute blood of the air,
Did she put on his knowledge with his power
Before the indifferent beak could let her drop?

EDWIN ARLINGTON ROBINSON

[1869–1935]

♦

Richard Cory

Whenever Richard Cory went down town,
We people on the pavement looked at him:
He was a gentleman from sole to crown,
Clean favored and imperially slim.

And he was always quietly arrayed,   5
And he was always human when he talked;
But still he fluttered pulses when he said,
"Good-morning," and he glittered when he walked.

And he was rich—yes, richer than a king—
And admirably schooled in every grace: 10
In fine, we thought that he was everything
To make us wish that we were in his place.

So on we worked, and waited for the light,
And went without the meat and cursed the bread;
And Richard Cory, one calm summer night,   15
Went home and put a bullet through his head.

Miniver Cheevy

Miniver Cheevy, child of scorn,
   Grew lean while he assailed the seasons;
He wept that he was ever born,
   And he had reasons.

Miniver loved the days of old   5
   When swords were bright and steeds were prancing;
The vision of a warrior bold
   Would set him dancing.

Miniver sighed for what was not,
   And dreamed, and rested from his labors;   10
He dreamed of Thebes and Camelot.
   And Priam's neighbors.

Miniver mourned the ripe renown
   That made so many a name so fragrant;
He mourned Romance, now on the town,   15
   And Art, a vagrant.

Miniver loved the Medici,
   Albeit he had never seen one;
He would have sinned incessantly
   Could he have been one.   20

Miniver cursed the commonplace
   And eyed a khaki suit with loathing;
He missed the mediaeval grace
   Of iron clothing.

---

[11]**Thebes** *Greek city famous in history and legend* / **Camelot** *the seat of King Arthur's court.*
[12]**Priam** *King of Troy during the Trojan War.*
[17]**the Medici** *family of powerful merchants and bankers, rulers of Florence in the 14th, 15th, and 16th centuries who were known for their patronage of the arts.*

Miniver scorned the gold he sought,   25
   But sore annoyed was he without it;
Miniver thought, and thought, and thought,
   And thought about it.

Miniver Cheevy, born too late,
   Scratched his head and kept on thinking;   30
Miniver coughed, and called it fate,
   And kept on drinking.

PAUL LAURENCE DUNBAR

[1872–1906]

♦

We wear the mask

We wear the mask that grins and lies,
It hides our cheeks and shades our eyes—
This debt we pay to human guile;
With torn and bleeding hearts we smile,
And mouth with myriad subtleties.   5

Why should the world be over-wise,
In counting all our tears and sighs?
Nay, let them only see us, while
   We wear the mask.

We smile, but, O great Christ, our cries   10
To thee from tortured souls arise.
We sing, but oh the clay is vile
Beneath our feet, and long the mile;
But let the world dream otherwise,
   We wear the mask!   15

WALTER DE LA MARE

[1873–1956]

♦

The Listeners

"Is there anybody there?" said the Traveler,
  Knocking on the moonlit door;
And his horse in the silence champed the grasses
  Of the forest's ferny floor:
And a bird flew up out of the turret,   5
  Above the Traveler's head:
And he smote upon the door again a second time;
  "Is there anybody there?" he said.
But no one descended to the Traveler;
  No head from the leaf-fringed sill   10
Leaned over and looked into his gray eyes,
  Where he stood perplexed and still.
But only a host of phantom listeners
  That dwelt in the lone house then
Stood listening in the quiet of the moonlight   15
  To that voice from the world of men:
Stood thronging the faint moonbeams on the dark stair,
  That goes down to the empty hall,
Hearkening in an air stirred and shaken
  By the lonely Traveler's call.   20
And he felt in his heart their strangeness,
  Their stillness answering his cry,
While his horse moved, cropping the dark turf,
  'Neath the starred and leafy sky;
For he suddenly smote on the door, even   25
  Louder, and lifted his head:—
"Tell them I came, and no one answered,
  That I kept my word," he said.

Never the least stir made the listeners,
    Though every word he spake   30
Fell echoing through the shadowiness of the still house
    From the one man left awake:
Ay, they heard his foot upon the stirrup,
    And the sound of iron on stone,
And how the silence surged softly backward,   35
    When the plunging hoofs were gone.

ROBERT FROST

[1874–1963]

♦

Mending Wall

Something there is that doesn't love a wall,
That sends the frozen-ground-swell under it,
And spills the upper boulders in the sun;
And makes gaps even two can pass abreast.
The work of hunters is another thing: 5
I have come after them and made repair
Where they have left not one stone on a stone,
But they would have the rabbit out of hiding,
To please the yelping dogs. The gaps I mean,
No one has seen them made or heard them made,   10
But at spring mending-time we find them there.
I let my neighbor know beyond the hill;
And on a day we meet to walk the line
And set the wall between us once again.
We keep the wall between us as we go.   15
To each the boulders that have fallen to each.
And some are loaves and some so nearly balls
We have to use a spell to make them balance:
'Stay where you are until our backs are turned!'
We wear our fingers rough with handling them.   20

Oh, just another kind of outdoor game,
One on a side. It comes to little more:
There where it is we do not need the wall:
He is all pine and I am apple orchard.
My apple trees will never get across   25
And eat the cones under his pines, I tell him.
He only says, 'Good fences make good neighbors.'
Spring is the mischief in me, and I wonder
If I could put a notion in his head:
'*Why* do they make good neighbors? Isn't it   30
Where there are cows? But here there are no cows.
Before I built a wall I'd ask to know
What I was walling in or walling out,
And to whom I was like to give offense.
Something there is that doesn't love a wall,   35
That wants it down.' I could say Elves' to him,
But it's not elves exactly, and I'd rather
He said it for himself. I see him there
Bringing a stone grasped firmly by the top
In each hand, like an old-stone savage armed.   40
He moves in darkness as it seems to me,
Not of woods only and the shade of trees.
He will not go behind his father's saying,
And he likes having thought of it so well
He says again, 'Good fences make good neighbors.'   45

The Death of the Hired Man

Mary sat musing on the lamp-flame at the table
Waiting for Warren. When she heard his step,
She ran on tiptoe down the darkened passage
To meet him in the doorway with the news
And put him on his guard. "Silas is back."   5
She pushed him outward with her through the door
And shut it after her. "Be kind," she said.

She took the market things from Warren's arms
And set them on the porch, then drew him down
To sit beside her on the wooden steps.   10

"When was I ever anything but kind to him?
But I'll not have the fellow back," he said.
"I told him so last haying, didn't I?
If he left then, I said, that ended it.
What good is he? Who else will harbor him   15
At his age for the little he can do?
What help he is there's no depending on.
Off he goes always when I need him most.
He thinks he ought to earn a little pay,
Enough at least to buy tobacco with,   20
So he won't have to beg and be beholden.
'All right,' I say, 'I can't afford to pay
Any fixed wages, though I wish I could.'
'Someone else can.' 'Then someone else will have to.'
I shouldn't mind his bettering himself   25
If that was what it was. You can be certain,
When he begins like that, there's someone at him
Trying to coax him off with pocket money,—
In haying time, when any help is scarce.
In winter he comes back to us. I'm done."   30

"Sh! not so loud: he'll hear you," Mary said.

"I want him to: he'll have to soon or late."

"He's worn out. He's asleep beside the stove.
When I came up from Rowe's I found him here,
Huddled against the barn door fast asleep,   35
A miserable sight, and frightening, too—
You needn't smile—I didn't recognize him—
I wasn't looking for him—and he's changed.
Wait till you see."

       "Where did you say he'd been?"

"He didn't say. I dragged him to the house,   40
And gave him tea and tried to make him smoke.
I tried to make him talk about his travels.
Nothing would do: he just kept nodding off."

"What did he say? Did he say anything?"

"But little."   45

                    "Anything? Mary, confess
He said he'd come to ditch the meadow for me."

"Warren!"

                    "But did he? I just want to know."

"Of course he did. What would you have him say?
Surely you wouldn't grudge the poor old man
Some humble way to save his self-respect.   50
He added, if you really care to know,
He meant to clear the upper pasture, too.
That sounds like something you have heard before?
Warren, I wish you could have heard the way
He jumbled everything. I stopped to look   55
Two or three times—he made me feel so queer—
To see if he was talking in his sleep.
He ran on Harold Wilson—you remember—
The boy you had in haying four years since.
He's finished school, and teaching in his college.   60
Silas declares you'll have to get him back.
He says they two will make a team for work:
Between them they will lay this farm as smooth!
The way he mixed that in with other things.
He thinks young Wilson a likely lad, though daft   65
On education—you know how they fought
All through July under the blazing sun,
Silas up on the cart to build the load
Harold along beside to pitch it on."

"Yes, I took care to keep well out of earshot." 70

"Well, those days trouble Silas like a dream.
You wouldn't think they would. How some things linger!
Harold's young college boy's assurance piqued him.
After so many years he still keeps finding
Good arguments he sees he might have used. 75
I sympathize. I know just how it feels
To think of the right thing to say too late.
Harold's associated in his mind with Latin.
He asked me what I thought of Harold's saying
He studied Latin, like the violin, 80
Because he liked it—that an argument!
He said he couldn't make the boy believe
He could find water with a hazel prong—
Which showed how much good school had ever done him.
He wanted to go over that. But most of all 85
He thinks if he could have another chance
To teach him how to build a load of hay—"

"I know that's Silas' one accomplishment.
He bundles every forkful in its place,
And tags and numbers it for future reference, 90
So he can find and easily dislodge it
In the unloading. Silas does that well.
He takes it out in bunches like big birds' nests.
You never see him standing on the hay
He's trying to lift, straining to lift himself." 95

"He thinks if he could teach him that, he'd be
Some good perhaps to someone in the world.
He hates to see a boy the fool of books.
Poor Silas, so concerned for other folk,
And nothing to look backward to with pride, 100
And nothing to look forward to with hope,
So now and never any different."

Part of a moon was falling down the west,
Dragging the whole sky with it to the hills.
Its light poured softly in her lap. She saw it 105
And spread her apron to it. She put out her hand
Among the harp-like morning-glory strings,
Taut with the dew from garden bed to eaves,
As if she played unheard some tenderness
That wrought on him beside her in the night. 110
"Warren," she said, "he has come home to die:
You needn't be afraid he'll leave you this time."

"Home," he mocked gently.

    "Yes, what else but home?
It all depends on what you mean by home.
Of course he's nothing to us, any more 115
Than was the hound that came a stranger to us
Out of the woods, worn out upon the trail."

"Home is the place where, when you have to go there,
They have to take you in."

    "I should have called it
Something you somehow haven't to deserve." 120

Warren leaned out and took a step or two,
Picked up a little stick, and brought it back
And broke it in his hand and tossed it by.
"Silas has better claim on us you think
Than on his brother? Thirteen little miles 125
As the road winds would bring him to his door.
Silas has walked that far no doubt to-day.
Why doesn't he go there? His brother's rich,
A somebody—director in the bank."

"He never told us that." 130

    "We know it though."

"I think his brother ought to help, of course.
I'll see to that if there is need. He ought of right
To take him in, and might be willing to—
He may be better than appearances.
But have some pity on Silas. Do you think   135
If he had any pride in claiming kin
Or anything he looked for from his brother,
He'd keep so still about him all this time?"

"I wonder what's between them."

        "I can tell you.
Silas is what he is—we wouldn't mind him—   140
But just the kind that kinsfolk can't abide.
He never did a thing so very bad.
He don't know why he isn't quite as good
As anybody. Worthless though he is,
He won't be made ashamed to please his brother."   145

"*I* can't think Si ever hurt anyone."

"No, but he hurt my heart the way he lay
And rolled his old head on that sharp-edged chair-back.
He wouldn't let me put him on the lounge.
You must go in and see what you can do.   150
I made the bed up for him there tonight.
You'll be surprised at him—how much he's broken.
His working days are done; I'm sure of it."

"I'd not be in a hurry to say that."

"I haven't been. Go, look, see for yourself.   155
But, Warren, please remember how it is:
He's come to help you ditch the meadow.
He has a plan. You mustn't laugh at him.
He may not speak of it, and then he may.
I'll sit and see if that small sailing cloud   160
Will hit or miss the moon."

231

It hit the moon.
Then there were three there, making a dim row,
The moon, the little silver cloud, and she.

Warren returned—too soon, it seemed to her,
Slipped to her side, caught up her hand and waited.   165
"Warren?" she questioned.

          "Dead," was all he answered.

The Tuft of Flowers

I went to turn the grass once after one
Who mowed it in the dew before the sun.

The dew was gone that made his blade so keen
Before I came to view the leveled scene.

I looked for him behind an isle of trees;   5
I listened for his whetstone on the breeze.

But he had gone his way, the grass all mown,
And I must be, as he had been,—alone,

"As all must be," I said within my heart,
"Whether they work together or apart."   10

But as I said it, swift there passed me by
On noiseless wing a bewildered butterfly,

Seeking with memories grown dim o'er night
Some resting flower of yesterday's delight.

And once I marked his flight go round and round,   15
As where some flower lay withering on the ground.

And then he flew as far as eye could see,
And then on tremulous wing came back to me.

I thought of questions that have no reply,
And would have turned to toss the grass to dry;   20

But he turned first, and led my eye to look
At a tall tuft of flowers beside a brook,

A leaping tongue of bloom the scythe had spared
Beside a reedy brook the scythe had bared.

The mower in the dew had loved them thus,   25
By leaving them to flourish, not for us,

Nor yet to draw one thought of ours to him,
But from sheer morning gladness at the brim.

The butterfly and I had lit upon,
Nevertheless, a message from the dawn,   30

That made me hear the wakening birds around,
And hear his long scythe whispering to the ground,

And feel a spirit kindred to my own;
So that henceforth I worked no more alone;

But glad with him, I worked as with his aid,   35
And weary, sought at noon with him the shade;

And dreaming, as it were, held brotherly speech
With one whose thought I had not hoped to reach.

"Men work together," I told him from the heart,
"Whether they work together or apart."   40

The Road Not Taken

Two roads diverged in a yellow wood,
And sorry I could not travel both
And be one traveler, long I stood
And looked down one as far as I could
To where it bent in the undergrowth;   5

Then took the other, as just as fair,
And having perhaps the better claim,
Because it was grassy and wanted wear;
Though as for that, the passing there
Had worn them really about the same,   10

And both that morning equally lay
In leaves no step had trodden black.
Oh, I kept the first for another day!
Yet knowing how way leads on to way,
I doubted if I should ever come back.   15

I shall be telling this with a sigh
Somewhere ages and ages hence:
Two roads diverged in a wood, and I—
I took the one less traveled by,
And that has made all the difference.   20

Birches

When I see birches bend to left and right
Across the lines of straighter darker trees,
I like to think some boy's been swinging them.
But swinging doesn't bend them down to stay
As ice-storms do. Often you must have seen them   5
Loaded with ice a sunny winter morning
After a rain. They click upon themselves

As the breeze rises, and turn many-colored
As the stir cracks and crazes their enamel.
Soon the sun's warmth makes them shed crystal shells   10
Shattering and avalanching on the snow-crust—
Such heaps of broken glass to sweep away
You'd think the inner dome of heaven had fallen.
They are dragged to the withered bracken by the load,
And they seem not to break; though once they are bowed   15
So low for long, they never right themselves:
You may see their trunks arching in the woods
Years afterwards, trailing their leaves on the ground
Like girls on hands and knees that throw their hair
Before them over their heads to dry in the sun.   20
But I was going to say when Truth broke in
With all her matter-of-fact about the ice-storm,
I should prefer to have some boy bend them
As he went out and in to fetch the cows—
Some boy too far from town to learn baseball,   25
Whose only play was what he found himself,
Summer or winter, and could play alone.
One by one he subdued his father's trees
By riding them down over and over again
Until he took the stiffness out of them,   30
And not one but hung limp, not one was left
For him to conquer. He learned all there was
To learn about not launching out too soon
And so not carrying the tree away
Clear to the ground. He always kept his poise   35
To the top branches, climbing carefully
With the same pains you use to fill a cup
Up to the brim, and even above the brim.
Then he flung outward, feet first, with a swish,
Kicking his way down through the air to the ground.   40
So was I once myself a swinger of birches.
And so I dream of going back to be.
It's when I'm weary of considerations,
And life is too much like a pathless wood
Where your face burns and tickles with the cobwebs   45
Broken across it, and one eye is weeping

From a twig's having lashed across it open.
I'd like to get away from earth awhile
And then come back to it and begin over.
May no fate willfully misunderstand me   50
And half grant what I wish and snatch me away
Not to return. Earth's the right place for love:
I don't know where it's likely to go better.
I'd like to go by climbing a birch tree,
And climb black branches up a snow-white trunk   55
Toward heaven, till the tree could bear no more,
But dipped its top and set me down again.
That would be good both going and coming back.
One could do worse than be a swinger of birches.

"Out, Out—"

The buzz saw snarled and rattled in the yard
And made dust and dropped stove-length sticks of wood,
Sweet-scented stuff when the breeze drew across it.
And from there those that lifted eyes could count
Five mountain ranges one behind the other   5
Under the sunset far into Vermont.
And the saw snarled and rattled, snarled and rattled,
As it ran light, or had to bear a load.
And nothing happened: day was all but done.
Call it a day, I wish they might have said   10
To please the boy by giving him the half hour
That a boy counts so much when saved from work.
His sister stood beside them in her apron
To tell them "Supper." At the word, the saw,
As if to prove saws knew what supper meant,   15
Leaped out at the boy's hand, or seemed to leap—
He must have given the hand. However it was,
Neither refused the meeting. But the hand!

The boy's first outcry was a rueful laugh,
As he swung toward them holding up the hand,   20
Half in appeal, but half as if to keep
The life from spilling. Then the boy saw all—
Since he was old enough to know, big boy
Doing a man's work, though a child at heart—
He saw all spoiled. "Don't let him cut my hand off—   25
The doctor, when he comes. Don't let him, sister!"
So. But the hand was gone already.
The doctor put him in the dark of ether.
He lay and puffed his lips out with his breath.
And then—the watcher at his pulse took fright.   30
No one believed. They listened at his heart.
Little—less—nothing!—and that ended it.
No more to build on there. And they, since they
Were not the one dead, turned to their affairs.

The Silken Tent

She is as in a field a silken tent
At midday when a sunny summer breeze
Has dried the dew and all its ropes relent,
So that in guys it gently sways at ease,
And its supporting central cedar pole,   5
That is its pinnacle to heavenward
And signifies the sureness of the soul,
Seems to owe naught to any single cord,
But strictly held by none, is loosely bound
By countless silken ties of love and thought   10
To everything on earth the compass round,
And only by one's going slightly taut
In the capriciousness of summer air
Is of the slightest bondage made aware.

Never Again Would Birds' Song Be the Same

He would declare and could himself believe
That the birds there in all the garden round
From having heard the daylong voice of Eve
Had added to their own an oversound,
Her tone of meaning but without the words.   5
Admittedly an eloquence so soft
Could only have had an influence on birds
When call or laughter carried it aloft.
Be that as may be, she was in their song.
Moreover her voice upon their voices crossed   10
Had now persisted in the woods so long
That probably it never would be lost.
Never again would birds' song be the same.
And to do that to birds was why she came.

The Gift Outright

The land was ours before we were the land's.
She was our land more than a hundred years
Before we were her people. She was ours
In Massachusetts, in Virginia,
But we were England's, still colonials,   5
Possessing what we still were unpossessed by,
Possessed by what we now no more possessed.
Something we were withholding made us weak
Until we found out that it was ourselves
We were withholding from our land of living,   10
And forthwith found salvation in surrender.
Such as we were we gave ourselves outright
(The deed of gift was many deeds of war)
To the land vaguely realizing westward,
But still unstoried, artless, unenhanced,   15
Such as she was, such as she would become.

238

Stopping by Woods on a Snowy Evening

Whose woods these are I think I know.
His house is in the village, though;
He will not see me stopping here
To watch his woods fill up with snow.

My little horse must think it queer   5
To stop without a farmhouse near
Between the woods and frozen lake
The darkest evening of the year.

He gives his harness bells a shake
To ask if there is some mistake.   10
The only other sound's the sweep
Of easy wind and downy flake.

The woods are lovely, dark and deep,
But I have promises to keep,
And miles to go before I sleep,   15
And miles to go before I sleep.

After Apple-Picking

My long two-pointed ladder's sticking through a tree
Toward heaven still,
And there's a barrel that I didn't fill
Beside it, and there may be two or three
Apples I didn't pick upon some bough.   5
But I am done with apple-picking now.
Essence of winter sleep is on the night,
The scent of apples: I am drowsing off.
I cannot rub the strangeness from my sight
I got from looking through a pane of glass   10
I skimmed this morning from the drinking trough
And held against the world of hoary grass.

It melted, and I let it fall and break.
But I was well
Upon my way to sleep before it fell,   15
And I could tell
What form my dreaming was about to take.
Magnified apples appear and disappear,
Stem end and blossom end,
And every fleck of russet showing clear.   20
My instep arch not only keeps the ache,
It keeps the pressure of a ladder-round.
I feel the ladder sway as the boughs bend.
And I keep hearing from the cellar bin
The rumbling sound   25
Of load on load of apples coming in.
For I have had too much
Of apple-picking: I am overtired
Of the great harvest I myself desired.
There were ten thousand thousand fruit to touch,   30
Cherish in hand, lift down, and not let fall.
For all
That struck the earth,
No matter if not bruised or spiked with stubble,
Went surely to the cider-apple heap   35
As of no worth.
One can see what will trouble
This sleep of mine, whatever sleep it is.
Were he not gone,
The woodchuck could say whether it's like his   40
Long sleep, as I describe its coming on,
Or just some human sleep.

Fire and Ice

Some say the world will end in fire,
Some say in ice.
From what I've tasted of desire
I hold with those who favor fire.
But if it had to perish twice,   5
I think I know enough of hate
To say that for destruction ice
Is also great
And would suffice.

Design

I found a dimpled spider, fat and white,
On a white heal-all, holding up a moth
Like a white piece of rigid satin cloth—
Assorted characters of death and blight
Mixed ready to begin the morning right,   5
Like the ingredients of a witches' broth—
A snow-drop spider, a flower like a froth,
And dead wings carried like a paper kite.

What had that flower to do with being white,
The wayside blue and innocent heal-all?   10
What brought the kindred spider to that height,
Then steered the white moth thither in the night?
What but design of darkness to appall?—
If design govern in a thing so small.

Desert Places

Snow falling and night falling fast, oh, fast
In a field I looked into going past,
And the ground almost covered smooth in snow,
But a few weeds and stubble showing last.

The woods around it have it—it is theirs.   5
All animals are smothered in their lairs.
I am too absent-spirited to count;
The loneliness includes me unawares.

And lonely as it is, that loneliness
Will be more lonely ere it will be less—   10
A blanker whiteness of benighted snow
With no expression, nothing to express.

They cannot scare me with their empty spaces
Between stars—on stars where no human race is.
I have it in me so much nearer home   15
To scare myself with my own desert places.

AMY LOWELL

[1874–1925]

♦

Patterns

I walk down the garden-paths,
And all the daffodils
Are blowing, and the bright blue squills.
I walk down the patterned garden-paths
In my stiff, brocaded gown.   5

With my powdered hair and jeweled fan,
I too am a rare
Pattern. As I wander down
The garden-paths.

My dress is richly figured,   10
And the train
Makes a pink and silver stain
On the gravel, and the thrift
Of the borders.
Just a plate of current fashion,   15
Tripping by in high-heeled, ribboned shoes.
Not a softness anywhere about me,
Only whalebone and brocade.
And I sink on a seat in the shade
Of a lime tree. For my passion   20
Wars against the stiff brocade.
The daffodils and squills
Flutter in the breeze
As they please.
And I weep;   25
For the lime-tree is in blossom
And one small flower has dropped upon my bosom.

And the plashing of waterdrops
In the marble fountain
Comes down the garden-paths.   30
The dripping never stops.
Underneath my stiffened gown
Is the softness of a woman bathing in a marble basin,
A basin in the midst of hedges grown
So thick, she cannot see her lover hiding,   35
But she guesses he is near,
And the sliding of the water
Seems the stroking of a dear
Hand upon her.
What is Summer in a fine brocaded gown!   40
I should like to see it lying in a heap upon the ground.
All the pink and silver crumpled up on the ground.

I would be the pink and silver as I ran along the paths,
And he would stumble after,
Bewildered by my laughter.   45
I should see the sun flashing from his sword-hilt and the
   buckles on his shoes.
I would choose
To lead him in a maze along the patterned paths,
A bright and laughing maze for my heavy-booted lover.
Till he caught me in the shade,   50
And the buttons of his waistcoat bruised my body as he
   clasped me,
Aching, melting, unafraid.
With the shadows of the leaves and the sundrops,
And the plopping of the waterdrops,
All about us in the open afternoon—   55
I am very like to swoon
With the weight of this brocade,
For the sun sifts through the shade.

Underneath the fallen blossom
In my bosom
Is a letter I have hid.   60
It was brought to me this morning by a rider from
   the Duke.
"Madam, we regret to inform you that Lord Hartwell
Died in action Thursday se'ennight."
As I read it in the white, morning sunlight,   65
The letters squirmed like snakes.
"Any answer, Madam," said my footman.
"No," I told him.
"See that the messenger takes some refreshment.
No, no answer."   70
And I walked into the garden,
Up and down the patterned paths,
In my stiff, correct brocade.
The blue and yellow flowers stood up proudly
   in the sun,
Each one.   75

I stood upright too,
Held rigid to the pattern
By the stiffness of my gown;
Up and down I walked,
Up and down: 80

In a month he would have been my husband.
In a month, here, underneath this lime,
We would have broke the pattern;
He for me, and I for him,
He as Colonel, I as Lady,   85
On this shady seat.
He had a whim
That sunlight carried blessing.
And I answered, "It shall be as you have said."
Now he is dead.   90

In Summer and in Winter I shall walk
Up and down
The patterned garden-paths.
The squills and daffodils
Will give place to pillared roses, and to asters,
    and to snow.   95
I shall go
Up and down
In my gown.
Gorgeously arrayed,
Boned and stayed.   100
And the softness of my body will be guarded from
    embrace
By each button, hook, and lace.
For the man who should loose me is dead,
Fighting with the Duke in Flanders,
In a pattern called a war.   105
Christ! What are patterns for?

RAINER MARIA RILKE

[1875–1926]

♦

Going Blind

She sat just like the others at the table.
But on second glance, she seemed to hold her cup
a little differently as she picked it up.
She smiled once. It was almost painful.

And when they finished and it was time to stand   5
and slowly, as chance selected them, they left
and moved through many rooms (they talked and laughed),
I saw her. She was moving far behind

the others, absorbed, like someone who will soon
have to sing before a large assembly;   10
upon her eyes, which were radiant with joy,
light played as on the surface of a pool.

She followed slowly, taking a long time,
as though there were some obstacle in the way;
and yet: as though, once it was overcome,   15
she would be beyond all walking, and would fly.

TRANSLATED BY STEPHEN MITCHELL

JOHN MASEFIELD

[1878–1967]

◆

Cargoes

Quinquireme of Nineveh from distant Ophir,
Rowing home to haven in sunny Palestine,
With a cargo of ivory,
And apes and peacocks,
Sandalwood, cedarwood, and sweet white wine.   5

Stately Spanish galleon coming from the Isthmus,
Dipping through the Tropics by the palm-green shores,
With a cargo of diamonds,
Emeralds, amethysts,
Topazes, and cinnamon, and gold moidores.   10

Dirty British coaster with a salt-caked smoke-stack,
Butting through the Channel in the mad March days,
With a cargo of Tyne coal,
Road-rails, pig-lead,
Firewood, iron-ware, and cheap tin trays.   15

[1]**Quinquireme** *ancient galley believed to have had five banks of oars or to have had each oar rowed by five men* / **Nineveh** *capital of ancient Assyria* / **Ophir** *biblical land rich in gold.*

CARL SANDBURG

(1878–1967)

♦

Chicago

Hog Butcher for the World,
Tool Maker, Stacker of Wheat,
Player with Railroads and the Nation's Freight Handler;
Stormy, husky, brawling,
City of the Big Shoulders: 5

They tell me you are wicked and I believe them, for I have
    seen your painted women under the gas lamps luring the
    farm boys.
And they tell me you are crooked and I answer: Yes, it is true
    I have seen the gunman kill and go free to kill again.
And they tell me you are brutal and my reply is: On the faces
    of women and children I have seen the marks of wanton
    hunger.
And having answered so I turn once more to those who sneer
    at this my city, and I give them back the sneer and say to
    them:
Come and show me another city with lifted head singing so
    proud to be alive and coarse and strong and cunning.   10
Flinging magnetic curses amid the toil of piling job on job,
    here is a tall bold slugger set vivid against the little soft
    cities;
Fierce as a dog with tongue lapping for action, cunning as a
    savage pitted against the wilderness,
      Bareheaded,
      Shoveling,
      Wrecking,   15
      Planning,
      Building, breaking, rebuilding,

Under the smoke, dust all over his mouth, laughing with
    white teeth,
Under the terrible burden of destiny laughing as a young man
    laughs,
Laughing even as an ignorant fighter laughs who has never
    lost a battle,   20
Bragging and laughing that under his wrist is the pulse, and
    under his ribs the heart of the people,
        Laughing!
Laughing the stormy, husky, brawling laughter of Youth,
    half-naked, sweating, proud to be Hog Butcher, Tool
    Maker, Stacker of Wheat, Player with Railroads and
    Freight Handler to the Nation.

WALLACE STEVENS

[1879–1955]

♦

Thirteen Ways of Looking at a Blackbird

I

Among twenty snowy mountains,
The only moving thing
Was the eye of the blackbird.

II

I was of three minds,
Like a tree   5
In which there are three blackbirds.

III

The blackbird whirled in the autumn winds.
It was a small part of the pantomime.

IV

A man and a woman
Are one.   10
A man and a woman and a blackbird
Are one.

V

I do not know which to prefer,
The beauty of inflections
Or the beauty of innuendoes,   15
The blackbird whistling
Or just after.

VI

Icicles filled the long window
With barbaric glass.
The shadow of the blackbird   20
Crossed it, to and fro.
The mood
Traced in the shadow
An indecipherable cause.

VII

O thin men of Haddam   25
Why do you imagine golden birds?
Do you not see how the blackbird
Walks around the feet
Of the women about you?

VIII

I know noble accents   30
And lucid, inescapable rhythms;
But I know, too,
That the blackbird is involved
In what I know.

IX

When the blackbird flew out of sight,   35
It marked the edge
Of one of many circles.

X

At the sight of blackbirds
Flying in a green light,
Even the bawds of euphony   40
Would cry out sharply.

XI

He rode over Connecticut
In a glass coach.
Once, a fear pierced him,
In that he mistook   45
The shadow of his equipage
For blackbirds.

XII

The river is moving.
The blackbird must be flying.

XIII

It was evening all afternoon.   50
It was snowing
And it was going to snow.
The blackbird sat
In the cedar-limbs.

Peter Quince at the Clavier

I

Just as my fingers on these keys
Make music, so the selfsame sounds
On my spirit make a music, too.

Music is feeling, then, not sound;
And thus it is that what I feel,   5
Here in this room, desiring you,

Thinking of your blue-shadowed silk,
Is music. It is like the strain
Waked in the elders by Susanna.

Of a green evening, clear and warm,   10
She bathed in her still garden, while
The red-eyed elders watching, felt

The basses of their beings throb
In witching chords, and their thin blood
Pulse pizzicati of Hosanna.   15

II

In the green water, clear and warm,
Susanna lay.
She searched
The touch of springs,
And found   20
Concealed imaginings.
She sighed,
For so much melody.

Upon the bank, she stood
In the cool   25
Of spent emotions.
She felt, among the leaves,

The dew
Of old devotions.

She walked upon the grass,   30
Still quavering.
The winds were like her maids,
On timid feet,
Fetching her woven scarves,
Yet wavering.   35

A breath upon her hand
Muted the night.
She turned—
A cymbal crashed,
And roaring horns.   40

III

Soon, with a noise like tambourines.
Came her attendant Byzantines.

They wondered why Susanna cried
Against the elders by her side;

And as they whispered, the refrain   45
Was like a willow swept by rain.

Anon, their lamps' uplifted flame
Revealed Susanna and her shame.

And then, the simpering Byzantines
Fled, with a noise like tambourines,   50

IV

Beauty is momentary in the mind—
The fitful tracing of a portal;
But in the flesh it is immortal.

The body dies; the body's beauty lives.
So evenings die, in their green going,   55
A wave, interminably flowing.
So gardens die, their meek breath scenting
The cowl of winter, done repenting.
So maidens die, to the auroral
Celebration of a maiden's choral.   60

Susanna's music touched the bawdy strings
Of those white elders; but, escaping,
Left only Death's ironic scraping.
Now, in its immortality, it plays
On the clear viol of her memory,   65
And makes a constant sacrament of praise.

WILLIAM CARLOS WILLIAMS

[1883–1963]

♦

The Red Wheelbarrow

so much depends
upon

a red wheel
barrow

glazed with rain   5
water

beside the white
chickens.

This Is Just to Say

I have eaten
the plums
that were in
the icebox

and which   5
you were probably
saving
for breakfast

Forgive me
they were delicious   10
so sweet
and so cold

The Dance

In Breughel's great picture, The Kermess,
the dancers go round, they go round and
around, the squeal and the blare and the
tweedle of bagpipes, a bugle and fiddles
tipping their bellies (round as the thick-   5
sided glasses whose wash they impound)
their hips and their bellies off balance
to turn them. Kicking and rolling about
the Fair Grounds, swinging their butts, those
shanks must be sound to bear up under such   10
rollicking measures, prance as they dance
in Breughel's great picture, The Kermess.

The Widow's Lament in Springtime

Sorrow is my own yard
where the new grass
flames as it has flamed
often before but not
with the cold fire   5
that closes round me this year.
Thirtyfive years
I lived with my husband.
The plumtree is white today
with masses of flowers.   10
Masses of flowers
load the cherry branches
and color some bushes
yellow and some red
but the grief in my heart   15
is stronger than they
for though they were my joy
formerly, today I notice them
and turned away forgetting.
Today my son told me   20
that in the meadows,
at the edge of the heavy woods
in the distance, he saw
trees of white flowers.
I feel that I would like   25
to go there
and fall into those flowers
and sink into the marsh near them.

Spring and All

By the road to the contagious hospital
under the surge of the blue
mottled clouds driven from the
northeast—a cold wind. Beyond, the
waste of broad, muddy fields   5
brown with dried weeds, standing and fallen

patches of standing water
the scattering of tall trees

All along the road the reddish
purplish, forked, upstanding, twiggy   10
stuff of bushes and small trees
with dead, brown leaves under them
leafless vines—

Lifeless in appearance, sluggish
dazed spring approaches—   15

They enter the new world naked,
cold, uncertain of all
save that they enter. All about them
the cold, familiar wind—

Now the grass, tomorrow   20
the stiff curl of wildcarrot leaf
One by one objects are defined—
It quickens: clarity, outline of leaf

But now the stark dignity of
entrance—Still, the profound change   25
has come upon them: rooted, they
grip down and begin to awaken

D. H. LAWRENCE

[1885–1930]

♦

Piano

Softly, in the dusk, a woman is singing to me;
Taking me back down the vista of years, till I see
A child sitting under the piano, in the boom of the tingling
    strings
And pressing the small, poised feet of a mother who smiles
    as she sings.

In spite of myself, the insidious mastery of song   5
Betrays me back, till the heart of me weeps to belong
To the old Sunday evenings at home, with winter outside
And hymns in the cosy parlour, the tinkling piano our guide.

So now it is vain for the singer to burst into clamour
With the great black piano appassionato. The glamour   10
Of childish days is upon me, my manhood is cast
Down in the flood of remembrance, I weep like a child
    for the past.

Snake

A snake came to my water-trough
On a hot, hot day, and I in pajamas for the heat,
To drink there.

In the deep, strange-scented shade of the great dark
    carob-tree
I came down the steps with my pitcher   5

And must wait, must stand and wait, for there he was at
  the trough before me.

He reached down from a fissure in the earth-wall in the
  gloom
And trailed his yellow-brown slackness soft-bellied down,
  over the edge of the stone trough
And rested his throat upon the stone bottom,
And where the water had dripped from the tap, in a small
  clearness,   10
He sipped with his straight mouth,
Softly drank through his straight gums, into his slack
  long body,
Silently.

Someone was before me at my water-trough,
And I, like a second comer, waiting.   15

He lifted his head from his drinking, as cattle do,
And looked at me vaguely, as drinking cattle do,
And flickered his two-forked tongue from his lips, and
  mused a moment,
And stooped and drank a little more,
Being earth-brown, earth-golden from the burning bowels
  of the earth   20
On the day of Sicilian July, with Etna smoking.

The voice of my education said to me
He must be killed,
For in Sicily the black, black snakes are innocent, the gold
  are venomous.

And voices in me said, If you were a man   25
You would take a stick and break him now, and finish
  him off.

But must I confess how I liked him,
How glad I was he had come like a guest in quiet, to drink
  at my water-trough

And depart peaceful, pacified, and thankless,
Into the burning bowels of this earth?   30

Was it cowardice, that I dared not kill him?
Was it perversity, that I longed to talk to him?
Was it humility, to feel so honored?
I felt so honored.

And yet those voices: 35
If you were not afraid, you would kill him!

And truly I was afraid, I was most afraid,
But even so, honored still more
That he should seek my hospitality
From out the dark door of the secret earth.

He drank enough   40
And lifted his head, dreamily, as one who has drunken,
And flickered his tongue like a forked night on the air,
   so black,
Seeming to lick his lips,
And looked around like a god, unseeing, into the air,
And slowly turned his head,   45
And slowly, very slowly, as if thrice adream,
Proceeded to draw his slow length curving round
And climb again the broken bank of my wall-face.

And as he put his head into that dreadful hole,
And as he slowly drew up, snake-easing his shoulders, and
   entered farther,   50
A sort of horror, a sort of protest against his withdrawing
   into that horrid black hole,
Deliberately going into the blackness, and slowly drawing
   himself after,
Overcame me now his back was turned.

I looked round, I put down my pitcher,
I picked up a clumsy log   55
And threw it at the water-trough with a clatter.

I think it did not hit him,
But suddenly that part of him that was left behind
   convulsed in undignified haste.
Writhed like lightning, and was gone

Into the black hole, the earth-lipped fissure in the
   wall-front,   60
At which, in the intense still noon, I stared with fascination.

And immediately I regretted it.
I thought how paltry, how vulgar, what a mean act!
I despised myself and the voices of my accursed human
   education.

And I thought of the albatross   65
And I wished he would come back, my snake.

For he seemed to me again like a king,
Like a king in exile, uncrowned in the underworld,
Now due to be crowned again.

And so, I missed my chance with one of the lords   70
Of life.
And I have something to expiate;
A pettiness.

EZRA POUND

[1885–1972]

◆

The Garden

En robe de parade.[†]
—SAMAIN

Like a skein of loose silk blown against a wall
She walks by the railing of a path in Kensington Gardens,
And she is dying piecemeal
    of a sort of emotional anemia.

And round about there is a rabble   5
Of the filthy, sturdy, unkillable infants of the very poor.
They shall inherit the earth.

In her is the end of breeding.
Her boredom is exquisite and excessive.
She would like some one to speak to her,   10
And is almost afraid that I
    will commit that indiscretion.

[†]This phrase, which means dressed as for a state occasion, is from a poem by the French poet Albert Samain (1858–1900).
[7]**They . . . earth** *See Matthew 5:5, "Blessed are the meek, for they shall inherit the earth."*

The River-Merchant's Wife: a Letter[†]

While my hair was still cut straight across my forehead
I played about the front gate, pulling flowers.
You came by on bamboo stilts, playing horse,
You walked about my seat, playing with blue plums.
And we went on living in the village of Chōkan: 5
Two small people, without dislike or suspicion.

At fourteen I married My Lord you.
I never laughed, being bashful.
Lowering my head, I looked at the wall.
Called to, a thousand times, I never looked back.   10

At fifteen I stopped scowling,
I desired my dust to be mingled with yours
Forever and forever and forever.
Why should I climb the look out?

At sixteen you departed,   15
You went into far Ku-tō-yen, by the river of swirling eddies,
And you have been gone five months.
The monkeys make sorrowful noise overhead.

You dragged your feet when you went out.
By the gate now, the moss is grown, the different mosses,   20
Too deep to clear them away!

The leaves fall early this autumn, in wind.
The paired butterflies are already yellow with August
Over the grass in the West garden;
They hurt me. I grow older.   25

[†]Pound translated this poem from the Chinese.

If you are coming down through the narrows of the
   river Kiang,
Please let me know before hand,
And I will come out to meet you
      As far as Chō-fū-Sa.   30

BY RIHAKU (LI T'AI PO)

HILDA DOOLITTLE (H. D.)

[1886–1961]

♦

Evening

The light passes
from ridge to ridge,
from flower to flower—
the hypaticas, wide-spread
under the light   5
grow faint—
the petals reach inward,
the blue tips bend
toward the bluer heart
and the flowers are lost.   10
The cornel-buds are still white,
but shadows dart
from the cornel-roots—
black creeps from root to root,
each leaf   15
cuts another leaf on the grass,
shadow seeks shadow,
then both leaf
and leaf-shadow are lost.

MARIANNE MOORE

[1887–1972]

♦

Poetry

I, too, dislike it: there are things that are important beyond
        all this fiddle.
Reading it, however, with a perfect contempt for it, one
discovers in it after all, a place for the genuine.
    Hands that can grasp, eyes
      that can dilate, hair that can rise   5
        if it must, these things are important not because a

high-sounding interpretation can be put upon them but
        because they are
useful. When they become so derivative as to become
unintelligible, the same thing may be said for all of
        us, that we
    do not admire what   10
      we cannot understand: the bat
        holding on upside down or in quest of something to

eat, elephants pushing, a wild horse taking a roll, a tireless
        wolf under
a tree, the immovable critic twitching his skin like a horse
        that feels a flea, the base-
ball fan, the statistician—   15
    nor is it valid
      to discriminate against "business documents and

school-books"; all these phenomena are important. One
        must make a distinction
however: when dragged into prominence by half poets, the
        result is not poetry,

nor till the poets among us can be   20
   "literalists of
   the imagination"—above
     insolence and triviality and can present

for inspection, "imaginary gardens with real toads in them,"
     shall we have
it. In the meantime, if you demand on the one hand,   25
the raw material of poetry in
   all its rawness and
   that which is on the other hand
     genuine, you are interested in poetry.

T. S. ELIOT

[1888–1965]

♦

The Love Song of J. Alfred Prufrock

S'io credesse che mia risposta fosse
A persona che mai tornasse al mondo,
Questa fiamma staria senza più scosse.
Ma per ciò che giammai di questo fondo
Non tornò vivo alcun, s'i'odo il vero,
Senza tema d'infamia ti rispondo.[†]

Let us go then, you and I,
When the evening is spread out against the sky
Like a patient etherized upon a table;
Let us go, through certain half-deserted streets,
The muttering retreats   5
Of restless nights in one-night cheap hotels
And sawdust restaurants with oyster-shells:
Streets that follow like a tedious argument
Of insidious intent
To lead you to an overwhelming question . . .   10
Oh, do not ask, "What is it?"
Let us go and make our visit.

In the room the women come and go
Talking of Michelangelo.

[†]Epigraph from Dante's *Inferno,* canto XXVII, 61–66. The words are spoken by Guido da Montelfetro when asked to identify himself: "If I thought my answer were given to anyone who could ever return to the world, this flame would shake no more: but since none ever did return above from this depth, if what I hear is true, without fear of infamy I answer thee."

The yellow fog that rubs its back upon the window-panes   15
The yellow smoke that rubs its muzzle on the window-panes
Licked its tongue into the corners of the evening,
Lingered upon the pools that stand in drains,
Let fall upon its back the soot that falls from chimneys,
Slipped by the terrace, made a sudden leap,   20
And seeing that it was a soft October night,
Curled once about the house, and fell asleep.

And indeed there will be time
For the yellow smoke that slides along the street,
Rubbing its back upon the window-panes;   25
There will be time, there will be time
To prepare a face to meet the faces that you meet;
There will be time to murder and create,
And time for all the works and days of hands
That lift and drop a question on your plate;   30
Time for you and time for me,
And time yet for a hundred indecisions,
And for a hundred visions and revisions,
Before the taking of a toast and tea.

In the room the women come and go   35
Talking of Michelangelo.

And indeed there will be time
To wonder, "Do I dare?" and, "Do I dare?"
Time to turn back and descend the stair,
With a bald spot in the middle of my hair—   40
[They will say: "How his hair is growing thin!"]
My morning coat, my collar mounting firmly to the chin,
My necktie rich and modest, but asserted by a simple pin—
[They will say: "But how his arms and legs are thin!"]
Do I dare   45
Disturb the universe?
In a minute there is time
For decisions and revisions which a minute will reverse.

For I have known them all already, known them all:
Have known the evenings, mornings, afternoons, 50
I have measured out my life with coffee spoons;
I know the voices dying with a dying fall
Beneath the music from a farther room.
   So how should I presume?

And I have known the eyes already, known them all— 55
The eyes that fix you in a formulated phrase,
And when I am formulated, sprawling on a pin,
When I am pinned and wriggling on the wall,
Then how should I begin
To spit out all the butt-ends of my days and ways? 60
   And how should I presume?

And I have known the arms already, known them all—
Arms that are braceleted and white and bare
[But in the lamplight, downed with light brown hair!]
Is it perfume from a dress 65
That makes me so digress?
Arms that lie along a table, or wrap about a shawl.
   And should I then presume?
   And how should I begin?
   . . . . .

Shall I say, I have gone at dusk through narrow streets 70
And watched the smoke that rises from the pipes
Of lonely men in shirt-sleeves, leaning out of windows? . . .

I should have been a pair of ragged claws
Scuttling across the floors of silent seas.
   . . . . .

And the afternoon, the evening, sleeps so peacefully! 75
Smoothed by long fingers,
Asleep . . . tired . . . or it malingers,
Stretched on the floor, here beside you and me.
Should I, after tea and cakes and ices,
Have the strength to force the moment to its crisis? 80

269

But though I have wept and fasted, wept and prayed,
Though I have seen my head [grown slightly bald] brought
    in upon a platter,
I am no prophet—and here's no great matter;
I have seen the moment of my greatness flicker,
And I have seen the eternal Footman hold my coat, and
    snicker,   85
And in short, I was afraid.

And would it have been worth it, after all,
After the cups, the marmalade, the tea,
Among the porcelain, among some talk of you and me,
Would it have been worth while,   90
To have bitten off the matter with a smile,
To have squeezed the universe into a ball
To roll it toward some overwhelming question,
To say: "I am Lazarus, come from the dead,
Come back to tell you all, I shall tell you all"—   95
If one, settling a pillow by her head,
    Should say: "That is not what I meant at all.
    That is not it, at all."

And would it have been worth it, after all,
Would it have been worth while,   100
After the sunsets and the dooryards and the sprinkled
    streets,
After the novels, after the teacups, after the skirts that
    trail along the floor—
And this, and so much more?—
It is impossible to say just what I mean!
But as if a magic lantern threw the nerves in patterns
    on a screen: 105
Would it have been worth while
If one, settling a pillow or throwing off a shawl,

---

[82]**head . . . platter** *John the Baptist was beheaded at the order of King Herod to please his wife and daughter. See Matthew 14:1–11.*
[94]**Lazarus** *Jesus raised him from the dead. See John 11:1–44.*

And turning toward the window, should say:
   "That is not it at all,
   That is not what I meant, at all."   110

. . . . .

No! I am not Prince Hamlet, nor was meant to be;
Am an attendant lord, one that will do
To swell a progress, start a scene or two,
Advise the prince; no doubt, an easy tool,
Deferential, glad to be of use,   115
Politic, cautious, and meticulous;
Full of high sentence, but a bit obtuse;
At times, indeed, almost ridiculous—
Almost, at times, the Fool.

I grow old . . . I grow old . . .   120
I shall wear the bottoms of my trousers rolled.

Shall I part my hair behind? Do I dare to eat a peach?
I shall wear white flannel trousers, and walk upon
   the beach.
I have heard the mermaids singing, each to each.

I do not think that they will sing to me.   125

I have seen them riding seaward on the waves
Combing the white hair of the waves blown back
When the wind blows the water white and black.

We have lingered in the chambers of the sea
By sea-girls wreathed with seaweed red and brown   130
Till human voices wake us, and we drown.

---

[117]sentence *sententiousness.*

JOHN CROWE RANSOM

[1888–1974]

♦

Piazza Piece

—I am a gentleman in a dustcoat trying
To make you hear. Your ears are soft and small
And listen to an old man not at all,
They want the young men's whispering and sighing.
But see the roses on your trellis dying   5
And hear the spectral singing of the moon;
For I must have my lovely lady soon,
I am a gentleman in a dustcoat trying.

—I am a lady young in beauty waiting
Until my truelove comes, and then we kiss.   10
But what grey man among the vines is this
Whose words are dry and faint as in a dream?
Back from my trellis, Sir, before I scream!
I am a lady young in beauty waiting.

ANNA AKHMATOVA

[1889–1966]

♦

Lot's Wife

And the just man trailed God's shining agent,
over a black mountain, in his giant track,
while a restless voice kept harrying his woman:
"It's not too late, you can still look back

at the red towers of your native Sodom,   5
the square where once you sang, the spinning-shed,
at the empty windows set in the tall house
where sons and daughters blessed your marriage-bed."

A single glance: a sudden dart of pain
stitching her eyes before she made a sound . . .   10
Her body flaked into transparent salt,
and her swift legs rooted to the ground.

Who will grieve for this woman? Does she not seem
too insignificant for our concern?
Yet in my heart I never will deny her,   15
who suffered death because she chose to turn.

TRANSLATED BY RICHARD WILBUR AND MAX HAYWARD

CLAUDE McKAY

[1890–1948]

♦

The Tropics in New York

Bananas ripe and green, and ginger-root,
    Cocoa in pods and alligator pears,
And tangerines and mangoes and grape fruit,
    Fit for the highest prize at parish fairs,

Set in the window, bringing memories   5
    Of fruit-trees laden by low-singing rills,
And dewy dawns, and mystical blue skies
    In benediction over nun-like hills.

My eyes grew dim, and I could no more gaze;
    A wave of longing through my body swept,   10
And, hungry for the old, familiar ways,
    I turned aside and bowed my head and wept.

ARCHIBALD MacLEISH

[1892–1982]

♦

Ars Poetica

A poem should be palpable and mute
As a globed fruit,

Dumb
As old medallions to the thumb,

Silent as the sleeve-worn stone   5
Of casement ledges where the moss has grown—

A poem should be wordless
As the flight of birds.

A poem should be motionless in time
As the moon climbs,   10

Leaving, as the moon releases
Twig by twig the night-entangled trees,

Leaving, as the moon behind the winter leaves,
Memory by memory the mind—

A poem should be motionless in time   15
As the moon climbs.

A poem should be equal to:
Not true.

For all the history of grief
An empty doorway and a maple leaf.   20

For love
The leaning grasses and two lights above the sea—

A poem should not mean
But be.

KIHACHI OZAKI

[b. 1892]

♦

A Word

I have to select a word for material.
It should be talked about in the smallest possible
    amount and
have a deep suggestiveness like nature,
bloom from inside its own self,   5
and at the edge of the fate encircling me
it will have to become darkly and sweetly ripened.

Of a hundred experiences it always
has to be the sum total of only one.
One drop of water dew   10
becomes the harvest of all dewdrops,
a dark evening's one red point of light
is the night of the whole world.

And after that my poem
like a substance entirely fresh,   15
released far away from my memory,
the same as a scythe in a field in the morning,
the same as the ice on a lake in spring,
will suddenly begin to sing from its own recollection.

TRANSLATED BY EDITH MARCOMBE SHIFFERT AND YŪKI SAWA

CÉSAR VALLEJO

[1892–1938]

♦

Our Daily Bread

(FOR ALEJANDRO GAMBOA)

Breakfast is drunk down . . . Damp earth
of the cemetery gives off the fragrance of the precious blood.
City of winter . . . the mordant crusade
of a cart that seems to pull behind it
an emotion of fasting that cannot get free!   5

I wish I could beat on all the doors,
and ask for somebody; and then
look at the poor, and, while they wept softly,
give bits of fresh bread to them.
And plunder the rich of their vineyards   10
with those two blessed hands
which blasted the nails with one blow of light,
and flew away from the Cross!

Eyelash of morning, you cannot lift yourselves!
Give us our daily bread,   15
Lord . . . !

Every bone in me belongs to others;
and maybe I robbed them.
I came to take something for myself that maybe
was meant for some other man; 20
and I start thinking that, if I had not been born,
another poor man could have drunk this coffee.
I feel like a dirty thief . . . Where will I end?

And in this frigid hour, when the earth
has the odor of human dust and is so sad, 25
I wish I could beat on all the doors
and beg pardon from someone,
and make bits of fresh bread for him
here, in the oven of my heart . . . !

TRANSLATED BY JAMES WRIGHT

E. E. CUMMINGS

[1894–1962]

♦

anyone lived in a pretty how town

anyone lived in a pretty how town
(with up so floating many bells down)
spring summer autumn winter
he sang his didn't he danced his did.

Women and men(both little and small) 5
cared for anyone not at all
they sowed their isn't they reaped their same
sun moon stars rain

children guessed(but only a few
and down they forgot as up they grew   10
autumn winter spring summer)
that noone loved him more by more

when by now and tree by leaf
she laughed his joy she cried his grief
bird by snow and stir by still   15
anyone's any was all to her

someones married their everyones
laughed their cryings and did their dance
(sleep wake hope and then)they
said their nevers they slept their dream   20

stars rain sun moon
(and only the snow can begin to explain
how children are apt to forget to remember
with up so floating many bells down)

one day anyone died i guess   25
(and noone stooped to kiss his face)
busy folk buried them side by side
little by little and was by was

all by all and deep by deep
and more by more they dream their sleep   30
noone and anyone earth by april
wish by spirit and if by yes.

Women and men(both dong and ding)
summer autumn winter spring
reaped their sowing and went their came   35
sun moon stars rain

my father moved through dooms of love

my father moved through dooms of love
through sames of am through haves of give,
singing each morning out of each night
my father moved through depths of height

this motionless forgetful where   5
turned at his glance to shining here;
that if (so timid air is firm)
under his eyes would stir and squirm

newly as from unburied which
floats the first who, his april touch   10
drove sleeping selves to swarm their fates
woke dreamers to their ghostly roots

and should some why completely weep
my father's fingers brought her sleep:
vainly no smallest voice might cry   15
for he could feel the mountains grow.

Lifting the valleys of the sea
my father moved through griefs of joy;
praising a forehead called the moon
singing desire into begin   20

joy was his song and joy so pure
a heart of star by him could steer
and pure so now and now so yes
the wrists of twilight would rejoice

keen as midsummer's keen beyond   25
conceiving mind of sun will stand,
so strictly (over utmost him
so hugely) stood my father's dream

his flesh was flesh his blood was blood:
no hungry man but wished him food;   30
no cripple wouldn't creep one mile
uphill to only see him smile.

Scorning the pomp of must and shall
my father moved through dooms of feel;
his anger was as right as rain   35
his pity was as green as grain

septembering arms of year extend
less humbly wealth to foe and friend
than he to foolish and to wise
offered immeasurable is   40

proudly and (by octobering flame
beckoned) as earth will downward climb,
so naked for immortal work
his shoulders marched against the dark

his sorrow was as true as bread: 45
no liar looked him in the head;
if every friend became his foe
he'd laugh and build a world with snow.

My father moved through theys of we,
singing each new leaf out of each tree   50
(and every child was sure that spring
danced when she heard my father sing)

then let men kill which cannot share,
let blood and flesh be mud and mire,
scheming imagine, passion willed,   55
freedom a drug that's bought and sold

giving to steal and cruel kind,
a heart to fear, to doubt a mind,
to differ a disease of same,
conform the pinnacle of am   60

though dull were all we taste as bright,
bitter all utterly things sweet,
maggoty minus and dumb death
all we inherit, all bequeath

and nothing quite so least as truth   65
—i say though hate were why men breathe—
because my father lived his soul
love is the whole and more than all

JEAN TOOMER

[1894–1967]

♦

Reapers

Black reapers with the sound of steel on stones
Are sharpening scythes. I see them place the hones
In their hip-pockets as a thing that's done,
And start their silent swinging, one by one.
Black horses drive a mower through the weeds,   5
And there, a field rat, startled, squealing bleeds,
His belly close to ground. I see the blade,
Blood-stained, continue cutting weeds and shade.

ROBERT GRAVES

[1895–1985]

♦

The Naked and the Nude

For me, the naked and the nude
(By lexicographers construed
As synonyms that should express
The same deficiency of dress
Or shelter) stand as wide apart   5
As love from lies, or truth from art.

Lovers without reproach will gaze
On bodies naked and ablaze;
The Hippocratic eye will see
In nakedness, anatomy;   10
And naked shines the Goddess when
She mounts her lion among men.

The nude are bold, the nude are sly
To hold each treasonable eye.
While draping by a showman's trick   15
Their dishabille in rhetoric,
They grin a mock-religious grin
Of scorn at those of naked skin.

The naked, therefore, who compete
Against the nude may know defeat;   20
Yet when they both together tread
The briary pastures of the dead,
By Gorgons with long whips pursued,
How naked go the sometime nude!

JORGE LUIS BORGES

[1899–1986]

♦

The Blind Man

I

He is divested of the diverse world,
of faces, which still stay as once they were,
of the adjoining streets, now far away,
and of the concave sky, once infinite.
Of books, he keeps no more than what is left him   5
by memory, that brother of forgetting,
which keeps the formula but not the feeling
and which reflects no more than tag and name.
Traps lie in wait for me. My every step
might be a fall. I am a prisoner   10
shuffling through a time which feels like dream,
taking no note of mornings or of sunsets.
It is night. I am alone. In verse like this,
I must create my insipid universe.

II

Since I was born, in 1899,   15
beside the concave vine and the deep cistern,
frittering time, so brief in memory,
kept taking from me all my eye-shaped world.
Both days and nights would wear away the profiles
of human letters and of well-loved faces.   20
My wasted eyes would ask their useless questions
of pointless libraries and lecterns.
Blue and vermilion both are now a fog,
both useless sounds. The mirror I look into

is gray. I breathe a rose across the garden,   25
a wistful rose, my friends, out of the twilight.
Only the shades of yellow stay with me
and I can see only to look on nightmares.

TRANSLATED BY ALASTAIR REID

FEDERICO GARCÍA LORCA

[1899–1936]

♦

Somnambule Ballad

Green, how much I want you green.
Green wind. Green branches.
The ship upon the sea
and the horse in the mountain.
With the shadow on her waist   5
she dreams on her balcony,
green flesh, hair of green,
and eyes of cold silver.
Green, how much I want you green.
Beneath the gypsy moon,   10
all things look at her
but she cannot see them.

Green, how much I want you green.
Great stars of white frost
come with the fish of darkness   15
that opens the road of dawn.
The fig tree rubs the wind
with the sandpaper of its branches,
and the mountain, a filching cat,
bristles its bitter aloes.   20

But who will come? And from where?
She lingers on her balcony,
green flesh, hair of green,
dreaming of the bitter sea.

—Friend, I want to change   25
my horse for your house,
my saddle for your mirror,
my knife for your blanket.
Friend, I come bleeding,
from the passes of Cabra.   30
—If I could, young man,
this pact would be sealed.
But I am no more I,
nor is my house now my house.
—Friend, I want to die   35
decently in my bed.
Of iron, if it be possible,
with sheets of fine holland.
Do you not see the wound I have
from my breast to my throat?   40
—Your white shirt bears
three hundred dark roses.
Your pungent blood oozes
around your sash.
But I am no more I,   45
nor is my house now my house.
—Let me climb at least
up to the high balustrades:
let me come! Let me come!
up to the green balustrades.   50
Balustrades of the moon
where the water resounds.

Now the two friends go up
towards the high balustrades.
Leaving a trail of blood,   55
leaving a trail of tears.

Small lanterns of tin
were trembling on the roofs.
A thousand crystal tambourines
were piercing the dawn.   60

Green, how much I want you green,
green wind, green branches.
The two friends went up.
The long wind was leaving
in the mouth a strange taste   65
of gall, mint and sweet-basil.
Friend! Where is she, tell me,
where is your bitter girl?
How often she waited for you!
How often did she wait for you,   70
cool face, black hair,
on this green balcony!

Over the face of the cistern
the gypsy girl swayed.
Green flesh, hair of green,   75
with eyes of cold silver.
An icicle of the moon
suspends her above the water.
The night became as intimate
as a little square.   80
Drunken civil guards
were knocking at the door.
Green, how much I want you green.
Green wind. Green branches.
The ship upon the sea.   85
And the horse on the mountain.

TRANSLATED BY STEPHEN SPENDER AND J. L. GILI

JACQUES PRÉVERT

[1900–1977]

♦

At the Florist's

A man enters a florist's
and picks out some flowers
the girl wraps up the flowers
the man puts his hand in his pocket
to get the money   5
money to pay for the flowers
but at the same time
suddenly
he clutches his heart
and he falls   10

At the same time that he falls
the money rolls on the ground
and then the flowers fall
at the same time as the man
at the same time as the money   15
and the girl stands there
with the rolling money
with the broken flowers
with the dying man
obviously that's all very sad   20
and she ought to do something
that florist
but she doesn't know how to set about it
she doesn't know
where to begin   25

There are so many things to do
with that dying man
those broken flowers
and that money
that money that rolls and rolls   30
and never stops rolling.

TRANSLATED BY CHARLES GUENTHER

Family Portrait

The mother knits
The son goes to war
She finds it all perfectly natural, Mama
And the father, what is he doing? Papa?
He is making little deals   5
His wife knits
His son goes to war
He is making little deals
He finds it all perfectly natural, Papa
And the son, the son   10
What does the son find?
The son finds absolutely nothing, the son
For the son the war his Mama the knitting his Papa little
     deals for him the war
When it is all over, that war
He will make little deals, he and his Papa   15
The war continues Mama continues she knits
Papa continues he carries on his activity
The son is killed he no longer carries on
Papa and Mama go to the cemetery
They find it all perfectly natural, Papa and Mama   20

Life continues life with knitting war little deals
Deals war knitting war
Deals deals activity
Life along with the cemetery.

TRANSLATED BY HARRIET ZINNES

ROBERT FRANCIS

[b. 1901]

♦

Pitcher

His art is eccentricity, his aim
How not to hit the mark he seems to aim at,

His passion how to avoid the obvious,
His technique how to vary the avoidance.

The others throw to be comprehended. He
Throws to be a moment misunderstood.

Yet not too much. Not errant, arrant, wild,
But every seeming aberration willed.

Not to, yet still, still to communicate
Making the batter understand too late.

LANGSTON HUGHES

[1902–1967]

♦

Dream Deferred

What happens to a dream deferred?

Does it dry up
like a raisin in the sun?
Or fester like a sore—
And then run?
Does it stink like rotten meat?   5
Or crust and sugar over—
like a syrupy sweet?

Maybe it just sags
like a heavy load.   10

Or does it explode?

Trumpet Player

The Negro
With the trumpet at his lips
Has dark moons of weariness
Beneath his eyes
Where the smoldering memory   5
Of slave ships
Blazed to the crack of whips
About his thighs.

The Negro
With the trumpet at his lips   10
Has a head of vibrant hair
Tamed down,
Patent-leathered now
Until it gleams
Like jet—   15
Were jet a crown.

The music
From the trumpet at his lips
Is honey
Mixed with liquid fire.   20
The rhythm
From the trumpet at his lips
Is ecstasy
Distilled from old desire—

Desire   25
That is longing for the moon
Where the moonlight's but a spotlight
In his eyes,
Desire
That is longing for the sea   30
Where the sea's a bar-glass
Sucker size.

The Negro
With the trumpet at his lips
Whose jacket   35
Has a *fine* one-button roll,
Does not know
Upon what riff the music slips
Its hypodermic needle
To his soul—   40

But softly
As the tune comes from his throat
Trouble
Mellows to a golden note.

RICHARD EBERHART

[b. 1904]

◆

The Groundhog

In June, amid the golden fields,
I saw a groundhog lying dead.
Dead lay he; my senses shook,
And mind outshot our naked frailty.
There lowly in the vigorous summer   5
His form began its senseless change,
And made my senses waver dim
Seeing nature ferocious in him.
Inspecting close his maggots' might
And seething cauldron of his being,   10
Half with loathing, half with a strange love,
I poked him with an angry stick.
The fever arose, became a flame
And Vigour circumscribed the skies,
Immense energy in the sun,   15
And through my frame a sunless trembling.
My stick had done nor good nor harm.
Then stood I silent in the day
Watching the object, as before;
And kept my reverence for knowledge   20
Trying for control, to be still,
To quell the passion of the blood;
Until I had bent down on my knees
Praying for joy in the sight of decay.

And so I left; and I returned 25
In Autumn strict of eye, to see
The sap gone out of the groundhog,
But the bony sodden hulk remained.
But the year had lost its meaning,
And in intellectual chains 30
I lost both love and loathing,
Mured up in the wall of wisdom.
Another summer took the fields again
Massive and burning, full of life,
But when I chanced upon the spot 35
There was only a little hair left,
And bones bleaching in the sunlight
Beautiful as architecture;
I watched them like a geometer,
And cut a walking stick from a birch. 40
It has been three years, now.
There is no sign of the groundhog.
I stood there in the whirling summer,
My hand capped a withered heart,
And thought of China and of Greece, 45
Of Alexander in his tent;
Of Montaigne in his tower,
Of Saint Theresa in her wild lament.

---

[46]**Alexander** *The Great, Greek military leader (4th century* B.C.*).*
[47]**Montaigne** *French essayist (1533–1592) whose study was in a small tower.*
[48]**Saint Theresa** *Catholic Saint and Spanish mystic (1515–1582), often portrayed experiencing an ecstastic combination of love and pain.*

PABLO NERUDA

[1904–1973]

◆

The Word

The word
was born in the blood,
grew in the dark body, beating,
and took flight through the lips and the mouth.

Farther away and nearer   5
still, still it came
from dead fathers and from wandering races,
from lands which had turned to stone,
lands weary of their poor tribes,
for when grief took to the roads   10
the people set out and arrived
and married new land and water
to grow their words again.
And so this is the inheritance;
this is the wavelength which connects us   15
with dead men and the dawning
of new beings not yet come to light.

Still the atmosphere quivers
with the first word uttered
dressed up   20
in terror and sighing.
It emerged
from the darkness
and until now there is no thunder
that ever rumbles with the iron voice   25
of that word,
the first
word uttered—

perhaps it was only a ripple, a single drop,
and yet its great cataract falls and falls. 30

Later on, the word fills with meaning.
Always with child, it filled up with lives.
Everything was births and sounds—
affirmation, clarity, strength,
negation, destruction, death— 35
the verb took over all the power
and blended existence with essence
in the electricity of its grace.

Human word, syllable, flank
of extending light and solid silverwork, 40
hereditary goblet which receives
the communications of the blood—
here is where silence came together with
the wholeness of the human word,
and, for human beings, not to speak is to die— 45
language extends even to the hair,
the mouth speaks without the lips moving,
all of a sudden, the eyes are words.

I take the word and pass it through my senses
as though it were no more than a human shape; 50
its arrangements awe me and I find my way
through each resonance of the spoken word—
I utter and I am and, speechless, I approach
across the edge of words silence itself.

I drink to the word, raising 55
a word or a shining cup;
in it I drink

the pure wine of language
or inexhaustible water,
maternal source of words, 60
and cup and water and wine
give rise to my song

because the verb is the source
and vivid life—it is blood,
blood which expresses its substance   65
and so ordains its own unwinding.
Words give glass quality to glass, blood to blood,
and life to life itself.

TRANSLATED BY ALASTAIR REID

ROBERT PENN WARREN

[b. 1905]

♦

Evening Hawk

From plane of light to plane, wings dipping through
Geometries and orchids that the sunset builds,
Out of the peak's black angularity of shadow, riding
The last tumultuous avalanche of
Light above pines and the guttural gorge,   5
The hawk comes.

     His wing
Scythes down another day, his motion
Is that of the honed steel-edge, we hear
The crashless fall of stalks of Time.   10

The head of each stalk is heavy with the gold of our error.

Look! look! he is climbing the last light
Who knows neither Time nor error, and under
Whose eye, unforgiving, the world, unforgiven, swings
Into shadow.   15

Long now,
The last thrush is still, the last bat
Now cruises in his sharp hieroglyphics. His wisdom
Is ancient, too, and immense. The star
Is steady, like Plato, over the mountain.   20
If there were no wind we might, we think, hear
The earth grind on its axis, or history
Drip in darkness like a leaking pipe in the cellar.

NAGASE KIYOKO

[b. 1906]

♦

Mother

I am always aware of my mother,
ominous, threatening,
a pain in the depths of my consciousness.
My mother is like a shell,
so easily broken.   5
Yet the fact that I was born
bearing my mother's shadow
cannot be changed.
She is like a cherished, bitter dream
my nerves cannot forget   10
even after I awake.
She prevents all freedom of movement.
If I move she quickly breaks,
and the splinters stab me.

TRANSLATED BY KENNETH REXROTH AND IKUKO ATSUMI

W. H. AUDEN

[1907–1973]

♦

Musée des Beaux Arts

About suffering they were never wrong,
The Old Masters: how well they understood
Its human position; how it takes place
While someone else is eating or opening a window or
    just walking dully along;
How, when the aged are reverently, passionately waiting   5
For the miraculous birth, there always must be
Children who did not specially want it to happen, skating
On a pond at the edge of the wood:
They never forgot
That even the dreadful martyrdom must run its course   10
Anyhow in a corner, some untidy spot
Where the dogs go on with their doggy life and the
    torturer's horse
Scratches its innocent behind on a tree.

In Breughel's *Icarus,* for instance: how everything turns
    away
Quite leisurely from the disaster; the ploughman may   15
Have heard the splash, the forsaken cry.
But for him it was not an important failure; the sun
    shone
As it had to on the white legs disappearing into the
    green
Water; and the expensive delicate ship that must
    have seen
Something amazing, a boy falling out of the sky,   20
Had somewhere to get to and sailed calmly on.

The Unknown Citizen

(To JS/07/M/378
This Marble Monument Is Erected by the State)

He was found by the Bureau of Statistics to be
One against whom there was no official complaint,
And all the reports on his conduct agree
That, in the modern sense of an old-fashioned word, he
    was a saint,
For in everything he did he served the Greater Community.   5
Except for the War till the day he retired
He worked in a factory and never got fired
But satisfied his employers, Fudge Motors Inc.
Yet he wasn't a scab or odd in his views,
For his Union reports that he paid his dues,   10
(Our report on his Union shows it was sound)
And our Social Psychology workers found
That he was popular with his mates and liked a drink.
The Press are convinced that he bought a paper every day
And that his reactions to advertisements were normal in
    every way.   15
Policies taken out in his name prove that he was fully
    insured,
And his Health-card shows he was once in hospital but
    left it cured.
Both Producers Research and High-Grade Living declare
He was fully sensible to the advantages of the Installment
    Plan
And had everything necessary to the Modern Man,   20
A phonograph, a radio, a car and a frigidaire.
Our researchers into Public Opinion are content
That he held the proper opinions for the time of year;
When there was peace, he was for peace; when there was
    war, he went.
He was married and added five children to the population,   25
Which our Eugenist says was the right number for a parent
    of his generation.

And our teachers report that he never interfered with their
   education.
Was he free? Was he happy? The question is absurd:
Had anything been wrong, we should certainly have heard.

In Memory of W. B. Yeats

[d. January 1939]

I

He disappeared in the dead of winter:
The brooks were frozen, the air-ports almost deserted,
And snow disfigured the public statues;
The mercury sank in the mouth of the dying day.
O all the instruments agree   5
The day of his death was a dark cold day.

Far from his illness
The wolves ran on through the evergreen forests,
The peasant river was untempted by the fashionable quays;
By mourning tongues   10
The death of the poet was kept from his poems.

But for him it was his last afternoon as himself,
An afternoon of nurses and rumours;
The provinces of his body revolted,
The squares of his mind were empty,   15
Silence invaded the suburbs,
The current of his feeling failed: he became his admirers.

Now he is scattered among a hundred cities
And wholly given over to unfamiliar affections;
To find his happiness in another kind of wood   20
And be punished under a foreign code of conscience.
The words of a dead man
Are modified in the guts of the living.

But in the importance and noise of to-morrow
When the brokers are roaring like beasts on the floor
    of the Bourse,   25
And the poor have the sufferings to which they are
    fairly accustomed,
And each in the cell of himself is almost convinced
    of his freedom;
A few thousand will think of this day
As one thinks of a day when one did something
    slightly unusual.

O all the instruments agree   30
The day of his death was a dark cold day.

II

You were silly like us: your gift survived it all;
The parish of rich women, physical decay,
Yourself; mad Ireland hurt you into poetry.
Now Ireland has her madness and her weather still,   35
For poetry makes nothing happen: it survives
In the valley of its saying where executives
Would never want to tamper; it flows south
From ranches of isolation and the busy griefs,
Raw towns that we believe and die in; it survives,   40
A way of happening, a mouth.

III

Earth, receive an honoured guest;
William Yeats is laid to rest:
Let the Irish vessel lie
Emptied of its poetry.   45

Time that is intolerant
Of the brave and innocent,
And indifferent in a week
To a beautiful physique,

[25]**Bourse** *stock exchange in Paris.*

Worships language and forgives 50
Everyone by whom it lives;
Pardons cowardice, conceit,
Lays its honours at their feet.

Time that with this strange excuse
Pardoned Kipling and his views, 55
And will pardon Paul Claudel,
Pardons him for writing well.

In the nightmare of the dark
All the dogs of Europe bark,
And the living nations wait, 60
Each sequestered in its hate;

Intellectual disgrace
Stares from every human face,
And the seas of pity lie
Locked and frozen in each eye. 65

Follow, poet, follow right
To the bottom of the night,
With your unconstraining Voice
Still persuade us to rejoice;

With the farming of a verse 70
Make a vineyard of the curse,
Sing of human unsuccess
In a rapture of distress;

In the deserts of the heart
Let the healing fountain start, 75
In the prison of his days
Teach the free man how to praise.

---

[55]**Kipling** *Rudyard Kipling (1865–1936), English writer with imperialistic views.*
[56]**Paul Claudel** *French Catholic writer (1868–1955) of extreme political conservatism.*
[58]**nightmare of the dark** *rising fears and tensions in Europe before the outbreak of World War II.*

THEODORE ROETHKE

[1908–1963]

♦

Elegy for Jane

MY STUDENT, THROWN BY A HORSE

I remember the neckcurls, limp and damp as tendrils;
And her quick look, a sidelong pickerel smile;
And how, once startled into talk, the light syllables leaped
    for her,
And she balanced in the delight of her thought,
A wren, happy, tail into the wind,   5
Her song trembling the twigs and small branches.
The shade sang with her;
The leaves, their whispers turned to kissing;
And the mold sang in the bleached valleys under the rose.

Oh, when she was sad, she cast herself down into such a
    pure depth,   10
Even a father could not find her:
Scraping her cheek against straw;
Stirring the clearest water.

My sparrow, you are not here,
Waiting like a fern, making a spiny shadow.   15
The sides of wet stones cannot console me,
Nor the moss, wound with the last light.

If only I could nudge you from this sleep,
My maimed darling, my skittery pigeon.
Over this damp grave I speak the words of my love: 20
I, with no rights in this matter,
Neither father nor lover.

The Premonition

Walking this field I remember
Days of another summer.
Oh that was long ago! I kept
Close to the heels of my father,
Matching his stride with half-steps   5
Until we came to a river.
He dipped his hand in the shallow:
Water ran over and under
Hair on a narrow wrist bone;
His image kept following after,—   10
Flashed with the sun in the ripple.
But when he stood up, that face
Was lost in a maze of water.

My Papa's Waltz

The whiskey on your breath
Could make a small boy dizzy;
But I hung on like death
Such waltzing was not easy.

We romped until the pans   5
Slid from the kitchen shelf;
My mother's countenance
Could not unfrown itself.

The hand that held my wrist
Was battered on one knuckle;   10
At every step you missed
My right ear scraped a buckle.

You beat time on my head
With a palm caked hard by dirt,
Then waltzed me off to bed   15
Still clinging to your shirt.

ROBERT FITZGERALD

[b. 1910]

♦

Cobb Would Have Caught It

In sunburnt parks where Sunday lies,
Or the wide wastes beyond the cities,
Teams in grey deploy through sunlight.

Talk it up, boys, a little practice.

Coming in stubby and fast, the baseman   5
Gathers a grounder in fat green grass,
Picks it stinging and clipped as wit
Into the leather: a swinging step
Wings it deadeye down to first.
Smack. Oh, attaboy, attaoldboy.   10

Catcher reverses his cap, pulls down
Sweaty casque, and squats in the dust:
Pitcher rubs new ball on his pants,
Chewing, puts a jet behind him;
Nods past batter, taking his time.   15
Batter settles, tugs at his cap:
A spinning ball: step and swing to it,
Caught like a cheek before it ducks
By shivery hickory: socko, baby:

Cleats dig into dust. Outfielder, 20
On his way, looking over shoulder,
Makes it a triple. A long peg home.

Innings and afternoons. Fly lost in sunset.
Throwing arm gone bad. There's your old ball game.
Cool reek of the field. Reek of companions. 25

ELIZABETH BISHOP

[1911–1979]

◆

The Fish

I caught a tremendous fish
and held him beside the boat
half out of water, with my hook
fast in a corner of his mouth.
He didn't fight. 5
He hadn't fought at all.
He hung a grunting weight,
battered and venerable
and homely. Here and there
his brown skin hung in strips 10
like ancient wallpaper,
and its pattern of darker brown
was like wallpaper:
shapes like full-blown roses
stained and lost through age. 15
He was speckled with barnacles,
fine rosettes of lime,
and infested
with tiny white sea-lice,
and underneath two or three 20
rags of green weed hung down.

While his gills were breathing in
the terrible oxygen
—the frightening gills,
fresh and crisp with blood,   25
that can cut so badly—
I thought of the coarse white flesh
packed in like feathers,
the big bones and the little bones,
the dramatic reds and blacks   30
of his shiny entrails,
and the pink swim-bladder
like a big peony.
I looked into his eyes
which were far larger than mine   35
but shallower, and yellowed,
the irises backed and packed
with tarnished tinfoil
seen through the lenses
of old scratched isinglass.   40
They shifted a little, but not
to return my stare.
—It was more like the tipping
of an object toward the light.
I admired his sullen face,   45
the mechanism of his jaw,
and then I saw
that from his lower lip
—if you could call it a lip—
grim, wet, and weaponlike,   50
hung five old pieces of fish-line,
or four and a wire leader
with the swivel still attached,
with all their five big hooks
grown firmly in his mouth.   55
A green line, frayed at the end
where he broke it, two heavier lines,
and a fine black thread

40isinglass *mica.*

still crimped from the strain and snap
when it broke and he got away.   60
Like medals with their ribbons
frayed and wavering,
a five-haired beard of wisdom
trailing from his aching jaw.
I stared and stared   65
and victory filled up
the little rented boat,
from the pool of bilge
where oil had spread a rainbow
around the rusted engine   70
to the bailer rusted orange,
the sun-cracked thwarts,
the oarlocks on their strings,
the gunnels—until everything
was rainbow, rainbow, rainbow!   75
And I let the fish go.

Sestina

September rain falls on the house.
In the failing light, the old grandmother
sits in the kitchen with the child
beside the Little Marvel Stove,
reading the jokes from the almanac,   5
laughing and talking to hide her tears.

She thinks that her equinoctial tears
and the rain that beats on the roof of the house
were both foretold by the almanac,
but only known to a grandmother.   10
The iron kettle sings on the stove.
She cuts some bread and says to the child,

It's time for tea now; but the child
is watching the teakettle's small hard tears
dance like mad on the hot black stove,   15
the way the rain must dance on the house.
Tidying up, the old grandmother
hangs up the clever almanac

on its string. Birdlike, the almanac
hovers half open above the child,   20
hovers above the old grandmother
and her teacup full of dark brown tears.
She shivers and says she thinks the house
feels chilly, and puts more wood in the stove.

It was to be, says the Marvel Stove.   25
I know what I know, says the almanac.
With crayons the child draws a rigid house
and a winding pathway. Then the child
puts in a man with buttons like tears
and shows it proudly to the grandmother.   30

But secretly, while the grandmother
busies herself about the stove,
the little moons fall down like tears
from between the pages of the almanac
into the flower bed the child   35
has carefully placed in the front of the house.

Time to plant tears, says the almanac.
The grandmother sings to the marvelous stove
and the child draws another inscrutable house.

First Death in Nova Scotia

In the cold, cold parlor
my mother laid out Arthur
beneath the chromographs:
Edward, Prince of Wales,
with Princess Alexandra,   5
and King George with Queen Mary.
Below them on the table
stood a stuffed loon
shot and stuffed by Uncle
Arthur, Arthur's father.   10

Since Uncle Arthur fired
a bullet into him,
he hadn't said a word.
He kept his own counsel
on his white, frozen lake,   15
the marble-topped table.
His breast was deep and white,
cold and caressable;
his eyes were red glass,
much to be desired.   20

"Come," said my mother,
"Come and say good-bye
to your little cousin Arthur."
I was lifted up and given
one lily of the valley   25
to put in Arthur's hand.
Arthur's coffin was
a little frosted cake,
and the red-eyed loon eyed it
from his white, frozen lake.   30

Arthur was very small.
He was all white, like a doll
that hadn't been painted yet.

Jack Frost had started to paint him
the way he always painted   35
the Maple Leaf (Forever).
He had just begun on his hair,
a few red strokes, and then
Jack Frost had dropped the brush
and left him white, forever.   40

The gracious royal couples
were warm in red and ermine;
their feet were well wrapped up
in the ladies' ermine trains.
They invited Arthur to be   45
the smallest page at court.
But how could Arthur go,
clutching his tiny lily,
with his eyes shut up so tight
and the roads deep in snow?   50

ROBERT HAYDEN

[1913–1980]

♦

Those Winter Sundays

Sundays too my father got up early
and put his clothes on in the blueblack cold,
then with cracked hands that ached
from labor in the weekday weather made
banked fires blaze. No one ever thanked him.   5

I'd wake and hear the cold splintering, breaking.
When the rooms were warm, he'd call,
and slowly I would rise and dress,
fearing the chronic angers of that house,

Speaking indifferently to him,   10
who had driven out the cold
and polished my good shoes as well.
What did I know, what did I know
of love's austere and lonely offices?

JULIA DE BURGOS

[1914–1953]

◆

To Julia de Burgos

The people are saying that I am your enemy,
  That in poetry I give you to the world.

  They lie, Julia de Burgos. They lie, Julia de Burgos.
The voice that rises in my verses is not your voice:
  it is my voice;
For you are the clothing and I am the essence;   5
Between us lies the deepest abyss.

  You are the bloodless doll of social lies
And I the virile spark of human truth;

  You are the honey of courtly hypocrisy; not I—
I bare my heart in all my poems.   10

  You, like your world, are selfish; not I—
I gamble everything to be what I am.

  You are only the serious lady. Señora. Doña Julia.
Not I. I am life. I am strength. I am woman.

You belong to your husband, your master. Not I: 15
I belong to nobody or to all, for to all, to all
I give myself in my pure feelings and thoughts.

You curl your hair and paint your face. Not I:
I am curled by the wind, painted by the sun.

You are the lady of the house, resigned, submissive,   20
Tied to the bigotry of men. Not I:
I am Rocinante, bolting free, wildly
Snuffling the horizons of the justice of God.

TRANSLATED BY GRACE SCHULMAN

OCTAVIO PAZ

[b. 1914]

♦

Between What I See and What I Say . . .

for Roman Jakobson

I

Between what I see and what I say,
between what I say and what I keep silent,
between what I keep silent and what I dream,
between what I dream and what I forget:
poetry.   5
      It slips
between yes and no,
                 says
what I keep silent,
              keeps silent   10
what I say,
         dreams
what I forget.

It is not speech:
it is an act.   15
It is an act
of speech.
Poetry
speaks and listens:
it is real.   20
And as soon as I say
it is real,
it vanishes.
Is it then more real?

II

Tangible idea,   25
intangible
word:
poetry
comes and goes
between what is   30
and what is not.
It weaves
and unweaves reflections.
Poetry
scatters eyes on a page,   35
scatters words on our eyes.
Eyes speak,
words look,
looks think.
To hear   40
thoughts,
see
what we say,
touch
the body of an idea.   45
Eyes close,
the words open.

TRANSLATED BY ELIOT WEINBERGER

Wind and Water and Stone

for Roger Caillois

The water hollowed the stone,
the wind dispersed the water,
the stone stopped the wind.
Water and wind and stone.

The wind sculpted the stone,   5
the stone is a cup of water,
the water runs off and is wind.
Stone and wind and water.

The wind sings in its turnings,
the water murmurs as it goes,   10
the motionless stone is quiet.
Wind and water and stone.

One is the other, and is neither:
among their empty names
they pass and disappear,   15
water and stone and wind.

TRANSLATED BY MARK STRAND

HENRY REED

[b. 1914]

♦

Naming of Parts

Today we have naming of parts. Yesterday,
We had daily cleaning. And tomorrow morning,
We shall have what to do after firing. But today,
Today we have naming of parts. Japonica

Glistens like coral in all of the neighboring gardens,   5
    And today we have naming of parts.

This is the lower sling swivel. And this
Is the upper sling swivel, whose use you will see,
When you are given your slings. And this is the piling swivel,
Which in your case you have not got. The branches   10
Hold in the gardens their silent, eloquent gestures,
    Which in our case we have not got.

This is the safety-catch, which is always released
With an easy flick of the thumb. And please do not let me
See anyone using his finger. You can do it quite easy   15
If you have any strength in your thumb. The blossoms
Are fragile and motionless, never letting anyone see
    Any of them using their finger.

And this you can see is the bolt. The purpose of this
Is to open the breech, as you see. We can slide it   20
Rapidly backwards and forwards: we call this
Easing the spring. And rapidly backwards and forwards
The early bees are assaulting and fumbling the flowers:
    They call it easing the Spring.

They call it easing the Spring: it is perfectly easy   25
If you have any strength in your thumb: like the bolt
And the breech, and the cocking-piece, and the point of
   balance,
Which in our case we have not got; and the almond-blossom
Silent in all of the gardens and the bees going backwards and
   forwards,
    For today we have naming of parts.   30

WILLIAM STAFFORD

[b. 1914]

◆

Traveling through the dark

Traveling through the dark I found a deer
dead on the edge of the Wilson River road.
It is usually best to roll them into the canyon:
that road is narrow; to swerve might make more dead.

By glow of the tail-light I stumbled back of the car   5
and stood by the heap, a doe, a recent killing;
she had stiffened already, almost cold.
I dragged her off; she was large in the belly.

My fingers touching her side brought me the reason—
her side was warm; her fawn lay there waiting,   10
alive, still, never to be born.
Beside that mountain road I hesitated.

The car aimed ahead its lowered parking lights;
under the hood purred the steady engine.
I stood in the glare of the warm exhaust turning red;   15
around our group I could hear the wilderness listen.

I thought hard for us all—my only swerving—,
then pushed her over the edge into the river.

DYLAN THOMAS

[1914–1953]

◆

Fern Hill

Now as I was young and easy under the apple boughs
About the lilting house and happy as the grass was green,
    The night above the dingle starry,
       Time let me hail and climb
    Golden in the heydays of his eyes,   5
And honored among wagons I was prince of the apple
   towns
And once below a time I lordly had the trees and leaves
      Trail with daisies and barley
    Down the rivers of the windfall light.

And as I was green and carefree, famous among the barns 10
About the happy yard and singing as the farm was home,
    In the sun that is young once only,
       Time let me play and be
    Golden in the mercy of his means,
And green and golden I was huntsman and herdsman,
   the calves   15
Sang to my horn, the foxes on the hills barked clear
   and cold,
      And the sabbath rang slowly
    In the pebbles of the holy streams.

All the sun long it was running, it was lovely, the hay
Fields high as the house, the tunes from the chimneys,
   it was air   20
    And playing, lovely and watery
      And fire green as grass.
    And nightly under the simple stars
As I rode to sleep the owls were bearing the farm away,

All the moon long I heard, blessed among stables,
  the night-jars
     Flying with the ricks, and the horses
       Flashing into the dark.

And then to awake, and the farm, like a wanderer white
With the dew, come back, the cock on his shoulder: it
  was all
     Shining, it was Adam and maiden,
       The sky gathered again
     And the sun grew round that very day.
So it must have been after the birth of the simple light
In the first, spinning place, the spellbound horses
  walking warm
     Out of the whinnying green stable
       On to the fields of praise.

And honored among foxes and pheasants by the gay house
Under the new made clouds and happy as the heart
  was long,
     In the sun born over and over,
       I ran my heedless ways,
     My wishes raced through the house high hay
And nothing I cared, at my sky blue trades, that time allow;
In all his tuneful turning so few and such morning songs
     Before the children green and golden
       Follow him out of grace,

Nothing I cared, in the lamb white days, that time would
  take me
Up to the swallow thronged loft by the shadow of my hand,
     In the moon that is always rising,
       Nor that riding to sleep
     I should hear him fly with the high fields
And wake to the farm forever fled from the childless land.
Oh as I was young and easy in the mercy of his means,
       Time held me green and dying
     Though I sang in my chains like the sea.

Do not go gentle into that good night

Do not go gentle into that good night,
Old age should burn and rave at close of day;
Rage, rage against the dying of the light.

Though wise men at their end know dark is right,
Because their words had forked no lightning they   5
Do not go gentle into that good night.

Good men, the last wave by, crying how bright
Their frail deeds might have danced in a green bay,
Rage, rage against the dying of the light.

Wild men who caught and sang the sun in flight,   10
And learn, too late, they grieved it on its way,
Do not go gentle into that good night.

Grave men, near death, who see with blinding sight
Blind eyes could blaze like meteors and be gay,
Rage, rage against the dying of the light.   15

And you, my father, there on the sad height,
Curse, bless, me now with your fierce tears, I pray.
Do not go gentle into that good night.
Rage, rage against the dying of the light.

MARGARET WALKER

[b. 1915]

◆

Lineage

My grandmothers were strong.
They followed plows and bent to toil.
They moved through fields sowing seed.

They touched earth and grain grew.
They were full of sturdiness and singing.   5
My grandmothers were strong.

My grandmothers are full of memories.
Smelling of soap and onions and wet clay
With veins rolling roughly over quick hands
They have many clean words to say.   10
My grandmothers were strong.
Why am I not as they?

GWENDOLYN BROOKS

[b. 1917]

◆

Kitchenette Building

We are things of dry hours and the involuntary plan,
Grayed in, and gray. "Dream" makes a giddy sound,
   not strong
Like "rent," "feeding a wife," "satisfying a man."

But could a dream send up through onion fumes
Its white and violet, fight with fried potatoes   5
And yesterday's garbage ripening in the hall,
Flutter, or sing an aria down these rooms

Even if we were willing to let it in,
Had time to warm it, keep it very clean,
Anticipate a message, let it begin?   10
We wonder. But not well! not for a minute!
Since Number Five is out of the bathroom now,
We think of lukewarm water, hope to get in it.

A *Song* in the Front Yard

I've stayed in the front yard all my life.
I want a peek at the back
Where it's rough and untended and hungry weed grows.
A girl gets sick of a rose.

I want to go in the back yard now   5
And maybe down the alley,
To where the charity children play.
I want a good time today.

They do some wonderful things.
They have some wonderful fun.   10
My mother sneers, but I say it's fine
How they don't have to go in at quarter to nine.
My mother, she tells me that Johnnie Mae
Will grow up to be a bad woman.
That George'll be taken to Jail soon or late   15
(On account of last winter he sold our back gate.)

But I say it's fine. Honest, I do.
And I'd like to be a bad woman, too,
And wear the brave stockings of night-black lace
And strut down the streets with paint on my face.   20

The Mother

Abortions will not let you forget.
You remember the children you got that you did not get,
The damp small pulps with a little or with no hair,
The singers and workers that never handled the air.
You will never neglect or beat   5
Them, or silence or buy with a sweet.
You will never wind up the sucking-thumb
Or scuttle off ghosts that come.
You will never leave them, controlling your luscious sigh,
Return for a snack of them, with gobbling mother-eye.   10

I have heard in the voices of the wind the voices of my dim
    killed children.
I have contracted. I have eased
My dim dears at the breasts they could never suck.
I have said, Sweets, if I sinned, if I seized
Your luck   15
And your lives from your unfinished reach,
If I stole your births and your names,
Your straight baby tears and your games,
Your stilted or lovely loves, your tumults, your marriages,
    aches, and your deaths,
If I poisoned the beginnings of your breaths,   20
Believe that even in my deliberateness I was not deliberate.
Though why should I whine,
Whine that the crime was other than mine?—
Since anyhow you are dead.
Or rather, or instead,   25
You were never made.

But that too, I am afraid,
Is faulty: oh, what shall I say, how is the truth to be said?
You were born, you had body, you died.
It is just that you never giggled or planned or cried. 30

Believe me, I loved you all.
Believe me, I knew you, though faintly, and I loved,
   I loved you all.

First fight. Then fiddle.

First fight. Then fiddle. Ply the slipping string
With feathery sorcery; muzzle the note
With hurting love; the music that they wrote
Bewitch, bewilder. Qualify to sing
Threadwise. Devise no salt, no hempen thing 5
For the dear instrument to bear. Devote
The bow to silks and honey. Be remote
A while from malice and from murdering.
But first to arms, to armor. Carry hate
In front of you and harmony behind. 10
Be deaf to music and to beauty blind.
Win war. Rise bloody, maybe not too late
For having first to civilize a space
Wherein to play your violin with grace.

ROBERT LOWELL

[1917–1977]

♦

The Drinker

The man is killing time—there's nothing else.
No help now from the fifth of Bourbon
chucked helter-skelter into the river,
even its cork sucked under.

Stubbed before-breakfast cigarettes   5
burn bull's-eyes on the bedside table;
a plastic tumbler of alka seltzer
champagnes in the bathroom.

No help from his body, the whale's
warm-hearted blubber, foundering down   10
leagues of ocean, gasping whiteness.
The barbed hooks fester. The lines snap tight.

When he looks for neighbors, their names blur in
   the window,
his distracted eye sees only glass sky.
His despair has the galvanized color   15
of the mop and water in the galvanized bucket.

Once she was close to him
as water to the dead metal.

He looks at her engagements inked on her calendar.
A list of indictments.   20
At the numbers in her thumbed black telephone book.
A quiver full of arrows.

Her absence hisses like steam,
the pipes sing . . .
even corroded metal somehow functions.   25
He snores in his iron lung,

and hears the voice of Eve,
beseeching freedom from the Garden's
perfect and ponderous bubble. No voice
outsings the serpent's flawed, euphoric hiss.   30

The cheese wilts in the rat-trap,
the milk turns to junket in the cornflakes bowl,
car keys and razor blades
shine in an ashtray.

Is he killing time? Out on the street,   35
two cops on horseback clop through the April rain
to check the parking meter violations—
their oilskins yellow as forsythia.

MAY SWENSON

[b. 1919]

♦

Women

Women   Or they
 should be   shoud be
 pedestals   little horses
 moving   those wooden
 pedestals   sweet   5
 moving   oldfashioned
 to the   painted
 motions   rocking
 of men   horses

the gladdest things in the toyroom.   10

The   feelingly
 pegs   and then
 of their   unfeelingly
 ears   To be
 so familiar   joyfully   15
 and dear   ridden
 to the trusting rockingly
 fists   ridden until
 To be chafed the restored

egos dismount and the legs stride away 20

Immobile   willing
 sweetlipped   to be set
 sturdy   into motion
 and smiling   Women
  women   should be   25
  should always pedestals
  be waiting to men

RICHARD WILBUR

[b. 1921]

♦

Juggler

A ball will bounce, but less and less. It's not
A light-hearted thing, resents its own resilience.
Falling is what it loves, and the earth falls
So in our hearts from brilliance,
Settles and is forgot.   5
It takes a skyblue juggler with five red balls

To shake our gravity up. Whee, in the air
The balls roll round, wheel on his wheeling hands,
Learning the ways of lightness, alter to spheres
Grazing his finger ends,   10
Cling to their courses there,
Swinging a small heaven about his ears.

But a heaven is easier made of nothing at all
Than the earth regained, and still and sole within
The spin of worlds, with a gesture sure and noble   15
He reels that heaven in,
Landing it ball by ball,
And trades it all for a broom, a plate, a table.

Oh, on his toe the table is turning, the broom's
Balancing up on his nose, and the plate whirls   20
On the tip of the broom! Damn, what a show, we cry:
The boys stamp, and the girls
Shriek, and the drum booms
And all comes down, and he bows and says good-bye.

If the juggler is tired now, if the broom stands   25
In the dust again, if the table starts to drop
Through the daily dark again, and though the plate
Lies flat on the table top,
For him we batter our hands
Who has won for once over the world's weight.   30

PHILIP LARKIN

[1922–1985]

♦

A *Study* of *Reading* *Habits*

When getting my nose in a book
Cured most things short of school,
It was worth ruining my eyes
To know I could still keep cool,
And deal out the old right hook   5
To dirty dogs twice my size.

Later, with inch-thick specs,
Evil was just my lark:
Me and my cloak and fangs
Had ripping times in the dark.   10
The women I clubbed with sex!
I broke them up like meringues.

Don't read much now: the dude
Who lets the girl down before
The hero arrives, the chap   15
Who's yellow and keeps the store,
Seem far too familiar. Get stewed:
Books are a load of crap.

LOUIS SIMPSON

[b. 1923]

♦

The Heroes

I dreamed of war-heroes, of wounded war-heroes
With just enough of their charms shot away
To make them more handsome. The women moved nearer
To touch their brave wounds and their hair streaked with
    gray.

I saw them in long ranks ascending the gang-planks;   5
The girls with the doughnuts were cheerful and gay.
They minded their manners and muttered their thanks;
The Chaplain advised them to watch and to pray.

They shipped these rapscallions, these sea-sick battalions
To a patriotic and picturesque spot;   10
They gave them new bibles and marksmen's medallions,
Compasses, maps, and committed the lot.

A fine dust has settled on all that scrap metal.
The heroes were packaged and sent home in parts
To pluck at a poppy and sew on a petal   15
And count the long night by the stroke of their hearts.

The Battle

Helmet and rifle, pack and overcoat
Marched through a forest. Somewhere up ahead
Guns thudded. Like the circle of a throat
The night on every side was turning red.

They halted and they dug. They sank like moles   5
Into the clammy earth between the trees.
And soon the sentries, standing in their holes,
Felt the first snow. Their feet began to freeze.

At dawn the first shell landed with a crack.
Then shells and bullets swept the icy woods.   10
This lasted many days. The snow was black.
The corpses stiffened in their scarlet hoods.

Most clearly of that battle I remember
The tiredness in eyes, how hands looked thin
Around a cigarette, and the bright ember   15
Would pulse with all the life there was within.

KENNETH KOCH

[b. 1925]

◆

Variations on a Theme
by William Carlos Williams

I

I chopped down the house that you had been saving to live
    in next summer.
I am sorry, but it was morning, and I had nothing to do
and its wooden beams were so inviting.

II

We laughed at the hollyhocks together
And then I sprayed them with lye.   5
Forgive me. I simply do not know what I am doing.

III

I gave away the money that you had been saving to live on
　　for the next ten years.
The man who asked for it was shabby
and the firm March wind on the porch was so juicy and cold.

IV

Last evening we went dancing and I broke your leg.　　　　10
Forgive me. I was clumsy, and
I wanted you here in the wards, where I am the doctor!

ROBERT CREELEY

[b. 1926]

◆

I Know a Man

As I sd to my
friend, because I am
always talking,—John, I

sd, which was not his
name, the darkness sur-　　　　　　5
rounds us, what

can we do against
it, or else, shall we &
why not, buy a goddamn big car,

drive, he sd, for　　　　　　　　10
christ's sake, look
out where yr going.

The Rain

All night the sound had
come back again,
and again falls
this quiet, persistent rain.

What am I to myself   5
that must be remembered,
insisted upon
so often? Is it

that never the ease,
even the hardness,   10
of rain falling
will have for me

something other than this,
something not so insistent—
am I to be locked in this   15
final uneasiness.

Love, if you love me,
lie next to me.
Be for me, like rain,
the getting out   20

of the tiredness, the fatuousness, the semi-
lust of intentional indifference.
Be wet
with a decent happiness.

ALASTAIR REID

[b. 1926]

◆

Curiosity

may have killed the cat. More likely,
the cat was just unlucky, or else curious
to see what death was like, having no cause
to go on licking paws, or fathering
litter on litter of kittens, predictably.   5

Nevertheless, to be curious
is dangerous enough. To distrust
what is always said, what seems,
to ask odd questions, interfere in dreams,
smell rats, leave home, have hunches,   10
does not endear cats to those doggy circles
where well-smelt baskets, suitable wives, good lunches
are the order of things, and where prevails
much wagging of incurious heads and tails.

Face it. Curiosity   15
will not cause us to die—
only lack of it will.
Never to want to see
the other side of the hill
or that improbable country   20
where living is an idyll
(although a probable hell)
would kill us all.
Only the curious
have if they live a tale   25
worth telling at all.

Dogs say cats love too much, are irresponsible,
are dangerous, marry too many wives,
desert their children, chill all dinner tables
with tales of their nine lives. 30

Well, they are lucky. Let them be
nine-lived and contradictory,
curious enough to change, prepared to pay
the cat-price, which is to die
and die again and again, 35
each time with no less pain.
A cat-minority of one
is all that can be counted on
to tell the truth; and what cats have to tell
on each return from hell 40
is this: that dying is what the living do,
that dying is what the loving do,
and that dead dogs are those who never know
that dying is what, to live, each has to do.

Oddments, Inklings, Omens, Moments

Oddments, as when
you see through skin,
when flowers appear
to be eavesdropping,
or music somewhere 5
declares your mood;
when sleep fulfils
a feel of dying
or fear makes ghosts
of clothes on a chair. 10

Inklings, as when
some room rhymes
with a lost time,
or a book reads
like a well-known dream;   15
when a smell recalls
portraits, funerals,
when a wish happens
or a mirror sees
through distances.   20

Omens, as when
a shadow from nowhere
falls on a wall,
when a bird seems
to mimic your name,   25
when a cat eyes you
as though it knew
or, heavy with augury,
a crow caws
cras cras from a tree.   30

Moments, as when
the air's awareness
makes guesses true,
when a hand's touch
speaks past speech   35
or when, in poise,
two sympathies
lighten each other,
and love occurs
like song, like weather.   40

RUTH EISENBERG

[b. 1927]

♦

Tomato Sestina

August again, the tomatoes are plump
and squirt with each bite.
In my kitchen, I measure redness
and think of Pop standing in the garden
with a salt shaker in one hand,   5
in the other, a tomato ready to split.

He needed no knife to split
that red skin. He would heft the plump
fruit with his hand,
polish it on his shirt, salt, then bite,   10
and seeds would spurt all over the garden.
In a ripe tomato there is redness

that nothing else can match. The redness
is not of the skin alone, for split
the fruit is just as red. In the garden   15
he grew beans too, and radishes, plump
as Christmas balls which he could not bite
when pulled. Instead, he'd hand

them to Mom to wash. She'd hand
them back, their dark redness   20
shining, stems and roots cut, and he would bite
into their white sharpness, his teeth splitting
each radish leaving a plump
half moon. Back he'd go to the garden

the 8 by 20 victory garden   25
in which with his suburban hand
he grew vegetables. Plump
he'd bend over the weeds, redness
flooding his cheeks. We thought he'd split
his pants, but no. There was no bite   30

in him then, a joy of earth. No bite,
no malice. A business man in his garden
growing tomatoes 'til they all but split
their skins. He'd lift them with his hand
as they turned from green to pink to redness   35
that outshone the sunset. That red and so plump.

From such plump memories, I take nibbling bites
in ripe redness the best of my garden
fondled with time's hand, whole memories not to
                                          be split.   40

GALWAY KINNELL

[b. 1927]

♦

To Christ Our Lord

The legs of the elk punctured the snow's crust
And wolves floated lightfooted on the land
Hunting Christmas elk living and frozen;
Inside snow melted in a basin, and a woman basted
A bird spread over coals by its wings and head.   5

Snow had sealed the windows; candles lit
The Christmas meal. The Christmas grace chilled
The cooked bird, being long-winded and the room cold.
During the words a boy thought, is it fitting
To eat this creature killed on the wing?   10

He had killed it himself, climbing out
Alone on snowshoes in the Christmas dawn,
The fallen snow swirling and the snowfall gone,
Heard its throat scream as the rifle shouted,
Watched it drop, and fished from the snow the dead.   15

He had not wanted to shoot. The sound
Of wings beating into the hushed air
Had stirred his love, and his fingers
Froze in his gloves, and he wondered,
Famishing, could he fire? Then he fired.   20

Now the grace praised his wicked act. At its end
The bird on the plate
Stared at his stricken appetite.
There had been nothing to do but surrender,
To kill and to eat; he ate as he had killed, with wonder.   25

At night on snowshoes on the drifting field
He wondered again, for whom had love stirred?
The stars glittered on the snow and nothing answered.
Then the Swan spread her wings, cross of the cold north,
The pattern and mirror of the acts of earth.   30

JAMES WRIGHT

[1927–1980]

♦

Mutterings Over the Crib of a Deaf Child

"How will he hear the bell at school
Arrange the broken afternoon,
And know to run across the cool
Grasses where the starlings cry,
Or understand the day is gone?"   5

Well, someone lifting cautious brows
Will take the measure of the clock.
And he will see the birchen boughs
Outside the sagging dark from the sky,
And the shade crawling upon the rock.   10

"And how will he know to rise at morning?
His mother has other sons to waken,
She has the stove she must build to burning
Before the coals of the night-time die,
And he never stirs when he is shaken."   15

I take it the air affects the skin,
And you remember, when you were young,
Sometimes you could feel the dawn begin,
And the fire would call you, by and by,
Out of the bed and bring you along.   20

"Well, good enough. To serve his needs
All kinds of arrangements can be made.
But what will you do if his finger bleeds?
Or a bobwhite whistles invisibly
And flutes like an angel off in the shade?"   25

He will learn pain. And, as for the bird,
It is always darkening when that comes out,
I will putter as though I had not heard,
And lift him into my arms and sing
Whether he hears my song or not.   30

A Blessing

Just off the highway to Rochester, Minnesota,
Twilight bounds softly forth on the grass.
And the eyes of those two Indian ponies
Darken with kindness.
They have come gladly out of the willows   5
To welcome my friend and me.
We step over the barbed wire into the pasture
Where they have been grazing all day, alone.
They ripple tensely, they can hardly contain their happiness
That we have come.   10
They bow shyly as wet swans. They love each other.
There is no loneliness like theirs.
At home once more,
They begin munching the young tufts of spring in the
    darkness.
I would like to hold the slenderer one in my arms,   15
For she has walked over to me
And nuzzled my left hand.
She is black and white,
Her mane falls wild on her forehead,
And the light breeze moves me to caress her long ear   20
That is delicate as the skin over a girl's wrist.
Suddenly I realize
That if I stepped out of my body I would break
Into blossom.

ANNE SEXTON

[1928–1974]

♦

Ringing the Bells

And this is the way they ring
the bells in Bedlam
and this is the bell-lady
who comes each Tuesday morning
to give us a music lesson   5
and because the attendants make you go
and because we mind by instinct,
like bees caught in the wrong hive,
we are the circle of the crazy ladies
who sit in the lounge of the mental house   10
and smile at the smiling woman
who passes us each a bell,
who points at my hand
that holds my bell, E flat,
and this is the gray dress next to me   15
who grumbles as if it were special
to be old, to be old,
and this is the small hunched squirrel girl
on the other side of me
who picks at the hairs over her lip,   20
who picks at the hairs over her lip all day,
and this is how the bells really sound,
as untroubled and clean
as a workable kitchen,
and this is always my bell responding   25
to my hand that responds to the lady
who points at me, E flat;
and although we are no better for it,
they tell you to go. And you do.

DONALD FINKEL

[b. 1929]

♦

Hunting Song

The fox came lolloping, lolloping,
Lolloping. His tongue hung out
And his ears were high.
He was like death at the end of a string
When he came to the hollow   5
Log. Ran in one side
And out of the other. O
He was sly.

The hounds came tumbling, tumbling,
Tumbling. Their heads were low   10
And their eyes were red.
The sound of their breath was louder than death
When they came to the hollow
Log. They held at one end
But a bitch found the scent. O   15
They were mad.

The hunter came galloping, galloping,
Galloping. All damp was his mare
From her hooves to her mane.
His coat and his mouth were redder than death   20
When he came to the hollow
Log. He took in the rein
And over he went. O
He was fine.

The log, he just lay there, alone in   25
The clearing. No fox nor hound
Nor mounted man
Saw his black round eyes in their perfect disguise
(As the ends of a hollow
Log). He watched death go through him,   30
Around him and over him. O
He was wise.

JOHN HOLLANDER

[b. 1929]

♦

Adam's Task

"And Adam gave names to all cattle, and to the fowl
of the air, and to every beast of the field . . . "
GEN. 2:20

Thou, paw-paw-paw; thou, glurd; thou, spotted
Glurd; thou, whitestap, lurching through
The high-grown brush; thou, pliant-footed,
Implex; thou, awagabu.

Every burrower, each flier   5
Came for the name he had to give:
Gay, first work, ever to be prior,
Not yet sunk to primitive.

Thou, verdle; thou, McFleery's pomma;
Thou; thou; thou—three types of grawl;   10
Thou, flisket; thou, kabasch; thou, comma-
Eared mashawk; thou, all; thou, all.

Were, in a fire of becoming,
Laboring to be burned away,
Then work, half-measuring, half-humming,   15
Would be as serious as play.

Thou, pambler; thou, rivarn; thou, greater
Wherret, and thou, lesser one;
Thou, sproal; thou, zant; thou, lily-eater.
Naming's over. Day is done.   20

Swan and Shadow

Dusk
Above the
water hang the
loud
flies
Here
O so
gray
then
What　　　　A pale signal will appear
When　　　Soon before its shadow fades
Where　　Here in this pool of opened eye
In us　　No Upon us As at the very edges
of where we take shape in the dark air
this object bares its image awakening
ripples of recognition that will
brush darkness up into light
even after this bird this hour both drift by atop the perfect sad instant now
already passing out of sight
toward yet-untroubled reflection
this image bears its object darkening
into memorial shades Scattered bits of
light　　　No of water Or something across
water　　　Breaking up No Being regathered
soon　　　Yet by then a swan will have
gone　　　Yes out of mind into what
vast
pale
hush
of a
place
past
sudden dark as
if a swan
sang

ADRIENNE RICH

[b. 1929]

♦

The Knight

A knight rides into the noon,
and his helmet points to the sun,
and a thousand splintered suns
are the gaiety of his mail.
The soles of his feet glitter   5
and his palms flash in reply,
and under his crackling banner
he rides like a ship in sail.

A knight rides into the noon,
and only his eye is living,   10
a lump of bitter jelly
set in a metal mask,
betraying rags and tatters
that cling to the flesh beneath
and wear his nerves to ribbons   15
under the radiant casque.

Who will unhorse this rider
and free him from between
the walls of iron, the emblems
crushing his chest with their weight?   20
Will they defeat him gently,
or leave him hurled on the green,
his rags and wounds still hidden
under the great breastplate?

GREGORY CORSO

[b. 1930]

♦

Marriage

Should I get married? Should I be good?
Astound the girl next door with my velvet suit and faustus
    hood?
Don't take her to movies but to cemeteries
tell all about werewolf bathtubs and forked clarinets
then desire her and kiss her and all the preliminaries   5
and she going just so far and I understanding why
not getting angry saying You must feel! It's beautiful to feel!
Instead take her in my arms lean against an old crooked
    tombstone
and woo her the entire night the constellations in the sky—

When she introduces me to her parents   10
back straightened, hair finally combed, strangled by a tie,
should I sit knees together on their 3rd degree sofa
and not ask Where's the bathroom?
How else to feel other than I am,
often thinking Flash Gordon soap—   15
O how terrible it must be for a young man
seated before a family and the family thinking
We never saw him before! He wants our Mary Lou!
After tea and homemade cookies they ask What do you do
    for a living?

Should I tell them? Would they like me then?   20
Say All right get married, we're losing a daughter
but we're gaining a son—
And should I then ask Where's the bathroom?

---

[2]**faustus hood** Dr. *Faustus, the central figure of Christopher Marlowe's play, sold his soul
to the devil.*

O God, and the wedding! All her family and her friends
and only a handful of mine all scroungy and bearded   25
just wait to get at the drinks and food—
And the priest! he looking at me as if I masturbated
asking me Do you take this woman for your lawful wedded
    wife?
And I trembling what to say say Pie Glue!
I kiss the bride all those corny men slapping me on the back   30
She's all yours, boy! Ha-ha-ha!
And in their eyes you could see some obscene honeymoon
    going on—
Then all that absurd rice and clanky cans and shoes
Niagara Falls! Hordes of us! Husbands! Wives! Flowers!
    Chocolates!
All streaming into cozy hotels   35
All going to do the same thing tonight

The indifferent clerk he knowing what was going to happen
The lobby zombies they knowing what
The whistling elevator man he knowing
The winking bellboy knowing   40
Everybody knowing! I'd be almost inclined not to do
    anything!
Stay up all night! Stare that hotel clerk in the eye!
Screaming: I deny honeymoon! I deny honeymoon!
running rampant into those almost climactic suites
yelling Radio belly! Cat shovel!   45
O I'd live in Niagara forever! in a dark cave beneath the Falls
I'd sit there the Mad Honeymooner
devising ways to break marriages, a scourge of bigamy
a saint of divorce—

But I should get married I should be good   50
How nice it'd be to come home to her
and sit by the fireplace and she in the kitchen
aproned young and lovely wanting my baby
and so happy about me she burns the roast beef
and comes crying to me and I get up from my big papa chair   55
saying Christmas teeth! Radiant brains! Apple deaf!

God what a husband I'd make! Yes, I should get married!
So much to do! like sneaking into Mr Jones' house late
   at night
and cover his golf clubs with 1920 Norwegian books
Like hanging a picture of Rimbaud on the lawnmower   60
like pasting Tannu-Tuva postage stamps all over the
   picket fence
like when Mrs Kindhead comes to collect for the Community
   Chest
grab her and tell her There are unfavorable omens in the sky!
And when the mayor comes to get my vote tell him
When are you going to stop people killing whales!   65
And when the milkman comes leave him a note in the bottle
Penguin dust, bring me penguin dust, I want penguin dust—

Yet if I should get married and it's Connecticut and snow
and she gives birth to a child and I am sleepless, worn,
up for nights, head bowed against a quiet window, the past
   behind me,   70
finding myself in the most common of situations a
   trembling man
knowledged with responsibility not twig-smear nor
   Roman coin soup—
O what would that be like!
Surely I'd give it for a nipple a rubber Tacitus
For a rattle a bag of broken Bach records   75
Tack Della Francesca all over its crib
Sew the Greek alphabet on its bib
And build for its playpen a roofless Parthenon

No, I doubt I'd be that kind of father
Not rural not snow no quiet window   80
but hot smelly tight New York City
seven flights up, roaches and rats in the walls

---

[60]Rimbaud *Arthur Rimbaud, French poet (1854–1891).*
[61]Tannu-Tuva *a republic in Siberia, part of the USSR.*
[74]Tacitus *Roman historian* (A.D. *55–117).*
[76]Della Francesca *Italian Renaissance painter (1420?–1492).*

a fat Reichian wife screeching over potatoes Get a job!
And five nose running brats in love with Batman
And the neighbors all toothless and dry haired   85
like those hag masses of the 18th century
all wanting to come in and watch TV

The landlord wants his rent
Grocery store Blue Cross Gas & Electric Knights of
    Columbus
Impossible to lie back and dream Telephone snow, ghost
    parking—   90
No! I should not get married I should never get married!
But—imagine if I were married to a beautiful sophisticated
    woman
tall and pale wearing an elegant black dress and long
    black gloves
holding a cigarette holder in one hand and a highball in
    the other
and we lived high up in a penthouse with a huge window   95
from which we could see all of New York and ever farther
    on clearer days
No, can't imagine myself married to that pleasant prison
    dream—

O but what about love? I forget love
not that I am incapable of love
it's just that I see love as odd as wearing shoes—   100
I never wanted to marry a girl who was like my mother
And Ingrid Bergman was always impossible
And there's maybe a girl now but she's already married
And I don't like men and—
but there's got to be somebody!   105
Because what if I'm 60 years old and not married,
all alone in a furnished room with pee stains on my
    underwear
and everybody else is married! All the universe married
    but me!

[83]Reichian *follower of psychoanalyst Wilhelm Reich (1897–1957).*

Ah, yet well I know that were a woman possible as I
   am possible
then marriage would be possible—   110
Like SHE in her lonely alien gaud waiting her Egyptian lover
so I wait—bereft of 2,000 years and the bath of life.

TED HUGHES

[b. 1930]

♦

Hawk Roosting

I sit in the top of the wood, my eyes closed.
Inaction, no falsifying dream
Between my hooked head and hooked feet:
Or in sleep rehearse perfect kills and eat.

The convenience of the high trees!   5
The air's buoyancy and the sun's ray
Are of advantage to me;
And the earth's face upward for my inspection.

My feet are locked upon the rough bark.
It took the whole of Creation   10
To produce my foot, my each feather:
Now I hold Creation in my foot

Or fly up, and revolve it all slowly—
I kill where I please because it is all mine.
There is no sophistry in my body: 15
My manners are tearing off heads—

---

[111]SHE *the heroine of H. Rider Haggard's novel,* She *(1887), who gains eternal youth by bathing in fire and who waits thousands of years for her lover's return.*

The allotment of death.
For the one path of my flight is direct
Through the bones of the living.
No arguments assert my right: 20

The sun is behind me.
Nothing has changed since I began.
My eye has permitted no change.
I am going to keep things like this.

GARY SNYDER

[b. 1930]

◆

Riprap

Lay down these words
Before your mind like rocks.
            placed solid, by hands
In choice of place, set
Before the body of the mind   5
            in space and time:
Solidity of bark, leaf, or wall
            riprap of things:
Cobble of milky way,
            straying planets,   10
These poems, people,
            lost ponies with
Dragging saddles—
            and rocky sure-foot trails.
The worlds like an endless   15
            four-dimensional
Game of *Go*.

ants and pebbles
In the thin loam, each rock a word
        a creek-washed stone   20
Granite: ingrained
        with torment of fire and weight
Crystal and sediment linked hot
        all change, in thoughts,
As well as things.   25

ETHERIDGE KNIGHT

[b. 1931]

♦

Haiku

I

Eastern guard tower
glints in sunset; convicts rest
like lizards on rocks.

II

The piano man
is sting at 3 am   5
his songs drop like plum.

III

Morning sun slants cell.
Drunks stagger like cripple flies
On Jailhouse floor.

IV

To write a blues song   10
is to regiment riots
and pluck gems from graves.

V

A bare pecan tree
slips a pencil shadow down
a moonlit snow slope.   15

VI

The falling snow flakes
Can not blunt the hard aches nor
Match the steel stillness.

VII

Under moon shadows
A tall boy flashes knife and   20
Slices star bright ice.

VIII

In the August grass
Struck by the last rays of sun
The cracked teacup screams.

IX

Making jazz swing in   25
Seventeen syllables AIN'T
No square poet's job.

PETER MEINKE

[b. 1932]

◆

Advice to My Son

The trick is, to live your days
as if each one may be your last
(for they go fast, and young men lose their lives
in strange and unimaginable ways)
but at the same time, plan long range   5
(for they go slow: if you survive
the shattered windshield and the bursting shell
you will arrive
at our approximation here below
of heaven or hell).   10

To be specific, between the peony and the rose
plant squash and spinach, turnips and tomatoes;
beauty is nectar
and nectar, in a desert, saves—
but the stomach craves stronger sustenance   15
than the honied vine.
Therefore, marry a pretty girl
after seeing her mother;
speak truth to one man,
work with another;   20
and always serve bread with your wine.

But, son,
always serve wine.

SYLVIA PLATH

[1932–1963]

◆

Metaphors

I'm a riddle in nine syllables,
An elephant, a ponderous house,
A melon strolling on two tendrils.
O red fruit, ivory, fine timbers!
This loaf's big with its yeasty rising.   5
Money's new-minted in this fat purse.
I'm a means, a stage, a cow in calf.
I've eaten a bag of green apples,
Boarded the train there's no getting off.

ROBERT WALLACE

[b. 1932]

◆

The Double-Play

In his sea lit
distance, the pitcher winding
like a clock about to chime comes down with

the ball, hit
sharply, under the artificial   5
banks of arc-lights, bounds like a vanishing string

357

over the green
to the shortstop magically
scoops to his right whirling above his invisible

shadows   10
in the dust redirects
its flight to the running poised second baseman

pirouettes
leaping, above the slide, to throw
from mid-air, across the colored tightened interval,   15

to the leaning-
out first baseman ends the dance
drawing it disappearing into his long brown glove

stretches. What
is too swift for deception   20
is final, lost, among the loosened figures

jogging off the field
(the pitcher walks), casual
in the space where the poem has happened.

YEVGENY YEVTUSHENKO

[b. 1933]

♦

People

No people are uninteresting.
Their fate is like the chronicle of planets.

Nothing in them is not particular,
and planet is dissimilar from planet.

And if a man lived in obscurity   5
making his friends in that obscurity
obscurity is not uninteresting.

To each his world is private,
and in that world one excellent minute.

And in that world one tragic minute.   10
These are private.

In any man who dies there dies with him
his first snow and kiss and fight.
It goes with him.

They are left books and bridges   15
and painted canvas and machinery.

Whose fate is to survive.
But what has gone is also not nothing:

by the rule of the game something has gone.
Not people die but worlds die in them.   20

Whom we knew as faulty, the earth's creatures.
Of whom, essentially, what did we know?

Brother of a brother? Friend of friends?
Lover of lover?

We who knew our fathers   25
in everything, in nothing.

They perish. They cannot be brought back.
The secret worlds are not regenerated.

And every time again and again
I make my lament against destruction.   30

TRANSLATED BY ROBIN MILNER-GULAND AND PETER LEVI

IMAMU AMIRI BARAKA

[b. 1934]

♦

An Agony. As Now.

I am inside someone
who hates me. I look
out from his eyes. Smell
what fouled tunes come in
to his breath. Love his   5
wretched women.

Slits in the metal, for sun. Where
my eyes sit turning, at the cool air
the glance of light, or hard flesh
rubbed against me, a woman, a man,   10
without shadow, or voice, or meaning.

This is the enclosure (flesh,
where innocence is a weapon. An
abstraction. Touch. (Not mine.
Or yours, if you are the soul I had   15
and abandoned when I was blind and had
my enemies carry me as a dead man
(if he is beautiful, or pitied.

It can be pain. (As now, as all his
flesh hurts me.) It can be that. Or   20
pain. As when she ran from me into
that forest.
                    Or pain, the mind
silver spiraled whirled against the
sun, higher than even old men thought
God would be. Or pain. And the other. The   25
yes. (Inside his books, his fingers. They

are withered yellow flowers and were never
beautiful.) The yes. You will, lost soul, say
'beauty.' Beauty, practiced, as the tree. The
slow river. A white sun in its wet sentences.   30

Or, the cold men in their gale. Ecstasy. Flesh
or souls. The yes. (Their robes blown. Their bowls
empty. They chant at my heels, not at yours.) Flesh
or soul, as corrupt. Where the answer moves too quickly.
Where the God is a self, after all.)   35

Cold air blown through narrow blind eyes. Flesh,
white hot metal. Glows as the day with its sun.
It is a human love, I live inside. A bony skeleton
you recognize as words or simple feeling.

But it has no feeling. As the metal, is hot, it is not,   40
given to love.

It burns the thing
inside it. And that thing
screams.

AUDRE LORDE

[b. 1934]

♦

Stations

Some women love
to wait
for life   for a ring
in the June light   for a touch
of the sun to heal them   for another   5
woman's voice   to make them whole

to untie their hands
put words in their mouths
form to their passages   sound
to their screams   for some other sleeper   10
to remember   their future   their past.

Some women wait for their right
train   in the wrong station
in the alleys of morning
for the noon to holler   15
the night come down.

Some women wait for love
to rise up
the child of their promise
to gather from earth   20
what they do not plant
to claim pain for labor
to become
the tip of an arrow   to aim
at the heart of now   25
but it never stays.

Some women wait for visions
that do not return
where they were not welcome
naked   30
for invitations to places
they always wanted
to visit
to be repeated.

Some women wait for themselves   35
around the next corner
and call the empty spot peace
but the opposite of living
is only not living
and the stars do not care.   40

Some women wait for something
to change   and nothing
does change
so they change
themselves.   45

MARK STRAND

[b. 1934]

♦

Eating Poetry

Ink runs from the corners of my mouth.
There is no happiness like mine.
I have been eating poetry.

The librarian does not believe what she sees.
Her eyes are sad   5
and she walks with her hands in her dress.

The poems are gone.
The light is dim.
The dogs are on the basement stairs and coming up.

Their eyeballs roll,   10
their blond legs burn like brush.
The poor librarian begins to stamp her feet and weep.

She does not understand.
When I get on my knees and lick her hand,
she screams.   15

I am a new man.
I snarl at her and bark.
I romp with joy in the bookish dark.

ROBERT MEZEY

[b. 1935]

◆

My Mother

My mother writes from Trenton,
a comedian to the bone
but underneath, serious
and all heart. "Honey," she says,
"be a mensch" and Mary too,   5
it's no good to worry, you
are doing the best you can
your Dad and everyone
thinks you turned out very well
as long as you pay your bills   10
nobody can say a word
you can tell them to drop dead
so save a dollar it can't
hurt—remember Frank you went
to highschool with? he still lives   15
with his wife's mother, his wife
works while he writes his books and
did he ever sell a one
the four kids run around naked
36 and he's never had,   20
you'll forgive my expression
even a pot to piss in
or a window to throw it,
such a smart boy he couldn't
read the footprints on the wall   25
honey you think you know all
the answers you don't, please try

⁵**mensch** *person.*

to put some money away
believe me it wouldn't hurt
artist shmartist life's too short   30
for that kind of, forgive me,
horsehit, I know what you want
better than you, all that counts
is to make a good living
and the best of everything,   35
as Sholem Aleichem said
he was a great writer did
you ever read his books dear,
you should make what he makes a year
anyway he says some place   40
Poverty is no disgrace
but its no honor either
that's what I say,
love,
Mother"   45

MARY OLIVER

[b. 1935]

♦

Poem for My Father's Ghost

Now is my father
A traveler, like all the bold men
He talked of, endlessly
And with boundless admiration,
Over the supper table,   5
Or gazing up from his white pillow—
Book on his lap always, until
Even that grew too heavy to hold.

Now is my father free of all binding fevers.
Now is my father   10
Traveling where there is no road.

Finally, he could not lift a hand
To cover his eyes.
Now he climbs to the eye of the river,
He strides through the Dakotas,   15
He disappears into the mountains. And though he looks
Cold and hungry as any man
At the end of a questing season,

He is one of *them* now:
He cannot be stopped.   20

Now is my father
Walking the wind,
Sniffing the deep Pacific
That begins at the end of the world.

Vanished from us utterly,   25
Now is my father circling the deepest forest—
Then turning in to the last red campfire burning
In the final hills,

Where chieftains, warriors and heroes
Rise and make him welcome,   30
Recognizing, under the shambles of his body,
A brother who has walked his thousand miles.

NATALIE SAFIR

[b. 1935]

♦

And She Did

I confess to my love
for Little Red Hen—
the quick pluck of her strut
level-headed squawks
her hard-boiled litany   5
the crackle of her resolve

We're not talking about winging it
We are talking about bread
about making it

This was no chicken—no   10
hysterical adolescent
issuing red alerts about the sky
No dumb cluck at the mercy
of barnyard poachers

This was a hard-working chick   15
who did and she did, and she did!

Survivors

In July we will go
to Grand Street
for a gravestone
Final edge of the chisel
will cut into its face   5
sister, beloved aunt,
love's widow—
a measure of words

By fall men will set the stone

Place it beside the day   10
her mother died
Sisters suddenly children
in her charge

In the cold company of stones
we will stand together   15
nieces, grand-nieces
and on down—a gathering
of monuments
she has raised

Women surviving   20
to face the inscription

And the dark
in my chest opens
missing her deep as the cavern
of earth brimming over   25
with her loss
Earth turned up, turns over
in my throat

LUCILLE CLIFTON

[b. 1936]

◆

Listen Children

listen children
keep this in the place
you have for keeping
always
keep it all ways   5

we have never hated black

listen
we have been ashamed
hopeless   tired   mad
but always   10
all ways
we loved us

we have always loved each other
children   all ways

pass it on   15

MARGE PIERCY

[b. 1936]

◆

A Work of Artifice

The bonsai tree
in the attractive pot
could have grown eighty feet tall
on the side of a mountain
till split by lightning.   5
But a gardener
carefully pruned it.
It is nine inches high.
Every day as he
whittles back the branches   10
the gardener croons,
It is your nature
to be small and cozy,
domestic and weak:
how lucky, little tree,   15
to have a pot to grow in.
With living creatures
one must begin very early
to dwarf their growth:
the bound feet,   20
the crippled brain,
the hair in curlers,
the hands you
love to touch.

BELLA AKHMADULINA

[b. 1937]

♦

The Bride

Oh to be a bride
Brilliant in my curls
Under the white canopy
Of a modest veil!

How my hands tremble,   5
Bound by my icy rings!
The glasses gather, brimming
With red compliments.

At last the world says yes;
It wishes me roses and sons.   10
My friends stand shyly at the door,
Carrying love gifts.

Chemises in cellophane,
Plates, flowers, lace . . .
They kiss my cheeks, they marvel   15
I'm to be a wife.

Soon my white gown
Is stained with wine like blood;
I feel both lucky and poor
As I sit, listening, at the table.   20

Terror and desire
Loom in the forward hours.
My mother, the darling, weeps—
Mama is like the weather.

. . . My rich, royal attire 25
I lay aside on the bed.
I find I am afraid
To look at you, to kiss you.

Loudly the chairs are set
Against the wall, eternity . . . 30
My love, what more can happen
To you and to me?

TRANSLATED BY STEPHAN STEPANCHEV

MICHAEL HARPER

[b. 1938]

♦

American History

Those four black girls blown up
in that Alabama church
remind me of five hundred
middle passage blacks,
in a net, under water 5
in Charleston harbor
so *redcoats* wouldn't find them.
Can't find what you can't see
can you?

Martin's Blues

He came apart in the open,
the slow motion cameras
falling quickly
neither alive nor kicking;
stone blind dead   5
on the balcony
that old melody
etched his black lips
in a pruned echo:
We shall overcome   10
some day—
Yes we did!
Yes we did!

CHARLES SIMIC

[b. 1938]

◆

Stone

Go inside a stone
That would be my way.
Let somebody else become a dove
Or gnash with a tiger's tooth.
I am happy to be a stone.   5

From the outside the stone is a riddle:
No one knows how to answer it.
Yet within, it must be cool and quiet
Even though a cow steps on it full weight,
Even though a child throws it in a river;   10

The stone sinks, slow, unperturbed
To the river bottom
Where the fishes come to knock on it
And listen.

I have seen sparks fly out   15
When two stones are rubbed,
So perhaps it is not dark inside after all;
Perhaps there is a moon shining
From somewhere, as though behind a hill—
Just enough light to make out   20
The strange writings, the star-charts
On the inner walls.

MARGARET ATWOOD

[b. 1939]

♦

This Is a Photograph of Me

It was taken some time ago.
At first it seems to be
a smeared
print: blurred lines and gray flecks
blended with the paper;   5

then, as you scan
it, you see in the left-hand corner
a thing that is like a branch: part of a tree
(balsam or spruce) emerging
and, to the right, halfway up   10
what ought to be a gentle
slope, a small frame house.

In the background there is a lake,
and beyond that, some low hills.

(The photograph was taken   15
the day after I drowned.

I am in the lake, in the center
of the picture, just under the surface.

It is difficult to say where
precisely, or to say   20
how large or small I am:

the effect of water
on light is a distortion

but if you look long enough,
eventually   25
you will be able to see me.)

Death of a Young Son by Drowning

He, who navigated with success
the dangerous river of his own birth
once more set forth

on a voyage of discovery
into the land I floated on   5
but could not touch to claim.

His feet slid on the bank,
the currents took him;
he swirled with ice and trees in the swollen water

and plunged into distant regions,   10
his head a bathysphere;
through his eyes' thin glass bubbles

he looked out, reckless adventurer
on a landscape stranger than Uranus
we have all been to and some remember.   15

There was an accident; the air locked,
he was hung in the river like a heart.
They retrieved the swamped body,

cairn of my plans and future charts,
with poles and hooks   20
from among the nudging logs.

It was spring, the sun kept shining, the new grass
leapt to solidity;
my hands glistened with details.

After the long trip I was tired of waves.   25
My foot hit rock. The dreamed sails
collapsed, ragged.

       I planted him in this county
       like a flag.

SEAMUS HEANEY

[b. 1939]

♦

Digging

Between my finger and my thumb
The squat pen rests; snug as a gun.

Under my window, a clean rasping sound
When the spade sinks into gravelly ground:
My father, digging. I look down   5

Till his straining rump among the flowerbeds
Bends low, comes up twenty years away
Stooping in rhythm through potato drills
Where he was digging.

The coarse boot nestled on the lug, the shaft   10
Against the inside knee was levered firmly.
He rooted out tall tops, buried the bright edge deep
To scatter new potatoes that we picked
Loving their cool hardness in our hands.

By God, the old man could handle a spade.   15
Just like his old man.

My grandfather cut more turf in a day
Than any other man on Toner's bog.
Once I carried him milk in a bottle
Corked sloppily with paper. He straightened up   20
To drink it, then fell to right away

Nicking and slicing neatly, heaving sods
Over his shoulder, going down and down
For the good turf. Digging.

The cold smell of potato mould, the squelch and slap   25
Of soggy peat, the curt cuts of an edge
Through living roots awaken in my head.
But I've no spade to follow men like them.

Between my finger and my thumb
The squat pen rests.   30
I'll dig with it.

Mid-Term Break

I sat all morning in the college sick bay
Counting bells knelling classes to a close.
At two o'clock our neighbors drove me home.

In the porch I met my father crying—
He had always taken funerals in his stride—   5
And Big Jim Evans saying it was a hard blow.

The baby cooed and laughed and rocked the pram
When I came in, and I was embarrassed
By old men standing up to shake my hand

And tell me they were "sorry for my trouble,"   10
Whispers informed strangers I was the eldest,
Away at school, as my mother held my hand

In hers and coughed out angry tearless sighs.
At ten o'clock the ambulance arrived
With the corpse, stanched and bandaged by the nurses.   15

Next morning I went up into the room. Snowdrops
And candles soothed the bedside; I saw him
For the first time in six weeks. Paler now,

Wearing a poppy bruise on his left temple,
He lay in the four foot box as in his cot.   20
No gaudy scars, the bumper knocked him clear.

A four foot box, a foot for every year.

JOSEPH BRODSKY

[b. 1940]

♦

Odysseus to Telemachus

My dear Telemachus,
          The Trojan War
is over now; I don't recall who won it.
The Greeks, no doubt, for only they would leave
so many dead so far from their own homeland.
But still, my homeward way has proved too long.   5
While we were wasting time there, old Poseidon,
it almost seems, stretched and extended space.

I don't know where I am or what this place
can be. It would appear some filthy island,
with bushes, buildings, and great grunting pigs.   10
A garden choked with weeds; some queen or other.
Grass and huge stones . . . Telemachus, my son!
To a wanderer the faces of all islands
resemble one another. And the mind
trips, numbering waves; eyes, sore from sea horizons,   15
run; and the flesh of water stuffs the ears.
I can't remember how the war came out;
even how old you are—I can't remember.

Grow up, then, my Telemachus, grow strong.
Only the gods know if we'll see each other   20
again. You've long since ceased to be that babe
before whom I reined in the plowing bullocks.
Had it not been for Palamedes' trick
we two would still be living in one household.
But maybe he was right; away from me   25
you are quite safe from all Oedipal passions,
and your dreams, my Telemachus, are blameless.

TRANSLATED BY GEORGE L. KLINE

SHARON OLDS

[b. 1942]

◆

Looking at My Father

I do not think I am deceived about him.
I know about the drinking, I know he's a tease,
obsessive, rigid, selfish, sentimental,
but I could look at my father all day
and not get enough: the large creased   5
ball of his forehead, slightly aglitter like the
sheen on a well-oiled baseball glove;
his eyebrows, the hairs two inches long,
black and silver, reaching out in
continual hope and curtailment; and most of   10
all I could look forever at his eyes,
the way they bulge out as if eager to see and
yet are glazed as if blind, the whites
hard and stained as boiled eggs
boiled in sulphur water, the irises   15
muddy as the lip of a live volcano, the
pupils glittering pure black,

magician black. Then there is his nose
rounded and pocked and comfy as the bulb of a
horn a clown would toot, and his lips   20
solid and springy. I even like to
look in his mouth, stained brown with
cigars and bourbon, my eyes sliding down the
long amber roots of his teeth,
right in there where Mother hated, and   25
up the scorched satin of the sides and
vault, even the knobs on the back of his
tongue. I know he is not perfect but my
body thinks his body is perfect, the
fine stretched coarse pink   30
skin, the big size of him, the
sour-ball mass, darkness, hair,
sex, legs even longer than mine,
lovely feet. What I know I know, what my
body knows it knows, it likes to   35
slip the leash of my mind and go and
look at him, like an animal
looking at water, then going to it and
drinking until it has had its fill and can
lie down and sleep.   40

The Signs

As I stand with the other parents outside the
camp bus, its windows tinted black
so we see our children, if we can find them, as
figures seen through a dark haze, like the dead,
I marvel at how little it takes to   5
tell me which is Gabriel—just a
tuft of hair, like the crest on the titmouse that
draws the titmice swiftly to its side.

Or all I see is the curve of a chin
scooped and pointed as some shining Italian   10
utensil for milk-white pasta with garlic,
that's my boy. All the other
mothers, too, can pick their kid by a
finger, a nose in the smoked mirror
as if we have come to identify their bodies   15
and take them home—such a cloud of fear and longing
hangs above the long drawn-out departure,
but finally it's over, each hand made of
just such genes and no others
waves its characteristic wave,   20
Gabey's thin finny hand
rotating like a windshield wiper, and they're
off in a Stygian stink of exhaust,
and then I would know his bus anywhere, in
any traffic jam, as it moves through the   25
bad air with the other buses,
its own smooth black shoulder
above the crowd, and when it turns the corner
I would know this world anywhere
as my son's world, I would love it any time in his name.   30

DAVE SMITH

[b. 1942]

♦

Desks

Piled on a loading dock where I walked,
    student desks battered, staggered
by the dozens, as if all our talk
    of knowledge was over,

as if there'd be no more thin blondes   5
    with pigtails, no math, no art,
no birds to stare at. Surplus now, those moulds
    we tried to sleep in, always hard

so it wouldn't be pleasant and we'd fall
    awake in time for the one question   10
with no answer. Quiet as a study hall,
    this big place, this final destination,

oblivious to whatever the weather is,
    hearing the creak of the wind's weight.
The desks are leg-naked, empty, as if   15
    we might yet come, breathless, late.

And all that time I thought of the flames
    I hadn't guessed, of a blonde
I had loved for years, how the names
    carved one into another would   20

all scar out the same, blunt, hard, in blue
    searing, like love's first pain.
I stood there like a child, scared, new,
    bird-eyed, not knowing why I came.

NIKKI GIOVANNI

[b. 1943]

♦

Ego Tripping

(THERE MAY BE A REASON WHY)

I was born in the congo
I walked to the fertile crescent and built
    the sphinx
I designed a pyramid so tough that a star
      that only glows every one hundred years falls   5
     into the center giving divine perfect light
I am bad

I sat on the throne
    drinking nectar with allah
I got hot and sent an ice age to europe   10
    to cool my thirst
My oldest daughter is nefertiti
    the tears from my birth pains
    created the nile
I am a beautiful woman   15

I gazed on the forest and burned
    out the sahara desert
    with a packet of goat's meat
    and a change of clothes
I crossed it in two hours   20
I am a gazelle so swift
    so swift you can't catch me

For a birthday present when he was three
I gave my son hannibal an elephant
   He gave me rome for mother's day   25
My strength flows ever on

My son noah built new/ark and
I stood proudly at the helm
   as we sailed on a soft summer day
I turned myself into myself and was   30
   jesus
     men intone my loving name
     All praises All praises
I am the one who would save

I sowed diamonds in my back yard   35
My bowels deliver uranium
   the filings from my fingernails are
   semi-precious jewels
     On a trip north
I caught a cold and blew   40
My nose giving oil to the arab world
I am so hip even my errors are correct
I sailed west to reach east and had to round off
   the earth as I went
     The hair from my head thinned and gold was laid   45
   across three continents
I am so perfect so divine so ethereal so surreal
I cannot be comprehended
   except by my permission

I mean . . . I . . . can fly   50
   like a bird in the sky . . .

ADEN ROSS

[b. 1943]

♦

Scraps

My mother always waited for potato skins,
chewed every melon into the rind,
lingered after dinner from plate to plate,
laughed how fat she'd grow as a waitress feasting
on leftover rolls and greasy lettuce leaves.   5

Waste not, want not, she cried,
and all those vitamins left behind!
She sopped each plate with bread crust,
saving for the end transparent thumbs
of beet fat, sucking them like gum.   10

When did she stop eating with us?
Or the family, grown to the outside, leave;
and mother, thinner and thinner, start to piece
stamplike scraps into quilt patterns
to throw across our growing bones?   15

J. D. McCLATCHY

[b. 1945]

♦

Hummingbird

There is no hum, of course, nor is the bird
That shiver of stained glass iridescence
Through which the garden appears—itself
In flight not from but toward an intensity
Of outline, color, scent, each flower   5
An imperium—as in a paragraph of Proust.

Mine is a shade of that branch it rests on
Between rounds: bark-wing, lichen-breast,
The butternut's furthest, hollow twig.
How to make from sow thistle to purslane?   10
So, into this airy vault of jewelweed,
Slipped past the drowsing bee watch,

Deep into the half-inch, bloodgold
Petal curve, tongue of the still untold.
Deaf to tones so low, the bees never mind   15
The dull grinding, these rusted gears
Pushed to the limit of extracting
From so many its little myth of rarity.

KRAFT ROMPF

[b. 1948]

♦

Waiting Table

To serve, I wait and pluck
the rose, brush crumbs, carry

madly trays of oysters and
Bloody Marys. Swinging through

doors, I hear them: mouths   5
open, eyes bugging, choking;

they beat a white clothed
table for caffeine piping

hot and sweet, sweet sugar.
Oh, I should pour it in   10

their eyes! And set their
tongues afire. How the chef

understands when I order
tartare and shout, "Let them

eat it raw!" Oh I would stuff   15
their noses with garlic

and the house pianist
could play the Hammer March

on their toes. But for a
tip—for a tip, for a tip   20

I would work so very, very
hard, and so gladly let

them shine into my soul,
and bow to them and laugh

with them and sing. I would   25
gladly give them everything.

Bicycle

Blue after blue
the harbor
drags

knotted currents under
barges and   5
tugs

drift over stars
in our
window

gushing vines and   10
viney spiders
and

where it shifts
so fast
from   15

night to day—
I miss
you.

Blue book, clouds,
gulls, gray   20
smoke-

wheeling ships, mud-
flapping spectacles,
airy

truths and rain.   25
And I
am

in love as
I bicycle
over   30

the jukebox, in
love with
the

messy sky, all
growth, all   35
that

falls up and
out of season.
And

when you slip   40
your arms
through

mine, I'm
suddenly beside
myself.   45

MICHAEL BLUMENTHAL

[b. 1949]

♦

I Have Lived This Way for Years and Do Not Wish to Change

I hope you'll forgive the black paint
on my windows, the smell of cat litter
in the kitchen. Guests complain sometimes
that my collection of Minoan cadavers spoils
their appetite, or that having the shower   5
in the living room creates too much moisture,
but I think you'll grow used to it
if we get to be friends.

Yes, it is kind of inconvenient
having the bed strapped to the ceiling,   10
but I've grown so accustomed to the view
of my Max Ernst carpet that I hardly think
I could sleep with gravity anymore.

Why thank you, it was a gift from my lover's husband
after our honeymoon in Cincinnati. I do think   15
it goes well with the orange bedroom set, the burgundy
    curtains.

See, you're feeling quite at home already.
Don't be shy.
Help yourself to the jellyfish, the goose down,
the chocolate-covered cotton balls.   20

RITA DOVE

[b. 1952]

♦

Geometry

I prove a theorem and the house expands:
the windows jerk free to hover near the ceiling,
the ceiling floats away with a sigh.

As the walls clear themselves of everything
but transparency, the scent of carnations   5
leaves with them. I am out in the open

and above the windows have hinged into butterflies,
sunlight glinting where they've intersected.
They are going to some point true and unproven.

GJERTRUD SCHNACKENBERG

[b. 1953]

♦

Signs

Threading the palm, a web of little lines
Spells out the lost money, the heart, the head,
The wagging tongues, the sudden deaths, in signs
We would smooth out, like imprints on a bed,

In signs that can't be helped, geese heading south,   5
In signs read anxiously, like breath that clouds
A mirror held to a barely open mouth,
Like telegrams, the gathering of crowds—

The plane's X in the sky, spelling disaster:
Before the whistle and hit, a tracer flare;   10
Before rubble, a hairline crack in plaster
And a housefly's panicked scribbling on the air.

VANESSA HALEY

[b. 1954]

◆

At *the Smithsonian*

The trumpeter swan's neck was curved
like something drawn to reflection
in wavering water, while flying
squirrels, fixed in flight,
stopped mid-air between the branches.   5

Laboring for years, the taxidermist's
hands bloomed with the touch of feathers
or animal fur, and yet in the end
they gnarled from caresses, trying
to make natural, poses of the dead.   10

And the hummingbirds are mourning,
wings spread like diadems, all blind:
Lazuline Sabrewing, Lucifer,
Magenta-throated Woodstar, hover
endlessly, never tasting columbines.   15

He forgot to give them eyes, too small
to bother with, or his hands had already
begun to stiffen. *Black-eared Fairy*
listens for nectar, its eyes
blank spheres of white, searching   20
in stillness for jewels of sight.

Appendix

꙰

Writing About Poetry

Reasons for Writing

Why write about poetry? For many reasons. First, writing about a poem encourages us to read it attentively and thus notice things we might miss during a more casual reading. Second, writing stimulates thinking, and thus can be an important way to discover what you think about a poem, how you feel about it, and why. Third, we can state our views in writing; we may write to endorse or refute a poem's values and ideas. And finally, writing gives us power over a poem, enabling us to absorb it into our storehouse of knowledge and experience.

An Approach to Writing About Poetry

Getting Started: Selecting a Topic The first step in writing about a poem is selecting a topic. This is sometimes done for you by your teacher, who may assign a specific writing topic. If you select your own topic, however, you should keep a few things in mind. First, make sure the topic is suited to the required length of the paper. If your essay will be less than 1,000 words long, you should probably focus on a single aspect of the poem. You might choose, for example, to write about a poem's language, its speaker and situation, its tone and ideas, or possibly about some aspect of its technique, such as rhythm and meter. You might choose to write, for example, about the situation of the speaker in Robert Frost's "Dust of Snow" (p. 4), or that of the speaker in Walt Whitman's "When

I heard the learn'd astronomer" (p. 73). Or you might write about the diction and imagery of Emily Dickinson's "The Bustle in a House" (p. 37) or of Adrienne Rich's "Aunt Jennifer's Tigers" (p. 16).

Whatever topic you choose, make sure it is one that interests you, one you are willing to invest time and effort exploring. Once you decide on your topic, think of a title that reflects its nature and focus. For example, if you were to write about the speaker and situation in "Dust of Snow" or in "When I heard the learn'd astronomer," you might choose one of these titles: "A Change of Heart: Nature and Man in Frost's 'Dust of Snow' "; "Education by Experience: The Importance of First-Hand Knowledge in Whitman's 'When I heard the learn'd astronomer.' " Or alternatively: "Language and Structure in Frost's 'Dust of Snow' "; "Contrast as a Structural Principle in Whitman's 'When I heard the learn'd astronomer.' " Deciding on a title can help clarify and focus your thinking. A clearly focused topic, moreover, can serve as a point of reference when you write and revise the paper, a reminder of your intention should you digress. In addition, a title targets the direction of your paper for a reader.

To find a topic that meets the criteria of suitability, specificity, and interest, reread your selected poem carefully a few times. If the poem appears in a book you own, or if you are working from a photocopy, mark the text as you read, underlining words and lines, noting significant details, and writing brief marginal notes. The following example shows the type of marginal annotations that can lead to the discovery of a subject, or a focused aspect of a work worth exploring in writing. This poem by Robert Hayden appears in the anthology on page 311.

Those Winter Sundays

This father gets up early *every* day—*even* on Sundays.

Sundays <u>too my father</u> got up early
and put <u>his</u> clothes on in the <u>blueblack</u>
 cold,

How can cold be "blueblack"?

then with cracked hands that ached
from labor in the weekday weather made

No one? Not other family members? Not the speaker?

banked fires blaze. <u>No one ever thanked</u>
 <u>him.</u>

Stanza 1 emphasizes the speaker's father; stanza 2 shifts emphasis to the speaker himself.

<u>I</u>'d wake and hear the cold splintering,
 breaking,
When the rooms were warm, <u>he</u>'d call,

Speaker remembers his *fear.* Fear of what? His father's anger? Was it directed at him?

and slowly <u>I</u> would rise and dress,
<u>fearing</u> the chronic angers of that house,

Father drives out the cold—warms the house, literally. Is the father himself a "warm" person, or "cold"?

Speaking <u>indifferently</u> to him,
who had driven out the <u>cold</u>
and polished my good shoes as well.

Repeats the question. Tone? Feeling? Speaker knows *now* what he did not know then.

<u>What did I know, what did I know</u> of
 <u>love</u>'s austere and <u>lonely</u> offices?

Father's loneliness/father's love.

Making general notes can help you discover what you think is interesting or important about a poem. As an alternative, you might want to focus on one aspect of a work and confine your marginal annotations to a particular poetic element or to a single issue or idea. You might decide, for example, to annotate John Updike's figures of speech in "The Mosquito" (pp. 27–28) or the imagery of William Wordsworth's "I wandered lonely as a cloud" (pp. 32–33).

Or you might analyze the structure of Edna St. Vincent Millay's sonnets (pp. 59, 61) or the sound play in Helen Chasin's "The Word *Plum*" (p. 72). Annotating a single feature of a poem can be excellent preparation for the later stages of the writing process—developing your ideas in a draft, organizing your thinking, and revising your draft.

If you do not own your text and cannot write in the margins, you can use an alternative method of note-making—the double-entry notebook. To create a double-entry notebook, divide a page in half vertically (or open a notebook so that you face two blank pages). On one side, *take* notes, summarizing the poem's action, situation, and ideas. On the other side, *make* notes, responding to the action, situation, and ideas. On the responding side of the notebook, record your own thinking about what you read: ask questions, speculate, make connections.

Here is an example of a double-entry notebook for Robert Hayden's "Those Winter Sundays":

DOUBLE-ENTRY NOTEBOOK

Summary and Observations	Responses and Reactions
The first stanza describes how the father would get up early every day (including Sundays) to light the fires that warmed the house for his family.	I remember my own father getting up at 5:00 AM to light the furnace so the house would be warm when the rest of the family got up. The images of this stanza stir my memory.
Stanza 1 ends with a short but important point: that no one ever thanked the father for what he did.	We all took my father's efforts for granted. We never thought of thanking him for what he did. Perhaps we should have— and not only for lighting the furnace.
Stanza 2 focuses on the speaker just as the first stanza focused on the father. The speaker	The poem's images here are evocative. You can feel the cold turning into warmth. You can

describes his memory of how the cold house became warm. He remembers how his father used to call him and how he would get up and get dressed in the now-warmed house.

Stanza 2 ends with a puzzling remark about how the speaker was fearful of what he calls the "angers" of the house. He says angers, not anger. And he describes those angers as "chronic" as well.

The third stanza continues to focus on the speaker. It mentions his indifference to his father's efforts, and it includes a memory of something else the father did for the son: polished his shoes for him.

Stanza 3 ends with a question, the only question in the poem. The question contains a repeated clause, "What did I know, what did I know," that suggests that the speaker feels he didn't know then what he knows now. The repetition also suggests how important his new knowledge is to him.

The speaker's final question focuses on the father's loneliness and also suggests his austerity. It doesn't give any reasons for this austerity; nor

hear the house waking up. And I can remember how my own father would come and wake us.

The speaker's fear is described in terms of the angers of the house. Perhaps he indicates a fear of his father. Was the speaker's father prone to displays of temper? Was his father critical of him?

A nice touch, those shoes. They suggest the father's thoughtfulness and attentiveness. When does a boy begin to polish his own shoes?

The poem seems to build toward this final pair of lines. I hear regret in them, regret for lost opportunities, regret for understanding too late the motive behind the father's attentions. Perhaps there is also regret for the distance that separated father and son from one another. Maybe the father was a bit austere—maybe more than a "bit." The lines suggest that love involves sacrifice, that it doesn't always—or perhaps even often—receive or require recognition. But perhaps the

does it explain any further the father's loneliness.

One thing seems clear, however: the son sees that the father's actions were motivated and sustained by love.

Another seems equally clear: the son regrets his earlier indifference, his lack of appreciation.

father needed some such appreciation. Perhaps it would have made him less remote, less distant. Why does the speaker realize these things now? Has he become a parent himself? Has his father's illness or death triggered these memories, feelings, and reflections?

After making these and other annotations, we could select a number of different subjects for writing: a memory of our father as compared with the speaker's memory of his, a discussion of the speaker's feelings about his father, an analysis of the poem's images or language or structure. Some titles for papers focusing on such subjects might include these: "A Small Boy's (Girl's) Memories of His (Her) Dad"; "Regret and Remorse in 'Those Winter Sundays' "; "The Cold Made Warm: Images of Life and Love in 'Those Winter Sundays' "; "The Structure of Thought and Feeling in 'Those Winter Sundays.' "

To gain practice in using these techniques, select an additional poem. Read it carefully; then annotate it and write a double-entry notebook page.

Drafting Your Paper—Developing and Organizing Your Ideas

Once you have arrived at a tentative subject and an angle of approach, you are ready to write a rough draft. The purpose of this draft is simply to write down your ideas and to see how they can be developed and supported. Think of the rough draft as an opportunity to discover what you think about the subject and to test and refine your ideas. Don't worry about having a clearly defined thesis or main idea before beginning. Instead, use your initial draft to find a thesis and sharpen it so that it eventually becomes clear.

In drafting the paper, consider your purpose. Are you writing to provide information and make observations about the poem? Are you writing to argue for a particular way of interpreting it? Ultimately, of course, all explanations of literary works are interpretations, and all interpretations are forms of argument. That is, interpretations are attempts to persuade other readers to see the poem one way rather than in other ways. When writing about a poem, you will often be attempting to convince others that what you see and say about it makes sense. You will be arguing for the validity of your way of seeing, not necessarily to the exclusion of other ways, but to demonstrate that your understanding of the poem is reasonable and valuable. Moreover, since readers will respond not only to your arguments themselves but also to how you present them, you will need to provide careful evidence for your ideas. Most often this evidence will come in the form of textual support—details of action, dialogue, structure, and language from the poem itself. See the analysis of "When I heard the learn'd astronomer" (pp. 73–78) as an example of this type of support. Additional evidence may come from secondary sources, books or journals in which you will find the comments of experienced readers whose observations and interpretations may influence and support your own thinking, or may contradict it.

After writing the draft, try to forget it for a while—at least for a day or two, and longer if possible. Upon returning to it, assess whether what you are saying makes sense, whether you have provided enough examples to clarify your ideas and presented sufficient evidence to make them persuasive. Read the draft critically, asking yourself what is convincing and what is not, what makes sense and what does not. Consider whether the draft centers on a single idea and stays on track. If the first draft does these things, you can begin thinking about how to tighten the paper's organization and polish its style. If, on the other hand, the draft contains frequent changes of direction and a number of different ideas, you will need to decide what to salvage and how to focus the paper more sharply.

When you have written an acceptable draft, you are then ready to view its organization. A general organizational framework would probably include an introductory section that clarifies your purpose and intention; a set of successive paragraphs that develop, explore, and explain your ideas; and a conclusion that rounds off the discussion. Within that framework, consider whether your ideas and examples have been arranged in a coherent and logical manner. Ask yourself whether the structure of your paper will be clear to readers. Consider also whether sufficient space (or perhaps too much space) has been allotted to clarifying and supporting your views. For these considerations, it may be advisable to ask someone to read your paper and make a few informal observations.

Perhaps the most important aspect of a paper's organization is that you as a writer have a clear sense of how your paper is structured. You should be able to identify each of the paper's parts and to explain how those parts are related and why you put them in the order you did. Consider the following example. In discussing the ironic tone of Stephen Crane's "War Is Kind" (pp. 48–49), you might focus on three or four ironic details. You might decide to discuss first the ironic quality of the title. The word *kind* is not usually associated with war; war is associated with suffering, waste, death, and destruction. The title, then, cannot be taken literally. Next you might decide to include Crane's speaker's advice to the lover, child, and mother of a slain soldier not to cry since war is "kind." And you might want to comment on how the horrifying details, such as the "field where a thousand corpses lie" and the soldier who "tumbled in the yellow trenches," stand alongside the more seemingly patriotic images, such as the regimental flag and the thundering drums.

Whatever details you ultimately select, and however many you choose, you will need to decide on a particular order in which to discuss them. Ask yourself how the ironic aspects of the poem can be related to one another. Consider what the ironic details contribute to the poem overall. You will probably view some details as more important than others; you may thus be able to subdivide and pair your examples, perhaps contrasting them. Or you may decide to consider them in order of increasing complexity or importance. It is necessary, though, to devise an organizational plan that makes sense to you and that will seem natural and evident to your readers.

Besides deciding on the order of ideas and examples in the paper and the amount of space allotted to each, you must consider also how to move from one example to another. You will need to link the sections of your discussion so that the writing flows smoothly. Generally, you can create transitions with phrases and sentences at the beginnings of paragraphs. (Examples include such words and phrases as "first, . . . second, . . ."; "on the other hand, . . ."; "in addition to . . ."; "another way in which. . . .") Sometimes, however, such an explicit mark of transition from one point to another will not be necessary. In such cases the careful ordering of the details that support your argument will be evidence enough of how one paragraph follows and is related to another.

Revising Your Paper   Revision is not something that occurs only once, at the end of the writing process. Redrafting your paper to consider the ordering of paragraphs and the use of examples is itself a significant act of revision. So, too, is rereading the poem and thinking about it again. Revision is a process that occurs throughout the entire span of reading and writing. It involves, essentially, reconsidering both your writing and your thinking. This reconsideration is made on three levels: conceptual, organizational, and stylistic.

Conceptual revision involves reconsidering your ideas. As you write a first or second draft, your understanding of the poem and what you plan to say about it may change. While accumulating textual evidence in support of one interpretation of the work, you may discover stronger evidence for a contrasting position. When this happens, you may need to go back to the note-taking stage to explore your revised vision of the work. You will then need to make major changes in the original draft. You may end up discarding much of it and beginning again with a stronger conviction about a different approach or a revised idea. In writing about Crane's "War Is Kind," for example, you may have started out with a literal interpretation, arguing that the poem is patriotic in impulse. Along the way, however, you may have become uneasy with certain details that counter this interpretation and prompt you to change your mind about what it means.

Organization, or structural, revision involves asking yourself whether the arrangement of the paper's parts best presents your line of thinking. Is the organizational framework readily discernible? Does it make sense? Have you written an introduction that clarifies your topic and intention? Have you organized your supporting details in a sensible and logical manner? Does your conclusion follow logically from your discussion and bring it to a satisfying close? Again, taking Crane's poem as an example, you might begin by identifying its general subject—war—and move toward suggesting that even though the poem contains some language that idealizes war, its details and its tone undermine such romanticized conceptions. From there you would move to the body of your argument, in which you would present the details that appear supportive of war's glories and show how other details of incident and language contradict them. In your conclusion, you would reiterate your main point, maybe responding personally to the poem and its meaning. You could also relate it to some other work you've read (by Crane or by another writer), and perhaps include an apt quotation that sums up your reading of the poem or its significance.

Stylistic revision concerns smaller-scale details, such as matters of syntax (word order), diction (word choice), tone, imagery, and rhythm. Even though you may think about these things in early drafts, it is better to defer critical attention to them until after writing a final draft, largely because such stylistic considerations may undergo significant alteration as you rethink and reorganize your paper.

You can focus on aspects of style that may require revision by using the following questions as guidelines:

1. Are your sentences concise and clear?
2. Can you eliminate words that are not doing their job?
3. Are your tone and voice consistent? (Do you shift from a formal to an informal, even colloquial, style?)
4. Is the level of language appropriate for your audience?
5. Do your words and sentences say what you want them to?
6. Are there any grammatical errors: inconsistencies in verb tenses, problems with subject-verb agreement, run-on sentences, and the like?
7. Are there any errors in spelling and punctuation?

As a final step, proofread the paper, making sure it conforms to all of your teacher's guidelines.

Some Ways of Writing About Poetry

Analysis   *Analysis* involves examining the relationships among the various elements of a work. When analyzing literary works, you study these elements to see what each reveals about the work overall. For example, you might analyze a poem's imagery or structure to see what each contributes to its meaning and effect.

Analysis is not an end in itself. We analyze literary works to better understand both *what* they mean and *how* they come to mean what they do. We take poems apart to reconstruct them, gaining along the way an enriched understanding of their significance and their artistry. The analytical comments on Dickinson's "Much Madness is divinest Sense" (pp. 11–12) and Rich's "Aunt Jennifer's Tigers" (pp. 16–19), along with the more extensive comments on Whitman's "When I heard the learn'd astronomer" (pp. 73–78), suggest how analysis of the elements of poetry enlarges our understanding of it.

Explication   A type of analysis frequently useful in explaining poems is *explication,* a careful line-by-line explanation of a passage in a poem. Explication involves the unfolding of the layers of meaning in a text. It provides a close-up look at the language of a passage with a view to explaining its meaning. To explicate is to interpret by means of careful, close reading. Because explication involves scrupulous attention to detail, it is usually reserved for specific sections or parts of longer poems, and sometimes even for parts of short poems as well.

Explication is particularly useful for revealing the meaning of a complex passage, something as long as a stanza or as short as a phrase. The analysis of the opening line of Dickinson's "Much Madness is divinest Sense" (p. 11) provides one example. Beginnings and endings of poems, in fact, are often worth considering in such careful detail because they provide the first and last opportunities for the poet to make and leave an impression on the reader.

For another example of explication, consider the following about the ending of Gerard Manley Hopkins's "Spring and Fall: To a Young Child." (Although only the last two lines are explicated here, the entire poem is reprinted. The accent marks were provided by the poet.)

Spring and Fall: To a Young Child

Márgarét, áre you gríeving
Over Goldengrove unleaving?
Leáves, like the things of man, you
With your fresh thoughts care for, can you?
Áh! ás the heart grows older
It will come to such sights colder
By and by, nor spare a sigh
Though worlds of wanwood leafmeal lie;
And yet you *will* weep and know why.
Now no matter, child, the name:
Sórrow's spríngs áre the same.
Nor mouth had, no nor mind, expressed
What heart heard of, ghost guessed:
It ís the blight man was born for,
It is Margaret you mourn for.

The poem's final couplet announces that Margaret is weeping not over the leaves of autumn, but over her own mortality. The older speaker clarifies what the child had subconsciously intuited: that beauty fades and life ends. Though weeping for her own mortality, Margaret is also weeping for the mortality of all humans and of nature, which mirrors human death in its own decay. The lines suggest that Margaret is mourning the loss of the innocence she possesses as a child, and the loss of life that inevitably awaits all living things. Sorrow, suffering, grief, loss—these are inevitable, inescapable. As we grow from childhood to adulthood, from innocence to knowledge, we experience a loss as well as a gain. Moreover, by calling life, and then death, the "blight" that we were "born for," the speaker suggests that we bring disease with us into the world—not only physical decay and death, but also sin, which "blights" our souls. It is the blight of original sin, the blight of failure, weakness, death. "Blight" is linked to the "Fall" of the poem's title, which, besides autumn, suggests the fall into experience, into sin, the fall from grace, perfection, and happiness; the "Spring" of the title, like springtime, suggests youth, vitality, innocence, life. Overall, the poem suggests that the values and virtues of innocence don't last, and it conveys a sadness at the inevitable end that awaits all living things.

Comparison and Contrast   Another useful approach in drafting a paper about a poem is the comparison and contrast of elements in a single work or of a particular aspect in different works. You might compare and contrast the differing perspectives on knowledge and learning of the astronomer and the speaker in Whitman's "When I heard the learn'd astronomer" (p. 73). Or you might compare the uses of irony in Crane's "War Is Kind" (p. 48) and Hardy's "Ah, are you digging on my grave?" (p. 207) Possible titles for papers exploring such comparative topics include: "Active and Passive Learning in Whitman's 'When I heard the learn'd astronomer' "; "Two Uses of Irony: Satire and Humor in Poems by Crane and Hardy."

Comparative analysis can sharpen your perception of the works under consideration. In looking at two works together, or at two aspects of a single work, you see what each lacks as well as what each possesses. In comparing two poems, you might notice, for example, that one includes rhyme and the other does not; that the action is external in one poem while in the other it is internal; or that the situations, speakers, imagery, or structures of the poems differ in significant and interesting ways. Such comparative observations will lead you to ask why those differences exist and why the writers developed their poems as they did.

When writing a comparative paper, keep the following guidelines in mind:

1. Compare two aspects of a poem that will reward your effort. By attending carefully to a poem's details, you will often find significant parallels and contrasts. Follow the leads the works provide.

2. Compare works that have a significant feature in common, such as authorship, style, subject, situation, or an aspect of technique. For example: the treatment of nature in two of Frost's or Dickinson's poems; the use of humor in Gregory Corso's "Marriage" and Robert Mezey's "My Mother" (pp. 348–352, 364–

365); versions of the sonnet form among the poems of Shakespeare, Frost, Milton, and Gwendolyn Brooks.

3. Make a point. Use comparison and contrast to support an idea, an argument, an interpretation. Your comparative analysis should lead to a conclusion, perhaps to an evaluation, not merely to a set of parallels. Your comparative and contrastive observations are important. But you must go beyond them to make connections, draw inferences, and reach conclusions, however provisional they might be.

4. Decide whether to organize your comparative discussion according to the "block" method—in which you discuss each subject separately—or according to the "alternating" method—in which you discuss the central ideas in point-by-point comparisons of specific characteristics. For example, if you are comparing the speakers in two poems according to the block method, you would devote the first half of your paper to one and the second half to the other. If you use the alternating method, you consider each speaker side by side, focusing on such features as their situations, manners of speaking, tones, attitudes, and physical and psychological characteristics.

Suggested Approaches to Papers About Poetry

1. Write a paper in which you recount your experience of reading a particular poem or a series of poems by the same author. You may want to compare your initial experience of reading the poem(s) with your experience in later readings.

2. Describe and characterize the speaker or another character from any poem. Present a sketch of this character by referring to the language of the poem. You may want to include poetic details about the speaker or character, things the speaker or character says along with the manner in which they are said.

3. Explicate the opening or closing lines of a poem. Explain the significance of the lines in the context of the poem overall.

4. Develop an alternative ending for a poem, changing the outcome of its action, altering its pattern of rhythm or rhyme, or making changes that are interesting to you. Be prepared to de-

fend your alternative version as a reasonable possibility. Consider why the author chose to end the poem as he or she did.

5. Select two or more brief passages from a long poem, passages that appear to be significant in their implications. They may be descriptive passages or passages in which a decisive action occurs. Establish the connections between the passages and explain their significance.

6. Read five or more poems by the same poet and discuss what features they have in common. Choose one as a typical example of the poet's work and identify the poem's salient characteristics.

7. Relate the action or situation of a poem to your own experience. Explain how the poem is relevant to your situation, and comment on how reading and thinking about it may have helped you view your own situation and experience more clearly.

8. Analyze the diction or word choices of a poem. Consider alternative possibilities the poet could have chosen. (See John Updike's "The Mosquito" on pages 27–28 for an example.) Examine the denotations and connotations of the words the poet actually did choose. Use your analysis of the diction to develop an interpretation of the poem.

9. Analyze the imagery of a poem. Make a list of all the poem's details, especially those that have an appeal to the senses. Look for connections among the details, and on the basis of what you find, write a paper explaining what the images contribute to the poem's meaning and feeling.

10. Analyze the figurative language of a poem. Identify and explain each figure of speech and discuss its function in the poem overall.

11. Discuss the ironic dimensions of a poem. Identify examples of irony, and explain their importance in the poem.

12. Explain the symbolic implications of the details of any poem. First explain the literal situation of the poem. Then explain the symbolic meaning of the literal details.

13. Identify the allusions in a poem and explain what they contribute to your understanding of the poem.

14. Analyze the structure of a poem. Consider both its overall structure and its small-scale structure—how the individual parts

themselves are organized. Identify the main parts of the work and comment on their relationship to each other.

15. Analyze the sound effects of a poem. Explain how sound contributes to the sense or meaning of the poem.

16. Analyze the rhythm and meter of a poem. Identify its prevailing metrical pattern. Acknowledge any deviations from this meter and comment on the significance of these deviations. Consider what the poem's rhythm and meter contribute to its overall meaning and feeling.

17. Evaluate a poem from the point of view of its merit or excellence—or lack thereof. Explain why you consider it to be an effective or ineffective poem.

18. Do a comparative evaluation of the poetic merit of any two poems. Explain what they share, how they differ, and why one is more effective than the other. (These may be by the same poet or by different poets.)

19. Discuss the values exemplified in one or more poems. Identify those values, relate them to your own, and comment on their significance and validity.

20. Write a few poems of your own. You can experiment with writing in free verse, as Whitman does in "When I heard the learn'd astronomer" (p. 73), or you can work in a tighter, more constrained form, such as the sonnet or the villanelle. Chances are you will read poems with a heightened attention after discovering what is involved in writing them.

Glossary

꙰

Allegory A symbolic narrative in which the surface details imply a secondary meaning, often both generalized and moral.

Alliteration The repetition of consonant sounds, especially at the beginning of words.

Allusion A reference to a person, event, or literary work outside the poem.

Anapest Two unaccented syllables followed by an accented one as in cŏmprĕhénd or ĭntĕrvéne.

Archetype An image, character, or event recurrent in literature and suggestive of mythological patterns of experience.

Assonance The repetition of similar vowel sounds in a sentence or a line of poetry as in "I rose and told him of my woe."

Aubade A love lyric in which the speaker complains about the arrival of the dawn, when he must part from his lover.

Ballad A narrative poem written in four-line stanzas, characterized by swift action and narrated in a direct style.

Blank verse A line of poetry or prose in unrhymed iambic pentameter.

Caesura A strong pause within a line of verse.

Closed form A type of form or structure in poetry characterized by regularity and consistency in such elements as rhyme, line length, and metrical pattern.

Conceit An extended metaphor that compares and links two apparently unrelated subjects in an unexpected combination; a philosophically intricate comparison.

Connotation The personal and emotional associations called up by a word.

Convention A customary feature of a literary work such as the use of iambic pentameter in the sonnet.

Couplet A pair of rhymed lines that may or may not constitute a separate stanza in a poem.

Dactyl A stressed syllable followed by two unstressed ones as in flúttĕrĭng or blúebĕrrў.

Denotation The dictionary meaning of a word.

Diction The selection of words in a literary work.

Dramatic monologue A type of poem in which a speaker addresses a silent listener.

Elegy A lyric poem that laments or memorializes the dead.

Elision The omission of an unstressed vowel or syllable to preserve the meter of a line of poetry.

Enjambment A run-on line of poetry in which logical and grammatical sense carries over from one line into the next. An enjambed line differs from an end-stopped line in which the grammatical and logical sense is completed within the line.

Epic A long narrative poem that records the adventures of a hero. Epics typically chronicle the origins of a civilization and embody its central values.

Epigram A brief witty poem, often satirical.

Falling meter Poetic meters such as trochaic and dactylic that move or fall from a stressed to an unstressed syllable.

Figurative language A form of language use in which writers and speakers intend something other than the literal meaning of their words. See *hyperbole, metaphor, metonymy, simile, synecdoche,* and *understatement.*

Foot A metrical unit composed of stressed and unstressed syllables. For example, an *iamb* or *iambic foot* is represented by ˘ ´, that is, by an unaccented syllable followed by an accented one. See the chart on p. 65.

Free verse   Poetry without a regular pattern of meter or rhyme.

Hyperbole   A figure of speech involving exaggeration.

Iamb   An unstressed syllable followed by a stressed syllable, as in tŏdáy.

Image   A concrete representation of a sense impression, a feeling, or an idea. Imagery refers to the pattern of related details in a work.

Irony   A contrast or discrepancy between what is said and what is meant or between what happens and what is expected to happen. In verbal irony characters say the opposite of what they mean. In irony of circumstance or situation the opposite of what is expected happens. In dramatic irony a character speaks in ignorance of a situation or event known to the audience or to other characters.

Literal language   A form of language in which writers and speakers mean exactly what their words denote.

Lyric poem   A type of poem characterized by brevity, compression, and the expression of feeling.

Metaphor   A comparison between essentially unlike things without a word such as *like* or *as* to designate the comparison. An example: "My love is a red, red rose."

Meter   The measured pattern of rhythmic accents in poems.

Metonymy   A figure of speech in which a closely related term is substituted for an object or idea. An example: "We have always remained loyal to the crown."

Narrative poem   A poem that tells a story.

Narrator   The voice and implied speaker (often called a *speaker*) of a literary work, to be distinguished from the actual living author.

Octave An eight-line unit, which may constitute a stanza or a section of a poem, as in the octave of a sonnet.

Ode A long, stately poem in stanzas of varied length, meter, and form. Usually a serious poem on an exalted subject.

Onomatopoeia The use of words to imitate the sounds they describe. *Buzz* and *crack* are onomatopoetic.

Open form A type of literary structure or form in poetry characterized by freedom from regularity and consistency in such elements as rhyme, line length, and metrical pattern.

Oxymoron A figure of speech consisting of two words that seem to contradict each other. An example: joyous pain.

Paradox A situation or phrase that appears contradictory but which contains a truth worth considering.

Parody A humorous, mocking imitation of a literary work.

Personification The endowment of inanimate objects or abstract concepts with animate or living qualities. An example: "The yellow leaves flaunted their color gaily in the wind."

Pyrrhic Two unaccented syllables together, as in ŏf thĕ. This serves as a substitute for iambic and trochaic feet and does not serve as a metrical norm.

Quatrain A four-line stanza in a poem.

Rhyme The matching of final vowel or consonant sounds in two or more words. Masculine rhymes end with a stressed syllable; feminine rhymes, with an unstressed one. Approximate or imperfect rhymes are called *slant* or *near* rhymes.

Rhythm The recurrence of accent or stress in lines of verse.

Rising meter Poetic meters such as iambic and anapestic that move or ascend from an unstressed to a stressed syllable.

Satire A literary form that criticizes human misconduct and ridicules vice, stupidity, and folly.

Sestet A six-line unit of verse constituting a stanza or section of a poem; the last six lines of an Italian sonnet.

Sestina   A poem of thirty-nine lines written in iambic pentameter. Its six-line stanzas repeat in an intricate and prescribed order the six last words of each line in the opening stanza. After the sixth stanza there is a three-line *envoi* (or envoy), which uses the six repeating words, two to a line.

Simile   A figure of speech involving a comparison between unlike things using *like, as,* or *as though.* An example: "My love is like a red, red rose."

Sonnet   A fourteen-line poem in iambic pentameter. The *Shakespearean* or *English sonnet* is arranged as three quatrains and a couplet, rhyming *abab cdcd efef gg.* The *Petrarchan* or *Italian sonnet* divides into two parts: an eight-line octave and a six-line sestet, rhyming *abbaabba cde cde* or *cd cd cd.*

Spondee   Two unaccented syllables together, as in kníck-knáck. This serves as a substitute for iambic and trochaic feet and does not serve as a metrical norm.

Stanza   A division or unit of a poem that is repeated in the same form—with similar or identical patterns of rhyme and meter.

Structure   The design or form of a literary work.

Style   The way an author chooses words, arranges them in sentences or in lines, and develops actions, ideas, and forms.

Symbol   An object or action in a literary work that means more than itself, that stands for something beyond itself.

Synecdoche   A figure of speech in which a part is substituted for the whole. An example: "Lend me a hand."

Synesthesia   An attempt to fuse different senses by describing one in terms of another.

Syntax   The grammatical order of words in a sentence or line of verse or dialogue.

Tercet   A three-line stanza.

Terza rima   Interlocking tercets rhyming *aba bcb cdc,* etc.

Theme   The idea of a literary work abstracted from its details of language, character, and action, and expressed in the form of a generalization.

Tone   The implied attitude of a poet toward the subject and materials of a poem.

Trochee A stressed syllable followed by an unstressed syllable, as in stórў.

Understatement A figure of speech in which a writer or speaker says less than what he or she means; the converse of exaggeration or *hyperbole.*

Villanelle A nineteen-line lyric poem that relies heavily on repetition. The first and third lines alternate throughout the poem, which is structured in six stanzas—five tercets and a final quatrain.

Index of
Poets and Poems

Index of
First Lines

COPYRIGHTS AND ACKNOWLEDGMENTS

Copyrights and Acknowledgments

Copyrights and Acknowledgments

Copyrights and Acknowledgments

Copyrights and Acknowledgments

Copyrights and Acknowledgments

ABOUT THE AUTHOR

Robert DiYanni is Professor of English at Pace University, Pleasantville, N.Y., where he is also Director of Interdisciplinary Studies. He received his B.A. from Rutgers and his Ph.D. from the City University of New York. His publications include articles and reviews on various aspects of English and American literature and on rhetoric and composition. Included also are a number of textbooks: *Connections: Reading, Writing, and Thinking* (Boynton/ Cook, 1985); *Reading Fiction: An Anthology of Short Stories* (Random House, 1988); *Literature: Reading Fiction, Poetry, Drama, and the Essay* (Random House, 1986); and *Modern American Poets: Their Voices and Visions* (Random House, 1987). He is currently working on a humanities textbook.